Kabir, Kabir

Purushottam Agrawal served as a member of the Union Public Service Commission of India from 2007 to 2013. Before this, he was professor and chairperson, Centre of Indian Languages, Jawaharlal Nehru University, New Delhi. He has been a visiting professor at Cambridge University, UK, and is a British Academy fellow at Wolfson College there. He has also been a visiting professor at El Colegio de Mexico.

A well-known panellist on TV debates, Agrawal also hosted 'Kitab', a unique show on books on Rajya Sabha TV. His published works in Hindi include *Akath Kahani Prem ki: Kabir ki Kavita aur Unka Samay* (2009), widely acclaimed as a path-breaking study on Kabir; *Majbooti ka Naam Mahatma Gandhi* (2005), which throws new light on issues of violence and power; *Hindi Serai: Astrakhan via Yerevan* (2013), a travelogue which traces the history of Indian traders who settled in Astrakhan, Russia, between the sixteenth and eighteenth centuries; and his debut novel *Nacohus*, a Kafkaesque fantasy on the politics of hurt sentiments. In English, his works include *Padmavat: An Epic Love Story*, a commentary on Malik Muhammad Jayasi's work, and *Who Is Bharat Mata?* (2019), a selection from Nehru's writings and speeches on history, culture and the idea of India.

Kabir,

The life and work of the early modern
poet-philosopher

Kabir

PURUSHOTTAM AGRAWAL

Introduction and Illustrations by

DEVDUTT PATTANAIK

WESTLAND
NON·FICTION

WESTLAND
NON-FICTION

First published in hardback by Westland Publications Private Limited in 2021

First published in paperback by Westland Non-Fiction, an imprint of Westland Books, a division of Nasadiya Technologies Private Limited, in 2023

No. 269/2B, First Floor, 'Irai Arul', Vimalraj Street, Nethaji Nagar, Alapakkam Main Road, Maduravoyal, Chennai 600095

Westland, the Westland logo, Westland Non-Fiction and the Westland Non-Fiction logo are the trademarks of Nasadiya Technologies Private Limited, or its affiliates.

ISBN: 9789395767576

10 9 8 7 6 5 4 3 2 1

Typeset by Special Effects Graphics Design Co., Mumbai
Printed at Nutech Print Services-India

In memoriam
Namvar Singh
(1926–2019)
Scholar and teacher extraordinaire

कबीर मन निरमल भया जैसा गंगा नीर।
तब पाछैं लगा हरि फिरै कहत कबीर, कबीर॥

I have made my mind as pure as Ganga water
Hari follows after, calling out 'Kabir, Kabir'

Contents

Introduction

Devdutt Pattanaik

I watched Purushottam Agrawal speak on the Kumbha Mela at the Jaipur Literature Festival in 2013. He refused to make the separation between the material and the spiritual as other scholars do. He did not see the grand gathering as exotic: he looked beyond the naked sadhus and the hygiene issues at the interconnectedness of the economic, the political, the historical, the cultural, the spiritual and the practical. This interconnectedness—of the context to the content, of the historical to the timeless, of the weaver to the poet, of the revolutionary thinker to the mystic—is seen in this book too. Hence the two Kabirs in the title.

I did not know that Agrawal was a Kabir scholar until I saw his passion, over coffee that day, as he explained how Western academics wanted to see the poet as a Muslim weaver, and so, wanted to distance him from any Brahminical influence, while at the same time, Kabir fans and followers strove hard to make him 'spiritual, not religious', for their own convenience. I bought his acclaimed book on Kabir the same day at the festival bookstore but found the Hindi too tough to follow. I begged him to translate or rewrite the book for an English reader like me. How long would we keep criticising Western scholars for approaching India using Western methodologies? Surely, we Indians should share Indian methodologies in a global world? He agreed.

But inspiration is one thing, implementation is another. It

took a long time for this manuscript to finally be ready after a pleasant detour—*Padmavat*, the book that I also had the privilege of inspiring, introducing and illustrating. *Kabir, Kabir*, however, is not a translation of the Hindi book. It is a new output, the result of his continued engagement with Kabir and Bhakti and its contemporary relevance.

We live in times when academics rarely engage with the public. Those who do are often trolled by politicians, as scholarly works challenge propaganda. We also live in times when academics study religion but insist they are not religious in order to assert their objectivity. Religious folk are busy being territorial about their faith and simultaneously terrified of critically examining their beliefs. But a book like this allows the general reader to enjoy the work of good scholarship: the warp of historical, political and literary facts and the weft of spiritual ideas—the full tapestry of Kabir. I call this the Indian way, the masala way, where all flavours explode simultaneously and provide insights both individually and collectively.

Kabir is a historical figure. But his ideas are not material; they are mystical, hence mythic. He believes in the spirit, a universal divinity present inside everyone, that he seeks and shares. Is this divine a measurable fact? No, it is not. It is therefore outside the purview of science. But it is a matter of faith, and faith is a construct, like gender, infinity, justice and equality. We need to outgrow the nineteenth-century binary of 'fact and fiction' and embrace twenty-first century ideas where we recognise that between fact (everybody's truth) and fiction (nobody's truth) is the realm of myth (somebody's truth). Kabir's truth was real for him and is real for those who engage with his poetry as seekers. The divine within seeks to make us decent human beings, tranquil and compassionate on the inside, just as ideas like justice and equality aspire to create a tranquil and compassionate society around us. One cannot exist without the other. Policy alone does not create paradise. Neither does poetry, on its own.

In the Vedas, divinity is called 'Brahman' and is as elusive as the meaning of a metaphor. Religion seeks to establish it outside, as god, formless in Islam, sculpted as fabulous imagery in Hinduism. Mystics establish it within, as spirit and soul, present here and there and everywhere. In his quest of this inner divinity, Kabir found no value in external religious forms or performances. Does that make him anti-religion and secular? Can a mystic be secular? Was Kabir's mysticism influenced by Islam or the Upanishads? Was he Hindu or Muslim? What were his influences? What was his caste? How did he deal with issues of class? Was he married? Did he have children, students, inheritors of his tradition? Somewhere in these academic and political enquiries and debates, the divine within is overlooked, even deliberately ignored.

Bhakti, or emotional response to the divine, is part of most religions and expressed in rituals and poetry of adoration. In Vedic times, the gods were invited through the ritual of yagna to partake of soma offerings and bestow blessings before departing. Emotion is embedded in the ritual of feeding. You cannot feed without emotion, unless you are a machine. The term 'bhakti' becomes explicit only in the Mahabharata, in the Bhagavad Gita narrative, when Krishna suggests Bhakti yoga as an approach to solve Arjuna's ethical dilemma just before the war. It is significant that after the war, when Arjuna tells Krishna to repeat his words, Krishna speaks of the intellectual and performative aspects of his discourse, Gyan yoga and Karma yoga, but not the emotional. Bhakti, it seems, is almost a last resort for the warrior.

Bhakti was also not the favoured response for Adi Shankara, the eighth-century Vedanta scholar, who, like the Buddhists he challenged, preferred the intellectual approach to the divine. Bhakti, as we know it, emerged in south India and was intimately linked with temple traditions. Alvars and Nayanars sang passionately about Vishnu and Shiva, but their Vishnu and Shiva were clearly housed in temples and had geographical anchors. In the eleventh century, Ramanuja linked Vedanta philosophy to bhakti and privileged the Sagun (god-with-form) bhakti of temples over the Nirgun (god-without-form) bhakti of the old yagna schools.

Islam's arrival in India in the twelfth century certainly privileged the idea of Nirgun bhakti over Sagun bhakti. Naturally, the centuries that followed saw a proliferation of mystic poets such as Kabir and Nanak who spoke of god as formless, unfettered by space and time. We also see greater importance given to holy texts over oral traditions—the composition of the *Ramcharitmanas* and the compilation of the Granth Sahib—to mirror the value placed on the Koran by Muslim rulers. But the Hindu temples continued to thrive. Poet-saints like Dnyaneshwara, Balaram Dasa and Annamacharya spoke passionately of devotion to Krishna, housed as Vitthala, Jagannath and Venkateshwara in their home towns of Pandharpur, Puri and Tirupati.

The new central Asian warlords were against idolatry and polytheism. They believed in one god. But this god was not merely outside idols; it was outside people. The Sufi idea of the divine within humans was seen as heresy. For the orthodox mulla, even creativity in the form of music, painting and theatre was heresy, as it sought to improve upon god's creation. By contrast, Hindus loved music, painting, sculpture and theatre. They were also comfortable with the idea of jiva-atma, the individual divine residing in the body, as well as param-atma, the cosmic divine residing in the image enshrined in the temple. But this was eclipsed by the attributes of the body—its gender, its caste, its desires. Not all bodies were considered pure enough to enter the Hindu temple. Adi Shankara once asked a 'low'-caste Chandala to move out of his path. The Chandala wanted to know why the body was being privileged over the soul. Adi Shankara, we are told, was humbled by the Chandala's wisdom but not enough to denounce the caste system, which continued to prevail in Indian society. Further, the celibate monk was privileged over the courtesan. Adi Shankara gave precedence to the hermit—like Buddhist bhikkus, Jain munis and Nath jogis—over the householder when he embraced the monastic path. Muslims were far more world-affirming and insisted on the importance of marriage. But they came with new forms of oppression: censorship against shrines, mystics and music.

For the politician, religion will always be a source of power. For the trader, religion will always be a source of income. For the seeker, religion will always be a source of wisdom. It was always so. It continues to be so. Kabir similarly will always be a literary figure, a political figure and a mystical figure. And his Ram will be simultaneously an expression of wisdom, a common greeting in the Gangetic plains and a Hindutva war cry. Everybody's truth is different. And to impose our truth on others is to carry the burden of other people's inadequacies.

So, rather than mourn about how the world and bhakti and the divine could be or should be, let us enjoy both Kabirs as presented in this book, reminding ourselves that:

Within infinite myths lies an eternal truth
Who sees it all?
Varuna has but a thousand eyes
Indra, a hundred
You and I, only two.

Kabir and I
A Note to the Reader

'Maybe Thomas Edison did a lot more to improve the world than Karl Marx and Neem Karoli Baba put together.'

Seemingly dismissive of attempts to understand the material basis of social dynamics on the one hand and of the spiritual pursuit on the other, this statement is attributed to Steve Jobs, one of the co-founders of Apple. He had come to India as a nondescript hippie with a friend in the early 1970s. The duo were amongst the thousands of Californians who landed here in search of 'spirituality'. After all, for centuries, India has been a favourite destination for this and the consequent 'balance and peace of mind'.

However, the search of these two young 'seekers' came to an abrupt end with their experiences with leeches, dysentery, scabies and their travellers' cheques being stolen. More distressing, however, according to Jobs's biographer Michael Moritz, was the young Californians' encounter with abject poverty, which shattered many illusions the entrepreneur had nurtured about India. As a middle-class American, Jobs could take for granted a certain level of freedom from deprivation, which perhaps allowed him to look for 'enlightenment'. But his worst nightmare of poverty would not have matched the stark reality of India of those days. He was 'struck by the incongruity between the country's condition and its airs of holiness'. Instead of some mysterious 'self-realisation', he came to this depressing observation.[1]

Jobs's reaction to this discord was perfectly justified. Poverty is not beautiful; it deserves to be eliminated, not glorified. His invocation of Neem Karoli Baba may or may not indicate his assessment of this particular guru, but it is certainly a telling comment on those who take spirituality as a euphemism for escape from the misery and degradation of poverty. The reference to Thomas Alva Edison underlines the vital importance of the material basis of 'seeking', by an individual or society, secular or spiritual. Without aiming for a certain level of well-being for *all* of humanity through technological advancement, there is no point in putting on a holy air of piety and spirituality. Incidentally, this is also what Marx stressed, and any serious student of sociology would agree with Jobs's focus on the material basis in human advancement.

At the same time, Jobs recognised the uniqueness of this country. He admired the 'Indian way of thinking' for its 'power of intuition and experiential wisdom'. Another biographer quotes him as having said, 'The people in Indian countryside don't use their intellect like we do, they use their intuition instead, and their intuition is far more developed than in the rest of the world.'[2]

Far from giving short shrift to 'desire'—of erotic and other kinds—the 'Indian way of thinking' accords it ethical soundness and validity. The much-hyped 'spirituality' detached from the mundane life, the so-called other-worldliness, is a characteristic not of real, historical India, but of the India fabricated through colonial scholarship. Interestingly, this colonial construct has been happily internalised by many 'proud' Indians.

Jobs encountered the shocking 'incongruity' in the land that had, in its philosophical moments, articulated the ideal fourfold goals of life—the purushartha chatushtya: only through ethical means (dharma), one must earn means (artha) to fulfil desires (kama), and along with this should strive for 'salvation' (moksha).

Moksha is the awareness of one's self and its place in the cosmic order. It is not something to be had only after this life is over or almost over; it is something to be achieved within this life, with all its hurly-burly. And, of course, achieving this kind of moksha is not the exclusive privilege of a believer or 'spiritualist'. An agnostic or even an atheist can attain and must strive for moksha.

Kabir, the fifteenth- to sixteenth-century poet-philosopher, has a wonderful expression for this awareness—jivanmrit, literally, being dead while alive. This poignant phrase reminds us that death is not a cancellation of life but its natural culmination, and is the only certainty in an otherwise uncertain existence, lending life itself perspective. Kabir categorically rejects all assurances of post-life moksha, salvation or god-realisation, insisting instead on infusing life with meaning and purpose to attain salvation when alive, so one dies with the satisfaction of having attained moksha, rather than with a desperate hope to reach it after death.

Albert Camus puts it succinctly in *The Myth of Sisyphus*, 'There is but one truly serious philosophical problem, and that is suicide. Judging whether life is or is not worth living amounts to answering the fundamental question of philosophy.'

'Worth living or not?'—how can one postpone this query about life until a supposed afterlife or rebirth?

Even if you do live another life after this one, be reborn, you will likely remember nothing of this life, have no good or bad qualities of the person you were. Then, clearly, it will be someone else's life, not yours, would it not?

Kabir is essentially a poet of such atma-khabar—literally, the news of self, or self-awareness—another of his favourite phrases. He recognises that we live only once and not forever. In his time too, there were people who imagined a binary opposition between jog, yoga or blissful union with the ultimate, and bhog, the pleasures of life. But Kabir, reiterating the essential idea of purushartha chatushtya, claims that his conception of bhakti combines jog and bhog.

His poetry as well as his life underline a basic truth: enlightenment is not a static achievement or a momentary flash but a constant process. The kind of instant enlightenment the hippies were looking for and some people go on looking forever is not to be found anywhere. Kabir would be utterly dismissive of any claim of enlightenment through some miracle-performing guru or similar 'exotic' methods. Through his experiences and experiments with the self and surroundings, he knew that the process of enlightenment has to be sustained by constant effort and perseverance.

By default, Kabir gives us another khabar, which is absolutely crucial to make sense of India's cultural experience and genius. He carried India's dialogue-oriented plurality on his person. Born into a Muslim weaver family, he, in the course of his search for the meaning of life, zeroed in on the liberal Vaishnava acharya Ramanand as a suitable guru. Before approaching him, Kabir had well-acquainted himself with philosophies and practices of the Sufis, Tantrikas and Nath panthis. His passage through all these avenues notwithstanding, Kabir remained an original, fiercely independent and brilliantly creative mind. He never became a Vaishnava or a Sufi or a Nath panthi in a sectarian sense. Borrowing words from varied lexicons, he composed his own poetic language system.

Kabir made a significant value-addition to the fourfold ideal by arguing for a rational conception of spirituality, an ethics of equality and an experience-based method of knowledge. His bhakti was a combination of these three, and to him, bhakti was the measure of everything. He assessed dharma on bhakti's touchstone, not the other way round. In the process, he interrogated all religious and social practices inconsistent with his bhakti; more than mere devotion, his bhakti is a call for constant reflection.

When we go through a rough patch, we are more likely to reflect on our choices, recall cautions and remember larger truths (including our mortality) and try to put the narrative of our lives in perspective. But, during better times, don't we tend to forget everything except the excitement of the moment? Knowing this, Kabir comments, 'Everyone reflects and remembers during a difficult time. If one does this constantly, there may perhaps be no difficult time at all.'

Ram is at the centre of Kabir's bhakti, not as an incarnation of Vishnu and the crown prince of Ayodhya, but as the most intimate and 'soothing' (that is what the word 'Ram' means) name given to cosmic consciousness, which, just like a 'flower's fragrance', is all pervasive, yet invisible.

Rejecting binaries imagined between jog and bhog, between the inner life and the outer one, the individual and the social, Kabir insists that an inner life of love with god and an outer life of keeping up with one's householder responsibilities and cultivating an awareness of one's self as well as the society around must complement each other in any serious pursuit of spirituality and morality. Celebrating hard work and honest profession, he seeks to put across this essential point throughout his poetry: making every moment of life a moment of bhakti, of moral self-awareness, helps one attain moksha in this very life.

My formal academic engagement with Kabir began in 1979 when I joined the PhD programme at Jawaharlal Nehru University (JNU) after my post-graduation in Hindi, under the supervision of the legendary scholar and teacher Namwar Singh. He was the ablest disciple of Hazari Prasad Dwivedi, a scholar extraordinaire of Kabir and Bhakti in general, an acharya in the true sense and also a first-rate novelist. As students of JNU, we had the good fortune of listening to the great acharya's last lectures in the summer of 1979, which he delivered at the invitation of our professor and his student Namwar Singh.

While pursuing my research, I also got the opportunity to have a number of long, enriching conversations with the eminent literary critic, historian and linguist Ram Vilas Sharma, who was then in Delhi, working on his monumental study of the British Raj and Marxism in India.

I realised the fondness that Professor Bipan Chandra of the Centre of Historical Studies at JNU had developed for me only

later, when as chairman of the National Book Trust, he persuaded
me to write an easy-to-access compilation of Kabir, published in
2007 as 'Kabir: Saakhi aur Sabad'. Professor Harbans Mukhia of
the same centre continues to be an encouraging and thought-
provoking conversationalist.

A paper I wrote, titled 'Kabir: The Poet of Protest', for Professor
Savitri Chandra's course on Bhakti poetry and its historical context
is what helped me choose Kabir as my topic of research. It was not
a career-oriented decision, not even a purely academic one. It was
an expected point in the journey that had begun in my childhood.

I was born in Gwalior, 300 kilometres south of Delhi. Even as a
child I was introverted, irritable, generally quiet but temperamental
enough to cause serious concern when I got angry. Deep down,
I was restless, filled with vexing questions and doubts about
everything. My parents believed all this indicated a continuation of
my inclinations from my previous birth as a sadhu. This, needless
to say, made me feel special.

But by the age of twelve, I knew the *'Jannat ki haqiqat'*, the
reality of the heavens, as the poet Ghalib puts it. Previous and
future lives are fascinating imaginations and nothing more; we live
only once, the only continuation of our lives is in the memories
of others, if at all. My restless inquisitiveness also led to reading
everything I could lay my hands on—from crime thrillers and
literary fiction to newspapers and even religious books, scriptures
and little didactic tracts from the Gita Press. I was obsessed with
questions like: What happens after I die? Can I see my own death?
How will others react to it? Will I really leave a void behind? This
curiosity to watch and record my own death still persists.

Despite the usual Indian middle-class parents' dreams to see
their child in a professional field, my mother stood by me in my
desire for padhai, literally, reading, or an education, for which I
am grateful. She ensured my stay at Gangadas-ji's shala (the word
means a centre of learning) for one year, because it was close to

Miss Hill's School where I studied. It was at this Vaishnava math that Lakshmibai, the Rani of Jhansi, was cremated by the then mahant Gangadas-ji in 1858. Here, I was under the watchful eyes of the mahant Jagannath Das-ji, an overbearing, almost fearsome personality who presided over an imposing property and huge patches of land, made possible due to the centuries of patronage from the Mughal court and the local ruling family, the Scindias.

Mahant-ji indulged me, in spite of his occasional desperation and indignation, like for instance, when he found me delving into *Satyarth Prakash* by Dayanand Saraswati, which contains a sharp critique of anything other than what Dayanand considered authentically Vedic. Mahant-ji's idol-worshipping, avatar-believing, Puranic faith was amongst the targets of the author's bitter polemics and sarcasm.

At this shala, I learnt much about Vaishnava rituals, rules of worship and code of discipline. Being a Ramanandi math, it was not fastidious about caste-related purity-pollution rules, and welcomed Kabir panthis too for short-term and even permanent stay. Also, celebrating its heritage of armed militant sadhus, the math worshipped its impressive collection of swords and spears on the day of Dussera.

It is partly due to this insider's knowledge of the Vaishnavas and other communities, that during my ongoing study of Kabir, other Bhaktas and Hinduism in general, I have found it difficult to reconcile with many an academic reconstruction of various sects and traditions.

I saw a Kabir-panthi sadhu for the first time in this shala— a sadhu without a janeu or caste, but with just a Tulsi-kanthi, a necklace made of tulsi wood, around his neck. He enjoyed equal status with the other sadhus, ate his meals with everyone else, moved freely in the campus, except the sanctum sanctorum and the kitchen, which was out of bounds for everyone, except Mahant-ji and the designated pujaris and cooks.

I strived for atma-gyan, self-knowledge, by talking about and listening to religious issues, participating in practices recommended only for sadhus, and, of course, reading widely. Alarmed by the interest I showed in the sadhu's way of life, my parents withdrew me from the shala. But my search for self-knowledge and similar desires remained.

Although Dayanand Saraswati's sharp prose had been a great pleasure to read, his self-righteous dismissal of everything did not really touch a chord with me. I found Vivekananda much closer to my heart. His life and work seemed far more open-minded, exciting and reassuring, and I visited the local branch of the Ram Krishna Mission quite regularly.

My spiritual quest went beyond Hinduism. I passed the Bible examination conducted by a Protestant church, attended sermons at a Catholic church and sessions at a Theosophical lodge, and often visited the Sufi shrine of Baba Kapur and some gurdwaras. I became quite active in Shri Ram Sharma's 'Gayatri Parivar', had a lengthy conversation with him during his Gwalior trip and learnt about the importance and mystery of the hallowed Gayatri Mantra. Then, there was a brief stint with the Nirankari Mission.

After all these years, I find it strange, even funny sometimes, that as a child and adolescent, I was in such a hurry to 'know' the mysteries of the self—individual and cosmic. It was a holistic search; attending all these 'spiritual' organisations and reading texts like the Upanishads and Darshans went side by side with reading creative and political literature and participating in social, intellectual and political activities.

I also actively explored some variants of 'new-age spirituality'. The Brahma Kumari centre was a novelty in the 1970s, and in a city like Gwalior, it attracted special attention, good and bad, due to the prominent role women played in its organisational structure and activities. Then there was Rajneesh (later Bhagwan and Osho), whose taped and published lectures were a kind of craze amongst even those, like myself, who did not consider him their guru. Some of my close friends were full-fledged 'sanyasis' of him, and I was an active member of the community, even if honorary, sometimes sceptical and even critical. Then there was the Bahá'í

Faith—an eclectic sect founded by the Persian mystic and preacher Bahá'u'lláh (1817–1892). The followers of this faith see it as a divinely sanctioned culmination of all religious traditions, and hence, instead of converting people, they simply expect others to recognise the spread and continuation of equally important divine messengers across nations and civilisations.

But after having gained some sense of a range of religious traditions and practices, instead of peace of mind, I came out armed with more doubts. The very idea of organised religion and deliberately constructed mystique around many practices and individuals made me more and more sceptical.

I had begun reading English tolerably well and came across J. Krishnamurti, who, due to his persistent questioning of received wisdom in all spheres, further fuelled my scepticism. In any case, I was now more inclined to social and political activism and thought of myself as an atheist by the time I turned twenty.

Quite interestingly, none of the spiritual gurus and organisations I had come across seemed particularly interested in Kabir, Rajneesh being the only exception. J. Krishnamurti, in any case, hardly cited or mentioned anyone. Kabir is usually referred to more by progressive intellectuals and left-wing political activists; however, for them, his spiritual or 'mystic' side was irrelevant or even 'reactionary'. However, during the course of my left-wing activism, I came in contact with only a minuscule community of Kabir panthis, almost invisible in the local cultural scene.

Even during my research work, I came in touch with hardly any Kabir panthis. My PhD thesis, submitted in 1985, was not about Kabir as the icon of a panth, but as a poet. It focussed on the issues raised in academic literary circles about his ideas and his place in the history of Hindi literature. It was only some time later that I got to know many Kabir panthis, including the prominent ones.

This was when I was immersed in anti-communalism activism alongside academic research. As a part of the Sampradayikta

Virodhi Andolan (SVA, between 1987 and 1992), as a consultant on the Oxfam project Violence Mitigation and Amelioration (1998–2003) and as a trustee of the Aman Trust (2003–2007), I travelled around the country, interacting with a cross-section of society, including Kabir panthis and members of other such panths. (Dilip Simeon, historian, philosopher and person of luminous moral and intellectual integrity, was instrumental in taking me to SVA, Oxfam and the Aman Trust. I remain deeply grateful for his friendship.)

During these decades, I benefitted from interactions with many Kabir-panthi acharyas, intellectuals and singers. I met some of them only once or twice, while I developed lasting relationships with others. Nawal Das, from the Parkah Marg branch of Kabir panth, whom I met in Varanasi in 1999, though not formally educated, epitomised 'Indian intuition' and 'experiential wisdom'. Talking with him reinvigorated my search for the real, ultimate truth. Conversations with him were, in fact, inner reflections on myself.

The year 1999 is also important to me because of the international conference on Kabir at the Heidelberg University, Germany. It was here that I met the much-admired Kabir scholars David Lorenzen and Linda Hess. Sometime later, I met John Hawley, another scholar, whose work on Surdas had convinced me to rethink many of my ideas. The professional meetings with these brilliant scholars and wonderful people soon matured into cherished personal friendships and fruitful academic collaboration, both formal and informal.

I remember fondly the late Abhilash Das, a great scholar and the head of the Parakh Marg. Listening to his persuasive voice addressing huge gatherings as well as talking with him in private were intellectually stimulating and emotionally soothing. Interactions with the present head of the Kabir Chaura math in Varanasi, Vivek Das—who, apart from his impressive scholarship, also possesses the zeal and courage of a social reformer and has done away with many traditional rituals of the panth—have always given me food for thought.

The stimulating friendships I earned with the celebrated Kabir singers Prahlad Singh Tipania (Malwa), the Bharti brothers (Chhattisgarh) and Mukhtiar Ali (Bikaner) continue till date. I recall with some satisfaction my role in organising Tipania's first concert in JNU in the early 1990s and seeing Mukhtiar Ali perform as a young boy in a programme organised by the Oxfam project.

During this period, my student at JNU, Kundan Yadav, a true 'Banarasi', helped me in my exploration of the Kabir panth and facilitated meetings with many memorable individuals. A senior officer with the Government of India now, Kundan continues to be a source of stimulating observations with a down-to-earth sense of humour. Abhisheka, a brilliant researcher who worked on Nabha Das's *Bhaktmal* with great insight and a wonderful interlocutor, is sorely missed.

Researching the vexed issue of the Kabir-Ramanand relationship, I consulted many archives, libraries and private collections, and met with Ramnareshacharya-ji, the head of Shri Ramanand Sampradaya, whose formidable scholarship of Nyaya, the Indian system of logic, is inspiringly complemented by his humility. It is always a pleasure to engage with a logician. During these years, I came to know the celebrated painter Gulam Mohammed Sheikh and benefited from the artist's insights too.

One of the outcomes of these relationships was a dialogue organised on the theme of 'Spiritually Beyond Organised Religion'. On this subject as well as on many others, conversations with the eminent poet Ashok Vajpeyi and the fascinating scholar Wagish Shukla have always been thought-provoking.

My travels and interactions with all these people and many more made me realise first-hand the incredible reach Kabir and his interrogative ideas had in those supposedly 'medieval' and 'stagnated' times: not just in Hindi-speaking areas and Punjab but across the country, from Odia- and Telugu-speaking regions to Gujarat and Maharashtra. Importantly, Kabir was and is admired not only by Kabir panthis but also by eminent Bhaktas like Dadu Dayal (from present-day Gujarat and Rajasthan), Tukaram (from Maharashtra), Shankardeva (from Assam) and Bhadrachala Ramadasu (from Telangana).

The spread of Kabir's influence sparkles through in the map on page fifty-one of the *Cultural Heritage Atlas of India* (ed. Prithvish Nag, National Atlas and Thematic Mapping Organisation of India, 2007). Dr. Nag, through his knowledge and experience, has also contributed a lot to my understanding of the people of India.

Direct encounters with vernacular wisdom shattered many of the maxims I held as self-evident truths as an academic, and it imbued my research and my search for moksha with a new perspective. I also came face to face with the irony of being culturally alien to one's own society, an existential reality of many liberal- and democratic-minded citizens concerned about the present and future of the country. On the other hand, I came to realise that not everything in the famed 'intuition of ordinary Indians' is praiseworthy either. Most depressing is the absence of a genuinely spontaneous and constant dialogue between these two segments of society.

In the light of my new discoveries, insights and realisations, I found my PhD thesis, submitted in 1985, to be quite inadequate. When my book on Kabir, *Akath Kahani Prem ki: Kabir ki Kavita aur Unka Samay* (The Indescribable Tale of Love: Kabir's Poetry and His Times) was finally published in 2009, Namwar Singh, presiding over its launch function, quipped, 'Not too many, Purushottam has taken only thirty-two years to write this book.'

It was indeed a result of thirty-two long, yet exciting years of constant travel, hard work, personal moments of gain and loss, researcher's excitement of new discoveries and the joy of gaining new friendships. Happily, it was well received by experts as well as general readers. The book you hold is not a translation of my Hindi work but a continuation of my reflections.

In the last eleven years, many things have changed, but some remain constant. I am much clearer and convinced about the idea of deshaj, or vernacular, modernity and the need to fully understand the human and cultural disaster colonialism was—not only for India and other non-Western countries but for all of humanity. I am even more insistent in my view that without getting rid of the habit of treating vernacular sources as mere translations and restatements of Sanskrit and Persian texts and without a genuine engagement with them, one can't make any sense of India's past and present or imagine a truly humane future.

And, most certainly, moksha is not to be postponed till the end of this life; we have to work for it *now*. The Nobel laureate and poet Joseph Brodsky gives words to this common human anxiety:

I sit in the dark. And it would be hard to figure out
which is worse: the dark inside, or the darkness out.

Kabir has an implicit suggestion for moving towards light from the 'dark inside' and the 'darkness out'. Basic, simple and helpful, but of course, as is characteristic of him, making some demands on the seeker:

Love has illuminated my body
My inner self has brightened
My words now have the fragrance of musk

पिंजर प्रेम प्रकास्या, आंतिर भया उजास।
मुख कस्तूरी महमही बानी फूटी बास॥

I

Approaching Kabir

A Rajput King Venerates a Muslim Weaver

Were it not for Kabir in this Kali yuga,
the ways of the world, joining forces
with Kali and the Vedas,
would have destroyed bhakti forever.

जो कलि नाम कबीर न होते।
लोक बेद और कलिजुग मिलि करि भगति रसातल देते॥[1]

A saviour of bhakti—this is how Pipa, a fifteenth-century Rajput king of Gagron in present-day Rajasthan, remembers Kabir, the weaver-poet from the holy north Indian city of Kashi. Pipa, a young contemporary of Kabir, did not lavish such praise even on their shared guru Ramanand.[2] Readers might be surprised to find a high-caste man, indeed of royal lineage, praising a humble, Muslim weaver in such moving words, though it says more about our own caste consciousness than theirs. Further in the song, Pipa's praise acquires an aspect of deep, personal gratitude:

The sweet tales of sagun
only add to human misery.
The Guru teaches the bitter truth of nirgun
without which life wastes away.
God, in order to uphold the glory of bhakti,
sent his own man:

Kabir,
who spread the true light everywhere,
so even humble Pipa could glimpse the truth.

श्रगुण कथि कथि मिष्ट खुवाया काया रोग बढ़ाया।
निर्गुण नींब पीया नहीं गुरगमि ताथैं आढ़ैं जीव बिकाया।
भगति प्रतापि राखिबे कारनि निज जन आप पठाया।
नांम कबीर साच प्रकासा तहां पीपै कुछ पाया।

The Hindu worldview considers the entirety of time as a cycle of four yugas. Kali yuga—which comes after Satya yuga, Treta yuga and Dwapara yuga—refers to an epoch in which the forces of dharma, or morally correct conduct, are weakest. We are, of course, mired in the social disintegration of the Kali yuga and will be for several millennia.

In this epoch, where the forces of moral decay, as Pipa puts it, have joined with lok and veda to defile and desecrate bhakti, Kabir is the first, divinely sanctioned line of defence. He uses the word 'veda' in a generic way to signify all orthodox, scriptural authority, the whole body of scholastic (that is to say, bookish) knowledge. 'Lok' refers to contemporary social conditions, dominant popular notions and prevalent practices—in other words, received wisdom.

A bhakti which needed to be saved from lok, veda and Kali yuga must have been more than merely a mode of worship, and this weaver from Kashi must have been some extraordinarily heroic soul to have saved this bhakti from catastrophe, earning such grateful praise from a Rajput king. Pipa is also careful to distinguish the robust, bracing medicine of his and Kabir's Nirgun bhakti from the seductive consolations of Sagun bhakti.

'Nirgun' means beyond attributes: the Nirgun panthis (henceforth referred to as Nirgunis), followers of this way, related to the divine without concern for images, idols and avatars. They also rejected, for the most part, ritualism and caste hierarchy. Sagun panthis (henceforth referred to as Sagunis), on the other hand, worshipped god through images and idols, believed in avatars and did not categorically reject caste; indeed, some of them, like the great poet Tulsidas, insisted on it.

Pipa was an influential Nirgun bhakta in his own right. The poem quoted above is found in the *Sarbangi* (an anthology of poems by several different poets) compiled in 1627 by Gopaldas.[3]

A society in which an upper-caste man from a feudal background could so openly eulogise a lowly weaver could not have been one in which caste was the only determinant of status and respect. Pipa's praise of Kabir, which undermines lazy conclusions about the social milieu of the time, cannot be explained away as an exception which proves the rule. In the course of this book, you will come across many people, events and situations that expose the notion of a static, caste-ridden pre-British India for what it is—a deliberate fabrication created by the colonial administration and its obliging scholars.

The prevalent notions about Indian society in the fifteenth and sixteenth centuries has been shaped by the British, whose interests it served to paint a picture of society beset by ceaseless Hindu-Muslim hostility at all levels until the Raj could intervene and bring some sanity. Many have argued that Indian society was entirely stagnant, with caste as the only determinant of one's status; of course, the caste structure, as imagined by these critics, was immune from any historical processes and evolution. Naturally enough, from such a perspective, the British Raj was necessary to jolt Indian society out of its inertia, to inject it with some dynamism.

British rule not only robbed India of its material wealth (the economist Utsa Patnaik estimates that the Raj had plundered US$ 45 trillion over 170 years) but also distorted Indian histories, memories and imaginations. Notwithstanding the excellent, pioneering work produced by many fine scholars working under the British dispensation, the colonial project of 'knowing' India was a key part of the larger project of controlling, exploiting and ultimately stealing its riches. The production of British scholarship in India was also tainted by cultural and racial prejudice, making

many unfounded, shoddily argued ideas part of the popular 'wisdom' about India.

Among these nuggets of wisdom is the 'otherworldliness' of Hindu traditions, which, in fact, produced texts like the *Kama Sutra* and *Arthashastra*, and revere Ram and Krishna, royal householders who never shirked challenges or sought to escape worldly problems. Dharma, morally correct conduct; artha, means of earning a living and participation in worldly responsibilities; kama, pleasure; and moksha, salvation, are fundamental to the Hindu conception of life. Far from creating a binary between spiritual and material fulfilment, these aims or principles of a full life encourage everyone to pursue opportunities and pleasures with moral discipline and social sensitivity.

Kabir's spiritual quest, too, was not a euphemism for an escape from the realities, pleasures and challenges of life. His sadhana, spiritual practice, was, in part, an attempt to transcend such oppositional binaries as inner against outer, personal against social, family against community and spiritual against material. Instead, in Kabir's poetry, Ram-bhavana, spiritual longing; samaj-bhavana, social concerns; and kama-bhavana, search for pleasure and fun, reinforce each other. Dismissing the supposed conflict between Ram and kama, the spiritual and the erotic, Kabir reminds us that the 'erotic takes you to the divine, provided you know the trick'. (काम मिलावे राम सूं, जे कोई जाने साध ...)

We have much to learn from this wise man. His voice touches chords deep within not only Indians but also people from all corners of the world. Kabir has evolved into a universally popular 'brand' that represents irreverent interrogation and irrepressible moral courage. His songs continue to be sung in villages and towns, even as young singers and musicians in metropolitan cities find novel ways to present his words and interpret his songs. Kabir, one could argue, is a millennial superstar, as adored and revered as he ever was in his own lifetime.

But he must be read with sensitivity to historical distance; we cannot wish away five centuries. Imposing ideas from our times on his and vice versa only leads to confusion, because of which many people see Kabir as an 'apostle' of Hindu-Muslim unity, while in fact he soars high above such unity between given, fixed religious identities. Kabir glories in the individuality and moral agency of a human being, not their religious identity.

That said, some of Kabir's other ideas (for example, his condemnation of women as an obstruction to sadhana) must be rejected. Or at least be read as part of a complicated process, for despite Kabir's condemnations of women in his didactic moods, he invariably adopts the persona of a woman in his poetic moments of love and longing for the beloved, for his Ram.

This apparent paradox needs to be placed in the context of a wider reflection on gender and sexuality of that time. It is crucial to put Indian historical experience in a comparative perspective.

We must, at the same time, not forget that with all the specific features of diverse cultural traditions, some concerns and desires are universal, common to all human beings. With reference to India, this point was succinctly made by the French scholar Raymond Schwab in *The Oriental Renaissance: Europe's Rediscovery of India and the East, 1680–1880*, first published in French in 1950 and translated into English only thirty-four years later. Many people—Europeans as well as Indians—while talking of the specific character and features of Indian civilisation, tend to turn them into 'exotica'. Right at the outset, Schwab reminds his European readers that: 'Unlike a unique model, India has always known the same problems as we, but has not approached them in the same way.'[4]

The 'uniqueness' of India lies not in its problems but in the way it sought and still seeks to handle them. The case of diversity is a telling example. While many Western societies show widespread uneasiness at perceived 'threats' to their homogeneity, India, for millennia, has been living meaningfully with manifold diversities of faiths, cultures, lifestyles and languages. Schwab's reminder points the way to a helpful perspective on comparison. Some thought-provoking questions could be: How did Europe in Kabir's time address issues of spirituality beyond organised religions, scriptural authority versus empirical wisdom, social hierarchy versus individual autonomy, and monopoly over ideas versus diversity of perspectives and lifestyles. How did it treat its internal critics and dissenters?

Kabir has been described as 'the Indian Luther' by some European scholars, just as Kalidasa has been described as the Indian Shakespeare and Kautilya as the Indian Machiavelli. One could just as easily reframe this question to: 'Who was the European Kabir?' so that we understand the role he played in his society, the impact he had, and ask if there is a European equivalent, rather than to glibly fit him, and the likes of Kalidasa and Kautilya, in European contexts.

But, to begin with, how do we get to the reality of Kabir's society to grasp its problems and dynamism? The straight answer: by taking deshbhasha, or vernacular, sources seriously and by engaging rigorously, critically and respectfully with a wide variety of them.

This, one could argue, is necessary not just to understand Kabir and his times but also to understand India in our own times.

'What Can He Say ... [Who] Has No Sanskrit': An Anecdote from Raju Guide's Life

There are two popular narratives about India's past. In one of these, India before the British Raj, despite some commerce, was characterised by limited economic activity. Its society was straitjacketed by the caste system which pervaded every sphere, not to mention such savage cultural practices as the burning of widows. India, in this view, lay outside history, unchanging and untouched by events elsewhere. In such a society, where is the question of any dynamics leading to the emergence of the idea of individual choice? People worked in their ancestral trades and followed meekly in the footsteps of their ancestors. British rule brought light and movement to this area of darkness.

In the other, diametrically opposed narrative, India before the arrival of the British, or rather, before the Muslims, was a veritable paradise on earth. There were no regressive social practices, no caste or gender prejudices or social tensions of any kind. All those cultural iniquities which embarrass us today were 'caused' by the aliens—Muslims and the British. Of course, this vision of Indian (read Hindu) glory is equally infantalising, for it suggests that not only can we not find it within ourselves to offer solutions to our problems but also lack even the ability to create those problems, dependent as we are on outsiders for everything.

Seemingly at odds with each other, both these descriptions stem from the same mindset that turns a blind eye to everyday practices as reflected in vernacular sources.

Colonial scholarship pertaining to India was underpinned by the prejudice that anything sensible and worthwhile that might exist in the Indian traditions could be found only in Sanskrit and Persian texts. India was, supposedly, well past its intellectual prime when it was colonised. Hence, everything in eighteenth-century India and its near past was of negligible intellectual value.

Meanwhile, this dismissal of deshbhasha sources has also been enthusiastically internalised by many 'proud' Hindus who now insist that all Hindu ideas and practices simply follow from ancient Sanskrit 'holy books'. That the Bhakti poets in the 'medieval' period were merely rehashing aspects of ancient wisdom in the idiom of love and devotion. That they just did not have the capacity to make any intellectual departures or innovations.

Not only lay people but also many scholars believe (at least implicitly) that deshbhasha works were either simply translated from or heavily influenced by Sanskrit or Persian sources. Consequently, vernacular works were, and still are, treated as secondary or confirmations of what is already available in Sanskrit texts. The indologist H.H. Wilson confidently wrote in 1819:

> It is an assertion that scarcely requires proof that the Hindu population of these extensive realms can be understood *only* through the medium of *Sanscrit* language: it alone furnishes us with the master spring of all the actions and passions, their prejudices and errors, and enables us to appreciate their vices or their worth.[5]

This is simply false. There is a lot of Hinduism and India outside the 'Sanscrit language'. But, having become part of the

scholarly 'narrative' and bolstered by institutional support, such misbegotten perceptions continue to dominate discussions about India's past and present. People blithely pass judgements on Kabir's India of the fifteenth and sixteenth centuries on the sole basis of texts composed centuries before. The historian Peter van der Veer astutely observes:

> The reference to the textual tradition is extremely problematic. In the first place, the texts are generally taken from the Vedic and classical periods of Hindu civilisation, i.e. texts dating from 1000 BC to AD 1200. Let us compare this with the study of modern Christianity. It is perfectly clear that the Bible and the interpretations of men like Augustine are of great importance to modern Christianity, but no one would even attempt to derive models from these texts to interpret the actual behaviour of Calvinists in a Dutch village. Such a method is based upon the assumption that before the arrival of Europeans, the traditional society was a kind of 'frozen' social reality, in which no change of any importance occurred.[6]

It is due to this strange method of describing Hinduism and India on the basis of Sanskrit texts alone, while deliberately ignoring the evidence of everyday practice found in vernacular sources, that the lowly status of middle castes and so-called untouchables is taken as a constant of Indian history. But the dynamics and prevalence of caste and other cultural practices differed from region to region. Brahmins did not enjoy the same sway in the north and west of India as they did in the south. Widow-burning was not as prevalent in other parts as it was in Bengal. It is thus crucial to look closely at the everyday practices of a given region before holding forth, unlike what the colonial scholars did, on the stagnation or dynamism of a society and culture.

Ravidas (or Raidas), a senior contemporary of Kabir, belonged to the 'untouchable' caste of hide-workers. How do you imagine he was treated by his contemporaries, particularly Brahmins? In

Ravidas's own words:

> Whose clan members even today work
> on leather-hides in and around Banaras,
> the same Raidas is revered
> and paid obeisance by pious Brahmins.

> जाके कुटुंब के ढेढ सब ढोर ढोवंत फिरहिं, अजहूं बनारसी आसा-पासा।
> आचार सहित विप्र करहिं दण्डौति, तिन तनै रैदास दासानुदासा ॥[7]

Many elites, belonging to higher castes, respected sants like Kabir and Ravidas who were considered to be their social inferiors. Indeed, Ravidas is believed to have been the guru of a Rajput queen just as Kabir was held in high regard by a Rajput king. It is misleading to see India between the fifteenth and eighteenth centuries solely through the prism of normative texts like the *Dharmashastra* of Manu. A normative text lays down laws and rules for social conduct and political governance. But reading such texts as indicative of ground realities and actual practices makes little sense. The US constitution, for instance, was adopted in 1776 and various amendments were passed over the years to guarantee constitutional liberties to all citizens, regardless of race, creed, religion, etc. But how credible would a reading of US history and society be on the sole basis of these declarations, ignoring the reality of legalised racist segregation past the middle of the twentieth century and the persistence of racial inequality into the twenty-first? Lest we forget, the Black Lives Matter slogan, 'I can't breathe', is a response to the events of the last half decade or so, nearly two and a half centuries after the US constitution came into being and well over two centuries since the Bill of Rights was ratified.

The *Dharmashastra* of Manu lays down many things, both good and bad. But the question is: how many of Manu's or others' normative injunctions were put to practice at which time and in which region of the Indian subcontinent? The internalisation of colonial methods of looking at Indian history has precluded such basic questions. For an authentic sense of evolving perceptions and changing attitudes, we must seriously engage with contemporaneous deshbhasha sources and drop our pernicious habit of treating these texts as mere translations of Sanskrit wisdom.

Let us take the *Ramayana* and the *Mahabharata* as examples. The *Ramcharitmanas* of Tulsidas is the most popular version of Ram's story in Hindi-speaking areas, and it can in no way be described as 'just' a translation of Valmiki's *Ramayana*. Naturally, it draws upon Valmiki's version. But other texts and sources too are essential to Tulsidas's poem, particularly the *Adhyatma Ramayana* composed a couple of centuries before it. Tulsidas omits the agonising events after Ram's victorious return to Ayodhya which occur in Valmiki's version. In *Ramcharitmanas*, having returned to Ayodhya, Ram and Sita simply 'live happily ever after'. Tulsidas makes the 'Utter Kand' (the seventh and last canto of his epic) a space to reflect on his own times. His description of the Kali yuga and suggestions to defeat its ill effects are put in a 'timeless' mythological frame, but it is a salvo in what was, for him, a very charged conflict—it is an expression of his profound disdain for the challenge presented by the Nirgun bhaktas to his cherished ideas.

Although one could debate the rights and wrongs of Tulsidas's views, the emphasis here is that Tulsidas did not render a vernacular version of a hallowed Sanskrit text for the 'less intelligent' and 'less educated'. He used the age-old Ramkatha as a vehicle for his own ideas. He engaged in a philosophical and theological debate with his peers. According to Pipa, the Kali yuga was in alliance with the doctrinaire veda and against bhakti; on the other hand, for Tulsidas, such a view represented not only a grave threat to bhakti as it should be correctly understood but also was an onslaught against all he held as holy and pious. Through his *Ramcharitmanas*, Tulsidas used a narrative deeply entrenched in the popular consciousness ('gadharudha pratyaya', to recall a term

from Sanskrit poetics) to attack the Nirgunis and to make his own
philosophical, social and political case.

The Malayalam poet Ezhuthachan and the Bengali poet
Krittibas also reconstructed the *Ramayana* to reflect their own
positions in the contemporary discourse.

In the fifteenth century, the Odia poet Sarala Dasa invented a
wonderful, innovative version of the *Mahabharata*. Some of the
twists and details he introduces, to fill gaps in the narrative, are
most moving and meaningful, for instance, revealing Shakuni's
motive for bringing the Kuru dynasty to its knees. Sarala Dasa also
establishes an Odia connection through Yudhishthira's marriage to
an Odia princess. Just like the Sanskrit version, his *Mahabharata*
is lengthy and copious, teeming over with details and plot points.
On the other hand, the fifteenth-century version of the epic
composed in Hindi by Vishnudas, a court poet of the Tomar king
of Gwalior, is a mere snippet in comparison. Vishnudas reduces
the seven hundred or so verses of the Gita to eight verses, but he
places it at a much more poignant moment. His Krishna tells the
eight-verse Gita not at the beginning of the battle, when Arjuna is
frozen in anticipation and indecision, but after the slaying of his
son Abhimanyu, when Arjuna is beside himself with grief.

There are also vernacular texts independent of the *Ramayana*
and the *Mahabharata*, musings on statecraft and ethics, for
example, reminding us that a tradition of scholarly rumination
continued in the vernacular and was not confined to Sanskrit
authors like Vyasa and Kautilya. Krishnadevaraya, the early-
sixteenth-century Vijayanagara king, composed *Amuktamalyada*
in Telugu. It is not only a poetic account of an avatar of Lord
Vishnu's marriage to the circa seventh-century Bhakti poet-saint
Andal, but also contains thoughts on the duties and dilemmas of
a king. It is unique because it was composed not by a disinterested
political thinker but a reigning king himself.

By defending the originality and importance of deshbhasha
texts, I am not denying the importance of Sanskrit and Persian
sources. Instead, I am calling for equal weight and emphasis to be

given to vernacular texts which, read carefully, offer a full portrait of Bhakti and its impact on society. Indian genius, after all, speaks in many tongues.

In the popular 1965 Hindi film *Guide*, directed by Vijay Anand and based on R.K. Narayan's eponymous novel, Raju, played by Devanand, after his release from prison, goes to a village where he is treated as a sadhu due to his calm, helpful nature. His popularity threatens the livelihood of the village priests. In order to expose him as a charlatan, the priests recite a mantra from the *Isha Upanishad* and challenge Raju to explain the verse. Poor Raju, having no Sanskrit, cannot respond. The priests crow about his ignorance. What can he say, they ask, he has no Sanskrit. Challenged, Raju bursts out in English. Now it is the priests who are nonplussed. What can they say, crows Raju, they have no English.

Those who spoke in languages, sometimes several of them, other than Sanskrit and Persian, also contributed significantly to the intellectual and sociopolitical life of India. For instance, Abul Fazl was no ordinary chronicler of events in Akbar's court but a scholar and philosopher. In his monumental *Akbarnama*, he refers to Kabir as a revered 'muwahid', the term broadly referring to a belief in the unity, the oneness of god. The historian Harbans Mukhia argues that the courtier's praise of Kabir was rooted in a 'new dichotomy Abul Fazl was constituting between denominational religions (Islam, Hinduism, Christianity, etc.,) on one hand and universal religiosity on the other'. In other words, Abul Fazl was putting organised religiosity on the one side and spirituality on the other. According to Mukhia, 'Kabir was a major inspiration to Abul Fazl for underlining this dichotomy and "resolving" it in the favour of "non-denominational" universal religiosity.'[8]

Bhakti: A Private Emotion and a Public Expression

The example of Abul Fazl, allied to such kings as Pipa and Birsingh Baghel, show the range of the 'high and mighty' who felt respect and reverence for Kabir. The poet, for his part, showed little diffidence:

> If you are a Brahmin, I am no less
> I am the weaver from Kashi
> I challenge you to explore my knowledge
> You are always running after kings and powerful people
> I am only concerned with Hari, with the divine

> तू बाम्हन मैं कासी का जुलहा, बूझहु मोर गियाना।
> तुम तौ पाचे भूपति राजे हरि सो मोर धियाना॥[9]

Kabir and other Nirgunis' rejection of the caste hierarchy led them to also distance themselves from the idea of avatar, as various avatars of god were supposed to have arrived among men to defend varnashrama. This compound word indicates a fourfold division of society and life—a hierarchical order with increasing disqualification and restriction as you go down the four varnas (Brahmin, Kshatriya, Vaishya and Shudra) combined with the four stages, ashrama, of life (Brahmacharya, Grihastha, Vanaprastha, Sanyasa). This practice of disqualifications and restrictions was a matter of unjust public humiliation in daily life for the supposedly 'lowborn'.

Bhakti was, along with being a deeply private emotion, also a public expression and activity, to both Sagunis and Nirgunis. This led to certain terms being shared between the sects but with conflicting usage and purposes. The best example is the name 'Ram'. Kabir insists that his Ram was neither born a prince of

Ayodhya, nor did he slay the king of Lanka; he is formless, beyond any particular attributes and so, Nirgun.

Many were uncomfortable with Kabir's 'offensive' ways of speaking about certain Hindu beliefs and traditions. Tulsidas, for instance, vehemently rejects Kabir's description of Ram as well as his criticism of caste hierarchy. Right at the beginning of *Ramcharitmanas*, Tulsidas makes Shiva say the following in response to Parvati's 'ignorant' query about Nirgun Ram being different from the Sagun version:

> Those who speak and hear such words are vile
> seized by the goblin of error
> hypocrites, averse to Hari's feet
> who cannot tell truth from falsehood
>
> Ignorant, blind, luckless fools,
> their mind-mirrors rusted by sensuality,
> wanton, duplicitous, thoroughly perverse,
> and who never dream of visiting saintly ones—
> they alone speak like this at odds with the Veda
> who have no inkling of true gain or loss.
> Their mirrors tarnished, lacking eyes,

how can such wretches see Ram's real form,
unable to discern god, with or without attributes,
they babble countless conceited teachings.
Driven by Hari's maya, they wander the world,
and there is nothing they will not say.
The mad, possessed and intoxicated,
do not think before they speak,
and to those who have drunk delusion's liquor,
one should never lend an ear.

(Translation by Philip Lutgendorf)

कहहिं सुनहिं अस अधम नर ग्रसे जे मोह पिसाच।
पाखंडी हरि पद विमुख जानहिं झूठ न साँच॥

अग्य अकोबिद अंध अभागी। काई विषय मुकुर मन लागी॥
लंपट कपटी कुटिल बिसेखी। सपनेहुँ संतसभा नहिं देखी॥
कहहिं ते बेद असंमत बानी। जिन्ह के सूझ लाभ नहिं हानी॥
मुकुर मलिन अरु नयन बिहीना। राम रूप देखहिं किमि दीना॥
जिन्ह के अगुन न सगुन बिबेका। जल्पहिं कल्पित बचन अनेका॥
हरिमाया बस जगत भ्रमाहीं। तिन्हहि कहत कछु अघटित नाहीं॥
बातुल भूत बिबस मतवारे। ते नहिं बोलहिं बचन बिचारे॥
जिन्ह कृत महामोह मद पाना। तिन्ह कर कहा करिअ नहिं काना॥[10]

In this dialogue between two mythological characters, we hear
loud and clear the frustration caused by the widespread public
influence of 'low-caste' people like Kabir and Ravidas.

Bhakti came to both Kabir and Tulsidas as a legacy from
the past; but far-reaching departures made by Bhakti poets
totally transformed the idea and practice of bhakti. The Nirgun
bhaktas were not merely elaborating upon ideas drawn from the
Upanishads and other ancient sources, but they were articulating
an intense, personal spirituality with an unprecedented emphasis
on social critique. Such departures and innovations were indicative
of the emergence of the idea of individuality and an interrogation

of birth-determined identity and hierarchy. Insistence on rational proof instead of scriptural citation was a natural corollary of such interrogation. Early modern Nirgun compositions in vernacular languages forcefully articulated individuality and rationality, today taken as defining characteristics of modernity, and left a perceptible impact on society. The poetry of Kabir and other vernacular poets indicate the emergence of an Indian vernacular modernity.

The significance of the transformative departures made in Bhakti practices in this era comes out most tellingly in the way Anantdas opens his account of the life of Namdev—a pioneer of Bhakti in Marathi in the late thirteenth to early fourteenth centuries. Written in 1588, Namdev was the first in the series of the many hagiographies of Bhakti poet-saints by Anantdas, including of Kabir, Pipa and Ravidas. It opens with:

> The first in the Kali yuga was Namdev,
> who had Hari, the lord, in his hand.

> कलिजुग प्रथम नामदे भइया।
> केसव अपने कर करि लइया ॥[11]

Although the Kali yuga became official with the departure of Lord Krishna after the Mahabharata war, millennia before Namdev's time, and countless Bhaktas must have walked on this earth in the intervening period, Anantdas recognises that Namdev brought something unprecedented to the table. Kabir agrees with Anantdas. He alludes and refers to many mythological events and persons, but mentions admiringly only three historical predecessors: Namdev, being the first, along with Jaidev and Trilochan. Obviously, Kabir was aware that he was speaking as part of a continuous tradition rather than in a vacuum.

For both Nirgunis and Sagunis (despite their contrasting positions on caste hierarchy), bhakti was not a method of worship alone (as it had thus far been considered), but a way of seeing the world, of looking at life and afterlife. Bhakti was a touchstone to determine the worth of personal relations and social attitudes, a perspective that gave meaning to one's everyday experiences and an expression of temporal and spiritual anguish. The spread of this conception of bhakti led to significant changes in social psychology, attitudes and everyday practices.

Communities of admirers and supporters coagulated around the ideas of various Nirgun and Sagun bhaktas. The practices of satsang, or the company of true, good people, and kirtan, or singing praises of god, played a crucial role in disseminating the debates and disputes around the various ideas of bhakti. They also provided a space for discussing everyday issues. Many of the Bhakti poets and enthusiasts established their own maths, or institutions, and panths, sects or communities. The Kabir panth is one such community—established not by Kabir himself, but by his followers. These communities provided Bhaktas with a network that was wider than one's family, caste and professional associations and was distinct and autonomous from the political space. A Bhakti gathering was (and remains) different from a family meeting or a caste panchayat. This notional space is a precursor of the modern public sphere created by newspapers and other mass media.

Nirgunis and Sagunis both consistently tried to 'win friends and influence people' by vigorously, vociferously putting forward their ideas, however polemical, and defending them in the public sphere.

This public sphere of Bhakti contributed to vernacular modernity in India.[12] I had first put forward and elaborated upon the notion of the Bhakti-inspired public sphere a decade ago in my 2009 study of Kabir and his times, *Akath Kahani Prem ki: Kabir ki Kavita aur Unka Samay*. Recently, some other scholars have been drawn to this idea, and in this book too, we will briefly discuss the intertwined phenomenon of vernacular modernity and the public sphere of Bhakti.[13]

'Blanket As Good As New …':
Four Keywords

Kabir wore his greatness lightly and did not take people's reverence as a license for excess. In his everyday life, nothing stood out. He was an 'extraordinarily ordinary' man, as the eminent Kabir scholar Hazari Prasad Dwivedi puts it. The poet continued to earn his living and look after his family as a weaver, treating his job not as an unwelcome burden but as a moral calling. He expected his god to provide him with enough not only to look after his family but also other noble souls:

साईं ऐता दीजिये जामें कुटुम समाय।
मैं भी भूखा न रहूं, साधु न भूखा जाय॥[14]

His work was an aesthetic performance. His artha and kama, instead of being mutually exclusive, complemented each other. His poetry abounds with metaphors and similes taken from his trade. His sadhana was an extension of an ethically conducted professional and family life. His self-confidence, that he was engaged in a holistic, moral life, is best reflected in this fabulous song:

Of what is the warp, of what the woof?
With what thread the blanket is woven?
Ingala is the warp and pingala the woof
With the thread Sushmana the blanket is woven

The eight-petalled lotus is the spinning wheel
with five tattvas and three gunas, He makes the blanket
For ten months, the Lord keeps weaving
Checking it well, He weaves the blanket

That blanket covers both gods and wise men
They wrap it round and the blanket gets dirty
Kabir has covered himself with care
He keeps his blanket as good as new.

(Translation by David Lorenzen)[15]

झीनी झीनी बीनी चदरिया।
काहे कै ताना काहे कै भरनी, कौन तार से बीनी चदरिया।
इंगला-पिंगला ताना भरनी, सुखमन तार से बीनी चदरिया।
आठ कंवल दल चरखा डोलै, पाँच तत्त गुन तीनी चदरिया।
सांई को सियत मास दस लागे, ठोंक ठोंक के बीनी चदरिया।
सो चादर सुर नर मुनि ओढ़े, ओढ़ के मैली कीनी चदरिया।
दास कबीर जतन से ओढ़िन, ज्यों की त्यों धरि दीनी चदरिया।

The five tattvas, or elements, are earth, water, fire, air and ether, while the three gunas, or attributes, that life comprises refer to sattava, true essence; rajas, will to possess and control; and tamas, the dark, baser instincts. The process of the human body taking shape is presented in this song through a picturesque arrangement of words and metaphors drawn from the weaving trade. The crucial thing here, however, is jatan—careful, attentive effort. Kabir is making the supremely confident declaration that while even the gods and wise, pious men have dirtied the blanket of life, he has lived every moment with such care that he can face the lord and return the used blanket as if it were brand new.

Living life with jatan implies being attentive to the totality of existence. In the traditional idiom of purushartha chatushtya, the fourfold ideal of human life, living with care means being constantly conscious of morality (dharma), while you make a living (artha) and fulfil your desires (kama). Such a conscious, self-aware life ensures eventual liberation (moksha).

Kabir provides us with clues to keep our own blankets as good as new. Reading him carefully, we can identify four keywords that put the fourfold ideal in a new perspective: prem, love; vivek, wisdom;

sahaj, a kind of natural serenity; and Ram, Kabir's favourite name for the innermost spiritual experience.

In the Hindu worldview, dharma is first in the fourfold ideal of life, but Kabir avoids using this word. He insists on bhakti instead and makes dharma subservient to his ideal of bhakti. The quintessentially accurate account of Kabir's ideas and his influence in Nabhadas's *Bhaktamal* (composed in the late sixteenth century) reads as follows: 'According to Kabir, bhakti is the crux of all the dharmas; each and every observance and ritual—yoga, yajna, fasting, charity is pointless if it is bereft of bhakti. He spoke for the good of everyone—Hindu or Muslim—without fear or favour, through his ramainis, sabdis and saakhis. That is why he is so highly regarded universally. Kabir did not bother himself with either the varnashrama or the six schools of philosophy.'

भक्तिविमुख जो धर्म सु सब अधर्म करि गाये।
योग यज्ञ व्रत दान भजन बिन तुच्छ दिखाये॥
हिंदू तुरक प्रमाण रमैनी सबदी साखी।
पक्षपात नहिं वचन सबन के हित की भाखी॥
आरूढ़ दशा है जगत पर मुख देखी नाहिंन भनी।
कबीर कानि रखी नहीं वर्णाश्रम षटदर्शनी॥[16]

'Saakhi' means witness and is used in the Nirgun bhakti
tradition for the metre called 'doha', a couplet, the idea being to
convey an authentic testimony of a deeply moving experience.
Sabdi or sabad is a pada, a longer poem, and the term 'sabad',
meaning word, is used to highlight the centrality of the idea of the
word in the Nirgun poetic universe. Ramaini is used for the metre
chaupai, a quatrain verse that uses a metre of four syllables, to
emphasise the specific idea of Ram. The six schools of philosophy
refer to the Vedic schools—Purva Mimamsa, Uttar Mimamsa (or,
as it is popularly known, Vedanta), Nyaya, Samkhya, Yoga and
Vaisheshika.

Why does Kabir enjoy such a preeminent status—in Nabhadas's
phrase, 'reigning over' or 'at the top of the world' (आरूढ़ दशा है जगत
पर)—in the public sphere of Bhakti?

We will explore this question and see how Kabir enriches the
traditional fourfold ideal, the purushartha chatushtya, with his
own shabd chatushtya, his four keywords. We will also discuss the
significance of Kabir making dharma subservient to bhakti and
the difference it makes to the fourfold ideal.

Prem has to be the first in the sequence of the fourfold ideal. In
Kabir's own words:

Love has illuminated my body
My inner self has brightened
My words now have the fragrance of musk

पंजरि प्रेम प्रकास्या, आंतरि भया उजास।
मुख कस्तूरी महमही, बानी फूटी बास ॥[17]

Love is at the root of Kabir's idea and practice of spirituality, to
expand the self through it rather than withdraw from the world.
Kabir is drawn to the paradox of love, its possessiveness and
jealousy on the one hand and, on the other, its self-effacement and
sacrifice. It is about ecstasy and also about pain, about togetherness
and about longing for togetherness. Kabir takes us on a tour of its

expanse, revealing to us love's pain and pleasure. He enables us to look at, listen to and speak about our own experience of love with a nuanced, rich language.

Kabir might reject the idea of the avatar because it is connected with the defence and preservation of birth-determined social hierarchy, but he freely uses names drawn from avatar narratives—Raghunath, Govind, Keshav, Madhav and so on, along with the core name, Ram. Every name gives an identification to the abstract Nirgun, placing it in a web of relationships. Kabir's Ram appears in his poems not only as god but also as parent and most frequently as friend and beloved. In such contexts where god is the beloved, love is articulated in the language of the erotic. In this way, the divide between the divine and secular is eliminated, and Kabir's audience realises the truth of what the Sufi poet Malik Muhammad Jayasi declares in his epic, *Padmavat*—'Love makes the human divine.' (मानुष प्रेम भयउ बैकुंठी ।)[18]

To Kabir, love is both the aim and measure of human life; living without experiencing love is like visiting a desolate house:

कबीर प्रेम न चाखिया, चाखि ना लिया साव।
सूने घर का पाहुना, ज्यों आवे त्यों जाव ॥[19]

Here, love must not be confused with inane sentiment. Kabir's love is not devoid of intellectual rigour and moral content. To reduce him as the spreader of such pabulum as 'universal love' for everyone and everything is to distort his ideas and emotions. While he celebrates the idea of love, he forcefully attacks what he perceives to be unjust and irrational, without being bothered about people's so-called 'hurt sentiments'. Kabir's love works in tandem with vivek. Rejecting the caste-related idea of purity, Kabir celebrates purity achieved through vivek:

I have made my mind as pure as Ganga water
Hari follows after, calling out 'Kabir, Kabir'

कबीर मन निरमल भया, जैसा गंगा नीर।
तब पाछैं लगा हरि फिरै, कहत कबीर कबीर ॥[20]

'Vivek', etymologically speaking, means the capacity to discriminate between the good and the bad. It is usually translated into English as 'discretion'. But rather than a pragmatic discretion, Kabir's vivek refers to a moral and intellectual enlightenment and also implies a sensitivity to the emotional aspects of the human psyche. A person with vivek will place everyday experiences in the wider framework of enlightened, rational understanding through reflection and interrogation; it is a constant negotiation with everything. This is precisely what Kabir does with his experience of caste-related insults and all kinds of empty ritualism. The English word 'wisdom', perhaps, better conveys the shades of vivek.

Vivek must evolve through human history and is the essence of conscious living. Although Kabir felt a deep affinity with Vaishnavas, he reminds them:

Having no sense of vivek,
showing your marks as a Vaishnava,
you are doing nothing but
hoodwinking people.

वैष्णव भया तो का भया, बूझा नहीं विवेक।
छापा तिलक बनाय के, दगध्या लोक अनेक ॥[21]

This sharp reminder applies equally to Kabir's admirers. We must constantly endeavour to add to our vivek and test everything, including Kabir's ideas.

Vivek has to be practised so persistently that it becomes sahaj, something with which one is born. In practice, it carries the connotation of 'with ease', 'natural'. One must constantly train and exercise one's vivek so that it becomes second nature, innate. Traits like compassion, curiosity, sensitivity and critical enquiry too must be practised regularly that they become reflexive rather than learnt behaviour. Given it is easier to retreat than to stand firm when confronted with a challenge, one cannot take vivek and sahaj for granted; constant self-monitoring and practice is the only way to remain on the right path. Kabir reminds us:

> People talk of sahaj, without ever knowing it;
> only those who can rid themselves
> of the compulsive, addictive habits of the mind
> can actually realise sahaj.

> सहज सहज सब कोई कहे, सहज न बूझै कोय।
> जिन सहजै विषया तजीं, सहज कहिजे सोय ॥[22]

If love and wisdom become ingrown and deep-rooted, you will have the capacity to talk of your anubhav, your innermost personal experiences as well as everyday social ones, without anbhay, fear. You have, through your merit, earned the right to transcend binaries, to experience the spiritual delight of listening to anhad, the unspoken and the unheard. In other words, when sahaj earned through the constant practice of vivek under a 'competent guru's direction becomes your swabhav, nature—you reach Ram'.

> कहै कबीर गुरि एक बुधि बताइ।
> सहज सुभाव मिले राम राई ॥[23]

In Chapter Four, we will return in some detail to the intertwined ideas of vivek and sahaj.

'Ram' as an adjective means soothing, pleasing. As a proper noun, it is the most popular name in north India for divinity—both in its Nirgun and Sagun versions. Kabir and other Nirgun poets insist on their Ram being neither a king of Ayodhya nor a slayer of Ravana. And yet, to give form to the abstract, they use numerous names (Raghav, Raghunath, etc.,) drawn from the narratives of Ram, an incarnation. Kabir also freely uses other names from Vaishnava and Islamic stock for god or divinity. He uses poetic adjectives to underline a specific quality and a specific relation in a given moment. To him, Ram, the soothing one, is also Jagjivan, the life-breath of the world, and Pak Parmanand, pious, ultimate bliss. Kabir naturally and delightfully brings together 'pak', an Arabic word meaning holy, and 'parmanand', an Indic term for divine bliss.

We have all experienced moments in life when we need to utter a name to enable us to remain steady, a name which has transformed abstract ideas like love, remembrance and gratitude into a palpable presence, a name that brings back memories of elevating moments and emotional commitments, a name that rekindles confidence and self-worth and thus activates inner strength.

Ram is such a name for Kabir. To him, Ram is an intimate, loving friend. Even while permeating every iota in the universe, Ram is deeply settled in Kabir's heart and soul. He is not a distant abstraction but the beloved of a possessive, even jealous, woman. Kabir longs for Ram, constantly utters his name, is immersed in the pleasures and pains of his love, but it is not unrequited love. Ram too needs Kabir's love and runs after him, uttering 'Kabir, Kabir ...'

Kabir's Ram is the name given to a transcendental experience. Ram refers to the creative interaction between human emotions and capacities for love, curiosity, wisdom and the expansion of self. It is indicative of a spirituality which goes beyond religiosity and is deeply rooted in morality and rationality. Kabir's spiritual pursuit is not insensitive to the human condition and its social context—it is characterised by the constant interaction and dialogue between the 'inside' and the 'outside'. Our era, with its technological marvels and the related condition of emotional and spiritual emptiness, is primed for Kabir's rational, moral and socially connected vision, for his shabd chatushtya of prem, vivek, sahaj and Ram.

Reading a Life through Legends: Keeping in Mind 'Lala-ji in Chandni Chowk'

What was the life of Kabir, this 'extraordinarily ordinary' man, like? How did he live? What did he look like? What kind of relationships did he have with his family and friends? What were the circumstances of his birth and death? Who were his followers and who were his detractors?

Kabir died in 1518 and did not leave any autobiographical notes. Besides Pipa and Nabhadas, other Bhakti poets mention Kabir with reverence, including the eminent Marathi sant Tukaram and Hariram Vyas from Bundelkhand. Despite being a Saguni, Vyas revered Kabir, counting him and other Nirgunis as members of his extended family. He was singing Kabir's praises in the middle of the sixteenth century, four decades after Kabir's demise.

In 1582–1583, within eighty years of Kabir's death, fifteen of his poems were included in a collection prepared in the region today known as Rajasthan, referred to by scholars as the *Fatehpur Manuscript*. Kabir's compositions were also included in the Adi Granth (1604), the first edition of the Granth Sahib, the central scripture of Sikhism.

The descendants of Birsingh Baghel of Bandhogarh (in Rewa, Madhya Pradesh), who was amongst Kabir's close circle, continue to look upon him as a family deity. Then, there are those who, even centuries after Kabir's death, claim to have been initiated by him. Garib Das of Haryana, born in the eighteenth century, and his contemporary Dariya Sahib of Bihar are cases in point. Dariya Sahib, in fact, claimed, without irony, to be an avatar of Kabir. In the south, Bhadrachala Ramadasu, a seventeenth-century devotee of Sagun Ram and a great composer of poetry and Carnatic music, claimed to have received his Taraka, or liberator, mantra from Kabir in person.

Obviously, Kabir was well known in his own lifetime and later became the subject of legend. Around 1600, Anantdas became the first person to put these legends together, titling his stories of the Bhakti saints *Kabir Parchai*—a feminine form of the word 'parcha' or 'parichay', meaning introduction. Idiomatically, 'parcha' also means proof. In the context of gods, goddesses and holy figures, it also suggests the capacity to perform miracles. A saying in Hindi goes: 'The poor goddess somehow carries on, but the priest insists on miracles.' (देवी दिन काटे, पंडा परचा माँगे।)

Hagiographies of saintly figures traditionally use their lives as a manifestation of their moral and spiritual message. Biographical facts are harnessed to shed light on their teachings. In the case of Kabir, such hard facts are thin on the ground. Anantdas highlights Kabir's miraculous spiritual achievements without burdening the reader with biographical detail. Still, reading various legends alongside contemporary accounts and some of Kabir's own poems provides us with a broad outline of his life and personality. This outline leaves enough space to exercise the 'fill in the blanks' option and a number of stories have been woven around the basic facts, such as they are.

There are references and allusions to some incidents in Kabir's life in his own poems but he, like others of his ilk, was more concerned with atma-khabr, self-assessment, in Kabir's own phrase, than with atma-katha, the self-revelation of autobiography. Any references to his personal life, rare as they are, must be 'read' in this light. Such references, by the poet or by others, come wrapped in the idiom of legends, which we need to absorb with a feel for the nuances of language and sensitivity to the cultural context of that time.

It is important to bear in mind that our own society, just like any society in the distant past, nurtures legends and myths. The power of traditional myths and legends continue to influence our decisions—in both personal and public life—and we continue to encounter new, evolving versions. We tell each other comforting, self-aggrandising stories about the power of technology to do good, for example, and our control over the future. We take recourse to various myths of national or civilisational superiority. We embroider legends around movie stars, athletes and even business tycoons and politicians. And these myths and legends, fuelled and spread by the media, are the staple diet of our national conversation. It is naturally easier to understand the content and orientation of contemporary legends, but what about legends around historical figures removed considerably from our own times?

Legends cannot be verified or falsified the way newspaper reports can be. Rather than their factual content, what is important is their moral orientation and what they are trying to 'tell' us. Legends are a kind of sandha-bhasha, enigmatic language. This expression—sandha-bhasha—was used to describe the esoteric and mystical sayings of Sidhhas, the Nath panthis and Nirgun bhaktas. It alludes to the moment of twilight, to a style of language in which something is said and something is left unsaid. Part of whatever is said is quite 'visible' to everyone who listens, while another part is shrouded in haze and has to be divined by use of the listener's own faculties. The choice is yours—you can either dismiss the wisdom contained in sandha-bhasha as mumbo jumbo or try to unravel its meaning.

Through this twilight language of legends, the collective consciousness of a society tries to preserve the essence of its significant memories and convey it to later generations. Some people take great pride in their cleverness in 'exposing' a legend as illogical and improbable. Such worthies forget that every society knows how to distinguish between myths and legends and quotidian reality. Those who 'believe' in the story of Hanuman having crossed the ocean in a single bound are intelligent enough to search for ways other than a Hanuman-sized leap. More importantly, they also know the other part of the story: Hanuman may have jumped across the ocean, Lord Ram and his army did not. They built a bridge.

Hanuman's jump is not intended as realistic description but is the use of sandha-bhasha to convey something more nuanced— his commitment and faith. Similarly, the point of the famous story in the Bible, of Jesus feeding hundreds of people with five loaves and two fishes, is not about how the crowd was fed but about the assurance being conveyed: Jesus is there not just to sate your spiritual yearning but also to help you meet your secular need for sustenance.

Myths and legends, when read sensitively, help us grasp aspects of historical experience that are generally hidden from view. In the case of India, a sensitive reading of legends is all the more crucial due to the role of oral tradition in communicating and preserving cultural memory, particularly in the light of colonial distortions. And what happens when we do not bother to learn the grammar, idiom and conventions of the source language— myths and legends—before translating it into our contemporary, 'realistic' language?

Well, here's a story.

Someone was once asked to translate the Hindi sentence 'लालाजी चांदनी चौक में टहल रहे थे (Lala-ji Chandni Chowk mein tahal rahe the)' into English. Quite ignorant of the grammar and conventions of either of the languages and blissfully innocent of his ignorance, the person translated the sentence word for word, perhaps using

Google Translate, and came up with, 'Bring bring heart ('La la, ji' rather than 'Lala-ji', a name) was walking in the moonlight yard (rather than in the famous Chandni Chowk area of Delhi).'

While reading legends, we must always keep poor Lala-ji in mind.

In the next chapter, I will focus on Kabir's life. Anantdas's *Kabir Parchai*, read alongside some of Kabir's poems, will be the main source for this reconstruction. Anantdas is unique in the annals of Bhakti for waxing lyrical about his subjects—Namdev, Kabir, Pipa, Raidas—but saying next to nothing about himself. His is an inspiring case of the selfless celebration of what he considered good and exemplary—the lives of these Bhaktas. The only hint he gives about himself is that he belonged to the Rasik branch of Ramanandi sadhus, who, unlike many others, worshipped Ram through the Rasik way of bhakti—sublimated erotic love. Followers of the Rasik path saw Ram not as a distant upholder of the social order but as an intimate lover. Rasik bhaktas imagined themselves to be the female beloveds and friends of Ram, the ultimate man.

Miracles are a feature of the legendary life of Kabir as told by Anantdas. They save Kabir from ordeals and sometimes serve to convince others of his essential goodness and positivity. These miracles, in the lives of Kabir and other Bhaktas, also emphasise the public nature of Bhakti. Miracles in all traditions are performed (or imagined, if you prefer) to make a point to an audience and are preserved in public memory.

But, can Kabir perform some miracles for our times?

Well, in the first place, in these increasingly insane times, a sane voice is in itself a miracle. Kabir's voice is reassuring and, at the same time, challenging. To him, neither is the social superficial nor the spiritual a sham. Neither is rationality burdensome nor emotions futile. Kabir's voice cautions us against falling prey to binaries and irrational exclusions in all spheres of our life. But, before we expect Kabir to perform miracles for us, let us ask ourselves: Are we ready to pause and reflect on our inner and outer worlds? Are we willing to rework ourselves or are just waiting for a quick-fix pill to come our way? Do we care to imagine and strive for a more humane and responsible social order? Are we thinking seriously of an inclusive and sustainable development model for the whole worlds? Do we take any responsibility for the plunder of nature that has precipitated global warming? Do we intend to rework our consumption patterns or blame 'others' while self-righteously absolving ourselves? Do we want to get rid of social injustice and various prejudices of race, caste and gender, or put down an unjust social structure as an 'act of god'? Do we dare to imagine a better system to organise our various social, economic and political activities?

Making a choice cannot be postponed any further. Global warming and water scarcity, the normalisation of cruel violence, the insensitivity to injustices built into our bureaucratic systems, the insanity of our public 'discourse', the overwhelming and weakening of so-called liberal and democratic structures worldwide—these are not rumours or paranoid speculations but very much a part of the stark reality that engulfs us.

It would be good to know something of Kabir's miraculous life, while asking the question: what have we done to ourselves?

II

'There Lived a Weaver in Kashi ...'

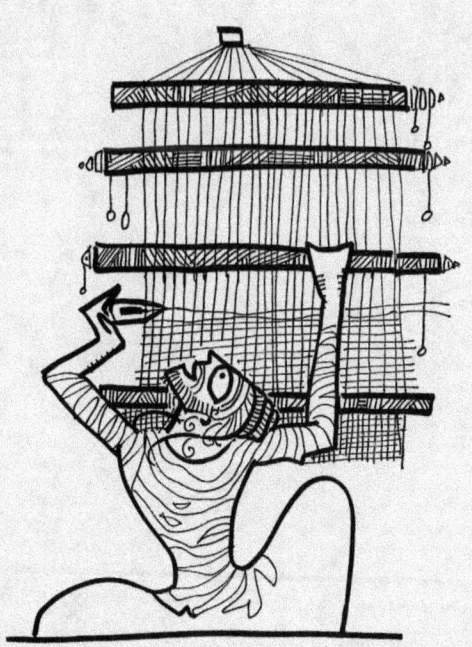

Chronicle of the
Last Rites Foretold

There are so many people gathered at the bank of the river. They are dancing and singing bhajans, not out of some ordinary joy but to express gratitude to their guru. Although they are also mourning his imminent demise, it is a celebration too, of his life, lived long and meaningfully. Just moments ago, though, they were arguing, on the verge of a physical conflict over how to administer their teacher's last rites. His Muslim followers argued, 'In whatever way the master might have lived, he was born a Muslim; his body must be buried.' The Hindus countered, 'So what if he was born a Muslim, he lived all his life as a Vaishnava. How dare you even think of giving him a Muslim burial?'

But throughout his life, their teacher had been critical of the shallowness and emptiness of ritualism and, above all, of the aggressive attitudes and violence that were excused and explained away as so-called religious sentiments. And now, here was the bitterest irony: his own students were frothing with anger and barely contained violence over the appropriate last rites for him. Although disheartening, this scene did not come as a surprise to the guru. He was wise enough to foresee and to actually put it down as a chronicle of his last rites foretold.

> Hindus insist on cremating my body, Muslims resist:
> 'How can you? He is, after all, our pir.
> He will receive a burial.'

Both are out fighting each other
The swan Kabir just looks on.

हिन्दू कहैं हमें ले जारो, तुर्क कहै मोर पीर।
दोउ आय दीनन में झगरौ, देखें हंस कबीर ॥[1]

In Indic tradition, the swan symbolises wisdom, in fact, the life force itself. Death is described as the 'swan's departure from the cage'. The wise are known as swans because, in folklore, the swan has the ability to separate milk from water, or the essential from the inessential.

Kabir, born into a family of Muslim weavers, took many a road, many a bylane and alleyway in fruitless search until he received the Ram mantra from the liberal Vaishnava preceptor Swami Ramanand. But he continued to be intellectually restless, questioning Hinduism, Islam and the very idea of organised religion. It was important to Kabir that he remained autonomous, that he held himself morally accountable.

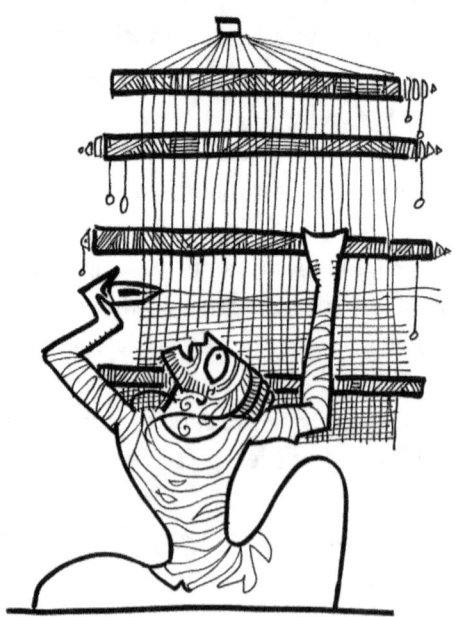

And now, in his last moments, he was faced with disciples who seemed to have missed the point of his teachings. Anantdas tells us of Kabir's ingenious solution to his dilemma:

> Kabir called for thirty-two measures of flowers
> to be arranged on a bed, on which he lay
> and covered himself with a sheet.
> Everybody came out celebrating the great life,
> chanting names of god, playing musical instruments.
> Kabir became immortal,
> without discarding his material body.
> Not taking recourse to a subtle one,
> he left for his heavenly abode.
> The astonished bhaktas could see
> only the flowers.

बोझ बतीस का फूल मंगाया।
तलैं ऊपर सैन कराया॥
सब संतन मिलि नाचैं गावैं।
ताल पखावज संख बजावैं॥
अमर भयौ छुट्यौ न सरीरू।
भयौ सैंदेही दास कबीरू॥
भगतन मांझ अचंभौ भइया।
फूल देखि अपने घर गईया॥[2]

This legend is sometimes read as a metaphor for Kabir's tragic failure—half the flowers were cremated and half were buried. His own disciples seemed to have failed him, reducing Kabir to the very boundaries he had sought to transcend. But in reality, the legend, or parable, is making a different point. Rather than an indication of the poet's ultimate failure, the story works not only as a solution to the immediate dilemma but also as a caution from the wise 'swan' Kabir.

A corpse has to be disposed of in a socially sanctioned manner, which is typically part of some religious tradition or the other.

What, then, could have been the funeral rites that would have been true to Kabir's personal philosophy as well as been satisfactory to his followers? Any alternative to traditional Hindu cremation or Muslim burial would have signalled the beginning of a new religious tradition. In other words, the arrival of another claim for control over the spiritual anguish inherent in the human psyche. This new entrant would have had its own 'divinely approved', hence unquestionable, power structure. Had this happened, Kabir would have ended up not as an interrogator of all organised religions and religiosity but as the founder of yet another religion and as a contributor to the ongoing strife amongst already existing ones. His solution, the story shows, was to effectively say—'Not a new religion please; last rites to the satisfaction of both sects.'

Back in the mid-seventeenth century, Mowbad Shah got it absolutely right. He was a Persian Shia Muslim (or maybe a Zoroastrian) and the author of *Dabistan-e-Mazahib*, a fascinating work of comparative religion. He gathered information about various subcontinental religious creeds and communities by travelling across India. He writes about Kabir extensively, describing him as a Vaishnava and a disciple of Ramanand and quotes a fakir saying this about Kabir's dual funeral:

'O friend, live so that after thy death, thy friends may bite their finger … Live so with good and bad that after thy death, the Muslims may wish to bury you and the Hindus to burn thee.'[3]

The legend of the dual funeral is a testimony to 'swan' Kabir's way of telling people, effectively, that the essential thing is to focus on the spiritual quest and moral life inherent in one's religion, not its power structure.

In *Kabir Parchai*, Anantdas, having mentioned the miraculous event, moves on to describe something historically and emotionally quite significant:

> Grieving over Kabir's death,
> some people did not eat, some were depressed.
> Kashi, engulfed in darkness,

looked like a starry sky with no moon.
The city was like a wedding party without the bridegroom,
a ghee-less feast without any taste.
Just as a body looks lacklustre without proper clothes,
Kashi lost its sheen without Kabir.

एक सुनि नाज न खाई।
एक लोग बहुत पछिताही॥
कबीर बिना कासी अंधियारा।
ज्यूं चंदा बिन दीसैं तारा॥
ज्यूं बरात में दूल्हा नाहीं।
ज्यूं घृत बिना जिवनार नसाहीं॥
ज्यूं बसतर बिना देह मलीना।
यूं कबीर बिन कासी हीनां॥[4]

Kabir, too, was bereft without Kashi (as we will see) in his last days. Though Kashi and he had 'quarrelled' amongst themselves, they were incomplete without each other.

Even if Kashi could be said to have no longer shone without him, Kabir's ideas, sadhana and persona continued to give off a brilliant glow. He inspired people, cutting across the divisions of belief systems. Anantdas underlines through a metaphor the universal respect Kabir received across the boundary lines of Nirgun/Sagun. In his description, Kabir, the interrogator of scriptural authority, was received in Vaikuntha most enthusiastically by Lord Vishnu himself; Vaikuntha is considered to be the highest divine abode, much higher than the heavens, the 'swarga' presided over by Indra. Anantdas writes in his *Kabir Parchai*:

Lord Vishnu tells Kabir,
'This Vaikuntha belongs to you.
I want you to stay here forever.'
The other pious souls
also shower affection on Kabir.
Kuber, the god of heavenly wealth,

wants to hand over all of it to him,
but Kabir will have none of it.
He prefers
the company of sages like Sanak and Sanandan.*
With Narada,
he develops a special bond of affection.
How far can I go in describing all this bliss?
Kabir has become immortal
even without discarding his material body.

*Sons of Brahma

बिसन कहै बैकुंठ तुम्हारौ।
बसौ सदा यहु भाव हमारौ॥
सिध सनेह करैं बहोतेरा।
सौंपन करै भंडार कुमेरा॥
सनकादिक मिलि बैठें संगा।
नारद सूं अति बाढ़यौ रंगा॥
कहौं कहां लग सब सुख जेता।
भयौ अब्यापी देह समेता॥5

That Kabir had developed a special bond with Narada, a dear bhakta of Vishnu, in Vaikuntha was quite natural, as while in this world, he had described his bhakti as 'Naradi'.

Kabir is supposed to have been born on the full moon day of Jeth, 1456 Vikrami Samvat, that is in the summer of 1398 in the Gregorian calendar, and is believed to have passed away in 1518, well over a century after his birth. Some modern scholars have tried to make his lifespan more 'credible' by putting his birth somewhere in the middle of the fifteenth century. In any case, there is a consensus amongst scholars that Kabir was active till the early sixteenth century, and the traditionally recognised date of his death conforms to this belief. While reaching the age of 120 is unusual, it is not impossible. It would be a mistake to think too literally about Kabir's age. It is a metaphor for a life well lived, an ideal and exemplary life.

The Pandit with a Bullock
on a Slippery Road

Anantdas opens his account of Kabir by telling us:

> There lived a weaver in Kashi
> who was steadfast in his bhakti of Hari.
> Having wasted a lot of time with the Shaktas,
> he now leans on Hari and sings his praises.

कासी बसै जुलाहा एक,
हरि भगति की पकड़ी टेक।
बहुत दिन साकत मैं गईया,
अब हरि का गुण ले निरबहिया ॥[6]

All the remarkable people Anantdas chose to celebrate in his parchais are historical figures, not mythological. To him, the most celebrated 'miracle' was that of the human spirit and a steadfast commitment to the moral values of bhakti. Everything else was built atop these foundations. In *Kabir Parchai*, the poet is received in Vaikuntha by Vishnu himself, even though he does not start off his life as an avatar or a messiah but as an inquisitive and sensitive, if humble, weaver from Kashi.

Anantdas's Kabir, thus, is a remarkable achiever who rose despite his humble origins. Kabir-panthi sources, on the other hand, project Kabir as the 'chosen one' since birth. In fact, to call their description of his arrival in this world as a 'birth' would be a misclassification. As with other incarnations of divinity, Kabir 'Sahib' or 'Sadguru' (as the Kabir bhaktas refer to him) appeared miraculously on a lotus leaf on the waters of the Ganga. He enjoyed 'guru' status in all the four yugas, even before he chose to come to us in the guise of Kabir. The Kabir-panthi stories about his previous 'arrivals' are similar to (possibly inspired by) the Buddhist Jataka stories which tell us about the miracles, achievements, teachings and adventures of Bodhisattva, before he was born as Siddhartha to finally become the Buddha.

Anantdas does not say anything about Kabir's birth, miraculous or otherwise. He obviously agrees with Kabir that it is not important how and into what family you are born—your worth, instead, depends on how you live and die. To recall Kabir's words:

> You cry as you enter this life,
> while everyone celebrates your birth.
> Live in such a way, says Kabir,
> that you depart joyously,
> while the world mourns for you.

> कबिरा जब जग में आए, जग हँसे आप रोए।
> ऐसी करनी कर चलो, आप हँसे जग रोए॥[7]

By the time Anantdas was writing his *Kabir Parchai*, the poet was already remembered gratefully and admiringly even by those who did not share his sharp critique of organised religion and its panoply of rituals. Anantdas neither claims to have 'discovered' Kabir nor to have rehabilitated a 'marginalised' voice. Kabir's poems and his fame had travelled to Punjab and what is today known as Rajasthan even before the time of Anantdas, who belonged to the latter region. Kabir was already venerated by Dadu (a Nirguni) in Rajasthan and Sankardev (not a Nirguni) in Assam.

I had mentioned Hariram Vyas (1510–1598) in the first chapter. Belonging to Orchha (a town in the Bundelkhand region of north India), he was a Sagun bhakta, a believer in the idea of avatars and somewhat accepting of the caste hierarchy. He celebrated the divine couple Radha and Krishna in life and in poetry. His theoretical position veered sharply away from Nirgun bhaktas. Still, while enumerating his notional, larger kutumba, or family, of fellow Bhaktas in a poem, he, at the very outset, mentions Kabir and other Nirgunis, including Sen the barber, Dhanna the peasant, Namdev the tailor, Pipa the king and Raidas the cobbler:

इतनौ है सब कुटुंब हमारौ,
सैन, धना अरु नामा, पीपा कबीर रैदास चमारौ।[8]

In the same period, we have Malik Muhammad Jayasi, a practising Muslim and revered Sufi, rating 'the weaver' higher than even Narada, the ultimate archetype of bhakti.

Narada calls out, crying,
'I have been defeated by a weaver.'

ना ना नारद रोय रोय पुकारा,
इक जुलाहे सों मैं हारा।[9]

Faith communities all over the world shroud the births of their central figures in miracle, particularly if they come from humble social backgrounds. The powerful and influential amongst the followers are instrumental in creating such fantastical origin stories in order to overcome their embarrassment of following a person of 'lowly' status. The spiritual achievement and consequent social recognition of these legendary figures are attributed to divine design, and they are projected as extraordinary from birth itself. Incarnation is one form of such projection; immaculate conception (Jesus being born to the virgin Mary) is another.

As already mentioned, some of the origin myths around Kabir rule out human parents. Other accounts—that circulate among followers and non-followers alike—suggest his mother was an embarrassed widow who left her newborn in god's hands. The very first mention of this unfortunate 'widowed mother' occurs as late as 1776, over two centuries after Kabir's death, in *Bhakti Gunadamchitrinitika* by Balakdas. This is a commentary on Nabhadas's *Bhaktamal* and is available only in manuscript form.

According to Balakdas, Kabir was born to a widowed Brahmin

woman, because the great sage Ramanand, unaware of her marital status, had blessed her in the standard way: 'May you be blessed with son.' (पुत्रवती भव।)

Once the Kabir panth became influential, it sought to underline the pre-destined divinity of the poet by claiming that he 'appeared' on a lotus leaf. The broader community of Bhaktas and admirers tried to accommodate the panth's sentiment, adjusting the story slightly to include a human mother blessed by none other than Ramanand. This way, Kabir's birth is saved both from being absolutely miraculous and from the inconvenient lineage of a weaver couple. Sadly, his parents, Neeru the weaver and his wife Nima, have had to pay the price for this bestowal of divinity on their son, having been turned from biological parents to foster ones.

But people closer in time to Kabir had no such compunctions about him being born to Muslim weavers. As mentioned already, Anantdas indeed does not even attempt to 'explain' Kabir's birth. He simply begins the poet's story with the line, 'There lived a weaver in Kashi.' In the third stanza, his Kabir wonders, 'How should I, a Muslim, be initiated?' and the poet's inner voice suggests the name of Ramanand, the liberal Vaishnava:

मुसलमांन हमारी जाती,
माला पाऊं कैसी भांती।
भीतौ बांणी बोल्या ऐह,
रामांनंद पैं दछया लेह।[10]

Later, the seventh stanza describes the response of Kabir's family and community to his spiritual experiments:

This lad has lost his mind and is discarding
his family ways and values:
Mecca, Medina, fasting and namaz.

कुटंब सजन समधी मिल रोवें,
बिकल भयौ काहे घर खोवे।
मका मदीना हमारा साजा,
कलमा रोज़ा और निवाजा।[11]

It has been argued in 'modern' Kabir scholarship that his family were recent converts to Islam. Well, it's true that Kabir was not born into a family of Chughtai Mughals or Seljuk Turks. People from his social strata in the subcontinent were 'recent converts', though we have no idea what is meant by 'recent'. Maybe just a generation earlier, maybe five? Who knows? All we do know, on the evidence of both Ravidas and Pipa, is that in Kabir's family 'Eid and Bakra Eid were observed, and a cow was slaughtered'.[12]

From sources other than Anantdas we learn that Kabir got his name when, following the Muslim custom, the maulvi opened the holy Koran to find a suitable name for the boy, and the word 'Kabir', meaning great or elder, caught his eye. The maulvi did not believe that providence could really have wanted this son of a weaver to be known as 'great'. So he tried again. And again. Each time, it was either Kabir or Akbar or some other synonym of 'great' that his eye fell upon. What could the poor maulvi do but submit to god's will?

Kabir does not name any of his relations or his guru, but in a couple of places alludes to his mother and wife. From the legends we know the names of, apart from his parents, his wife, Loi; son, Kamaal; and daughter, Kamaali. These three women—mother, wife and daughter—play significant (in some places poignant, in yet others even ironical) roles in Kabir's life. In one incident, we find Kamaali cautioning (in a way on behalf of Kabir) a scholar against the arrogant, scholastic hubris of bookish knowledge disconnected from life.

And this is how the story goes: There was a great pandit in the south with formidable erudition and powers of persuasion and was so successful in shastrartha, or scriptural and philosophical debates, that he was given the sobriquet 'Sarvajit', universal winner. But his own mother would consider him an all-conquering winner

only if he defeats the weaver of Kashi in argument. Sarvajit leaves
for Kashi, loading practically his entire reference library onto a
sturdy bullock. Reaching after an arduous journey, he spots a girl
at a well and asks for some water for his bullock and directions to
Kabir's home.

This girl is Kamaali, who instantly realises the purpose of the
pandit's visit and comes up with a profoundly witty reply:

> Kabir dwells in a high place;
> the way is too slippery even for ants.
> And some people want to negotiate it
> on a loaded bullock.

> जन कबीर का सिखरि घर, राह सलैली गैल।
> पांव न टिके पिपीलिका, लोगन लादे बैल॥[13]

He eventually meets the poet. The proud pandit who wanted
to prove a point to his mother and defeat Kabir in debate is so
charmed by his unassuming humility and the immensity of his
wisdom that he becomes the disciple instead. Sarvajit became
known as Surati Gopal Sahib, a cherished follower of Kabir and
the founder of the Chaura (Varanasi) branch of Kabir panth.

Kamaali's contempt for Sarvajit and his book-laden bullock
is instructive. Knowledge, she seems to be telling us, is useful for
winning shastrartha, among other things, but to gain the wisdom
necessary to achieve atmartha, it must be detached from arrogance,
from performative scholasticism, and allied to humility and
openness to dialogue. Kabir's four keywords—prem, vivek, sahaj
and Ram—are his essential tools to explore the meaning of the self.

It appears that Kabir began his spiritual journey in the company
of Shaktas, worshippers of the divine energy in the female form.
Anantdas reports Kabir's lament: 'I have wasted many days with
Shaktas.' (बहुत दिन साकत मैं गईया।) Shakta styles of worship included
animal sacrifice, the consumption of meat and intoxicating
substances, and distinct sexual practices. Theoretically, the point

was to be able to transcend the baser human instincts under the guidance and observation of a guru who had already made the transition. More often than not, though, this end was used to justify the unbridled pursuit of hedonistic indulgences and an amoral life. Shaktas were also known for intimidating people with claims of performing miracles. Other sects, particularly the Vaishnavas, detested them.

From Kabir's poems, we know that Shaktas were the one group of people for whom he had little sympathy and even less hope. When he speaks of Shaktas, he is uncharacteristically angry, dismissive, even cruel:

What is the point of talking
about something important to a dog?
What is the point of talking
of Hari to a Shakta?
Why feed camphor to a crow?
Why feed milk to a venomous snake?
A Shakta and a dog are kin;
one keeps denigrating, just as the other keeps barking.
Even if you irrigate a neem sampling with nectar,
it will not turn sweet.

का सुनहां को सुमृत सुनांयैं। का साषित पैं हरि गुन गायैं॥
का कऊवा को कपूर खवांयैं। का विषहर को दूध पिलांयैं॥
साषित सुनहां दोनों भाई। वौ नींदै वो भौंकत जाई॥
अंमृत ले ले नींब सिचाई। कहै कबीर वाकी बांनि न जाई॥[14]

Kabir must have been 'denigrated' by many, but it is only the calumny of Shaktas that so provokes him. The reason for his passionate dislike could have been his former closeness to the Shaktas; he had tried to make himself part of their group but could not suppress his need to find his own path. He was rejected as a renegade, and he took his revenge with the vehemence of a disenchanted insider. In one poem, Kabir clearly confirms what

Anantdas says about his past, calling the memories of his 'Shakta days' embarrassing and painful. He sees those days as precious time wasted in immaturity. He states clearly that 'till the age of twelve, I did not understand anything, and till the thirtieth year of life, did not worship the lord'. It was only after this that Kabir, with his guru's blessings, earned the grace of Hari and 'was overwhelmed with the desire for Gopal and left the temple of the goddess forever'. (आई तलब गोपालराय की माइआ मंदिर छोड़ि चलिओ ।)[15]

Elsewhere, Kabir extends the Shaktas a rather amusing left-handed compliment. Blissfully describing the achievement of his sadhana, he says, 'Now my foes have turned to friends; even Shaktas have turned into nice human beings!' (बैरी उलटि भये हैं मीता, साखत उलटि सजन भये चीता ।)[16]

This shows that Kabir can laugh at himself, can recognise his own prejudices and biases. This clear-sightedness means he never compromises his principles, chief among which is his faith in the individual rather than in group identity. For instance, despite his closeness to the Vaishnavas and his dislike for the Shaktas, Kabir writes that a Shakta householder as chaste as a virgin is better than a vicious Vaishnava, who ought to be avoided by pious people.

संसारी साकत भला, कुंवारी के भाइ।
दुराचारी बैसनव बुरा, हरिजन तहां न जाइ ॥[17]

Strangely, Kabir scholars have ignored this aspect of his biography. Indeed, Charlotte Vaudeville, the renowned French scholar of Kabir, makes Anantdas say something quite different. She 'reads' the relevant passage as, 'Having spent his childhood in error, i.e. as a Muhammadan ...'[18]

This is a telling example of the misleading binary of Hindu versus Muslim imposed by colonial scholarship on Indian history. In this binary, all the complexity and fluidity of social identities and their interactions are lost. Being in 'error' for Anantdas and Kabir did not mean being a 'Muhamaddan'. Vaudeville's reading is a gross error, although she is not alone. Many find it hard to imagine that people like Kabir, who were born Muslims, even some from elite backgrounds, came to be recognised as *both* Muslim and Vaishnava without being condemned either for discarding Islam or 'sullying the purity' of Hinduism. Mowbad Shah in *Dabistan-e-Mazahib* mentions at least two Muslim nobles amongst his own personal acquaintances—Mirza Saleh and Mirza Hyder—who had 'adopted the Vaishnava faith and practices'.[19] Mahmud Wali Balkhi (from Balkh in Afghanistan), who travelled in India between 1625 and 1631, left behind a voluminous account of his journeys. Historians Muzaffar Alam and Sanjay Subrahmanyam have analysed its contents along with those of some other travelogues. In Banaras, on the bank of the Ganga, Balkhi saw twenty-three Muslims 'wearing sacred thread and marks ("qashqa") on their forehead in order to pursue their puja. On being questioned, they raised their hands towards the sky, and placing a finger on their foreheads, signalled that it was thus written in their fate.'[20]

Tensions between Hindus and Muslims did, of course, exist, but the flat, perpetual binary did not. The fact of Muslim nobles adopting Vaishnava practices was not unheard of, nor was it so alien that a Muslim weaver might become impressed by and then disenchanted with Shakta practices. Anantdas did not write with

an agenda to promote 'Hindu-Muslim unity', nor did he write from the perspective of Hindus and Muslims being locked in perennial conflict. He was not surprised that Kabir found succour and favour among Vaishnavas, and he records, again without particular bias, that the poet felt sorry and angry about his Shakta past; this was misread, because of colonial-inflected biases, as Kabir being filled with regret about being born a Muslim.

Kabir started off as a Shakta, then learnt a lot through eager interactions with various sects and spiritual practices. This resulted in his liberal use of technical terms, metaphors and allusions from Tantrik, Nath-panthi, Vaishnava and Islamic traditions. He critically and, above all, autonomously examined the available interpretations of the 'truth' and other significant matters, both spiritual and secular. He was original, constructing his own ideas with a vocabulary borrowed from varied sources.

He has broadly been seen as a Vaishnava initiated by Ramanand, who himself had rebelled against a very conservative, brahminical Sri Vaishnava sect and used deshbhasha as his medium of expression. In the early modern period, the term 'Vaishnava' referred to followers of a particular Vaishnava school and acharya, or a venerated scholar and teacher, but it also referred to a person who was comparatively liberal in matters of faith and caste and abjured the destruction of all life, hence being a vegetarian. Mowbad Shah writes: 'In Hindostan it is known that whosoever abstains from eating meat and hurting living animals is esteemed a Vaishnava without regard to the doctrine before-said.'[21] This connotation still lingers in everyday use. The adjective 'Vaishnava' on a sign at a highway dhaba is not an invitation for initiation into a religious sect but a signal that vegetarian food is available on the premises. On a more poetic note, the words in the fifteenth-century Gujarati Bhakti poet Narsi Mehta's song (Mohandas Karamchand Gandhi's favourite) reinforce this popular conception of the Vaishnava: '*Vaishnava jana to tene kahiye/ je pida parayi jane re*'—only those who empathise with the pain of others are fit to be called Vaishnavas.

Kabir was a Vaishnava in this broad, non-sectarian sense.

He harboured as much love for Vaishnavas as he did disdain for Shaktas. He even describes a Vaishnava as 'one of his two very helpful, constant companions'. The other was Ram himself.

As we have seen, though Kabir did not believe in avatars, he did not hesitate to use names like Raghunath (the lord of the house of Raghu) and Raghava (in the line of Raghu) for his Ram. In a poem, he recalls that it was Raghunath who took care of his well-being when his life was seriously threatened. More about this poignant poem later. Raghu is said to be the most illustrious ancestor of Dasharatha, the father of Ram. Kabir also uses alternative names of Krishna, like Hari, Govinda and Madhava.

It might seem paradoxical that someone opposed to avatars as a concept should be so comfortable using the names and stories of avatars. But, it is also understandable. You use a name to anchor your emotions. With name comes the narrative. It gives a form to an abstraction. You can philosophise about the nirgun, but can only love someone or something with form. Moreover, various avatar stories were integral to the ecology of Kabir's language and also to his mindscape.

Now, let us come to the story of Kabir's 'initiation' into the way of Ram.

Kabir, after his falling out with the Shaktas, was in search of a suitable guru. His inner voice suggested Ramanand. Although Ramanand was liberal, it would be unlikely that he would initiate a Muslim in the ways of Ram. So, one day, Kabir lay on the steps leading down to the Ganga along the route that Ramanand took for his morning ablutions. In the pre-dawn darkness, Ramanand's foot struck Kabir, and the saint cried out the name of Ram. Kabir claimed Ramanand's shocked utterance as a 'guru-mantra', or initiation. From then on, he began to identify himself as a disciple of Ramanand. When the news reached the saint, he was surprised and called for Kabir. Speaking from behind a curtain, his standard practice when talking to 'impure' Muslims, Ramanand asked Kabir: 'When did I initiate you? Why make false claims?'

'You gave me the touch of your piety and the name of Ram,

even if by chance. What else is required for initiation?' responded Kabir.

Moved by the young man's devotion, Ramanand emerged from behind his curtain and embraced Kabir, declaring him a worthy disciple. The Ramanandi sampradaya continues to venerate Kabir, alongside Ravidas and others born into 'low-caste families', as worthy disciples of the great guru Ramanand.

The story of how Ramanand became Kabir's guru is a parable that makes a profound pedagogical point: overcoming emotional prejudices and intellectual limitations is not a one-way traffic. The teacher and the taught, the guru and the disciple, must learn from each other. A dialogue between open minds, not a self-righteous monologue, is the pathway to genuine learning in the spiritual as well as secular spheres of life.

A Mother's Agony, Death Threats and the Honeytrap

Kabir's closeness to Vaishnavas and their way of life annoyed his mother, provoking bitter recriminations. 'Who has ever uttered the name of Ram in our family!' Kabir reports her exclaiming in anger. 'Ever since this niputa has unthinkingly taken to the Mundi, there has been no happiness around. I wish that those misleading my son lose their sons as well. In fact, I fervently wish death upon these Mundis.'

हमरे कुल कउने राम कहिओ।
जब की माला लई निपूते, तब से सुख न भइओ।
सुनहु जेठानी, सुनहु देरानी, अचरजु एक भइओ।
सात सूत न मुंडीए खोए, इह मुंडीआ किए न मुइओ।

The word 'niputa' means a person not blessed with a son. It is used in north India as a strong rebuke, especially by women. In this usage above, it means a worthless fellow. 'Mundi' was a word used colloquially for a Vaishnava. Here, Kabir's mother seems to be venting her frustrations about her son to other women in the neighbourhood. In the same poem, Kabir records his response, the tone he takes with his mother both sage-like and filial: 'For everyone, the lord—Hari—is the same; my guru has introduced me to him. The lord took care of Prahlada and killed his father Hiranyakashyapa, the demon king. Having acquired the "word" from that guru, I am not interested in family heritage and tradition anymore. Listen, Mother, Kabir is telling you—the company of sants will take away all sins.'

सर्व सखा का एक हरि स्वामी, सो गुरु नाम दयो।
संत प्रहलाद की पैज निज राखी, हरनाखसु नख विदरयो।
घर के देव पितर की छोड़ो, गुरु को सबद लयो।
कहत कबीर सकल पाप खंडन, संतह से उधरयो।[22]

Kabir hardly refers to his father, but the poet is in constant, if agonised, dialogue with his mother. Obviously, the bond between mother and son was too strong to be snapped even by his 'waywardness'. Their relationship takes an ironic and tragic turn when Nima is made to lead a delegation to the sultan Sikandar Lodhi against her own son. We will soon hear more from Anantdas about these events, but for the moment let us continue with the dialogue between mother and son.

In another moving poem, Kabir's mother is concerned about his indifference to the family trade: 'O God [she uses the Islamic word, 'khuda'], how is this boy going to survive … He has inscribed the name of Ram all over his body.' For Kabir, 'attachment to the thread on the loom' would have led to snapping the 'love-thread' that tied him to Ram. Not surprisingly, this explanation makes poor Nima weep. A confident Kabir reassures her, 'Listen, dear Mother, the lord of the three worlds will take care of your son's needs.'

तनना बुनना तज्या कबीर । राम नाम लिख लिया सरीर ॥
जब लग करौं नली का नेह । तब लग टूटै राम सनेह ॥
ठाढ़ी रोवै कबीर की माइ । ए लरिका क्यूं जीवै खुदाइ ॥
कहै कबीर सुनहु री माइ । पूरनहारा त्रिभुवन राइ ॥[23]

Kabir, in yet another poem, describes a dramatic scene. A mother is crying and loudly begging passers-by to save her son from drowning in the river. According to the stories about Kabir and some hints dropped by the poet himself, he was nearly drowned in the Ganga as punishment for the maverick ideas he sought to spread. In this particular poem, he turns this attempted murder into a metaphor of immersion in bhakti. Addressing a notional sakhi, or a female companion, in the language a woman would use, the poet conveys the bliss of union with his lord, his beloved. The numerous voices Kabir adopts and the quick movement of moods and metaphors turn the lines into a feat of poetic genius:

Sant Kabir has drowned in the river;
his mother is desperately calling out for help.
But what is the point?
The sant himself is thirsty for the nectar
raining from the clouds that look and sound like Ram.
O, my sakhi, the river Ganga is overflowing;
my whole existence is drinking from it.
Sanak and Sanandan have already drowned themselves in it;
and it is for this that Rudra meditates.
Kabir has realised his true self, has earned bamek;*
he has become one with the clouds filled with nectar.

* Vivek or wisdom

कबीरा संत नदी गयौ बहि रे ।
ठाढ़ी माइ कराड़ै टेरै, है कोई ल्यावै गहि रे ॥
बादल बानी राम घन उनया बरिषै अमृत धारा ।
सखी नीर गंग भरि आई, पीवै प्रान हमारा ॥
जहाँ बहि लागे सनक-सनंदन, रुद्र ध्यान धरि बैठे ।

सुयं प्रकास आनंद बमेक मैं घन आनंद कबीर ह्वै पैठे ॥[24]

Threatened by Kabir's increasing influence and jealous of his popularity, his detractors try to destroy his reputation by all means, including public humiliation and even trying to lay a honeytrap. Anantdas tells of an incident that (amusingly) underlines the Brahmins' sense of entitlement and is indicative of the 'threat' Kabir represented to power. A rumour is set afloat that Kabir has prepared a feast for everyone. People begin arriving at the appointed hour, much to Kabir's astonishment. Unable to do something, he slips away and hides. But his Hari takes charge and assuming Kabir's form, fills everybody's plate to the brim, even giving them food to take back home. When Kabir slinks back from his hiding place and asks his family how they had coped with a hungry and, no doubt, angry crowd, they are surprised: 'Why talk in this strange way? Were you not here all this time?' Kabir immediately understands and is deeply grateful to his lord.

Having spread the rumour of Kabir's feast amongst the Shudras, the Brahmins and sanyasis keep away, waiting for news of Kabir's public humiliation to spread. The miracle leaves them fuming. They show up in large numbers and harangue Kabir for feeding the Shudras and ignoring 'respectable' society. The Brahmins come armed with curses, but the sanyasis have more potent weapons at hand, like swords. 'Leave the city,' they scream at Kabir, 'or you are going to be killed right here.' In desperation, the poet asks the murderous mob: 'But what have I done? I just do my work and remember Ram. Whose property have I snatched? Which woman have I ogled?' The 'respectables' are unmoved. Eventually, Kabir's lord must perform the miracle of the feast all over again. Even then, some of these angry gentlemen, while praising the sumptuous food, suspect foul play: 'This wretched weaver must be making money through questionable sources. He must be reported to the authorities.'

If this story is almost comical, exposing the venality and towering self-regard of the 'respectables' who see fit to rule over

the impropriety and respectability of others, the story of the honeytrap, as told by Anantdas and also mentioned by Kabir, is deeply moving. The two well-known Kabir poems alluding to this attempted seduction refer to the two women assigned to the job simply as 'Maya', illusion. In the first poem, Maya requests Kabir to at least have a look and offers herself in all her manifestations to him. Her erotic charms are supplemented by her offer of access to all manner of wealth and power, what Hindus know as the ashta siddhis and nava nidhis, that is, eight varieties of superpower and nine treasures. 'I am happy with my life,' Kabir tells her tersely, 'made meaningful by the grace of guru.' But Maya persists, and in the subsequent poem we come to understand that she has come in the form of not one but two enchanting women.

Although in Anantdas's description, there is only one woman. Uninhibited and bold, she invites Kabir to satisfy his lust with her 'at least for a few days, for why waste life without enjoying it with a willing damsel like me?' (जब लग लीया न सुख हमारा। तब लग झूठा जनम तुम्हारा। इतनी मानौ बात हमारी। बहुत नहीं तो राखौ दिन चारी।) Kabir's response, found in his own poem, has been partly repeated verbatim by Anantdas. After the initial harsh sarcasm, Kabir becomes reflective and then compassionate, inviting the women to join him in his unceasing sadhana for Ram:

Sisters, please go back
The kohl in your eyes looks like poison
I have discarded anjan*, adopted nirnajan#
I must really, however,
admire those who have sent you to seduce me
You are inviting me to have a look
at your well made-up selves,
claiming to have come from paradise
just to make me your man
But to me, one of you is mother and the other sister
Please tell me, what calamity made you leave
your paradise for my Kali yuga of suffering?
I am Kabir the weaver,
uninterested in whatever you have to offer
Please go back to your paradise
of pleasures, fine garments and exhilarating fragrances
What are you going to get from this lowly weaver?
I am accountable to my lord
Try however hard, this stone will not melt
Listen, I am Kabir, born as a weaver
If you really care for me, as you claim,
please join me as my mother and my maternal aunt
in my wanderings in the forests.

* kohl   # the unmarked

तुम घर जाहु हमारी बहनाँ। विष लागै तुम्हरै नैनाँ॥
अंजन छाँड़ि निरंजन रातें, नाँ किसहीं का दैनाँ।
बलि जाऊँ ताकी जिन तुम्ह पठाई, एक माइ एक बहना॥
राती खांडी देखि कबीरा, देखि हमारा सिंगारौ।
सरग लोक थैं हम चलि आईं, करन कबीर भतारौ॥
सरग लोक में क्या दुख पड़िया, तुम आईं कलि मांहीं।
जाति जुलाहा नाम कबीरा, अजहूँ पतीजौ नाँहीं॥
तहाँ जाहु जहाँ पाट पटंबर, अगर चंदन घसि लीनाँ।
आइ हमारै कहा करोगी, हम तो जात कमीनाँ॥
साहिब मेरा लेखा माँगे, लेखा क्यूंकर दीजे।

जे तुम जतन करौ बहुतेरा, पाहन नीर न भीजै ॥
जाति जुलाहा नाम कबीरा, बन बन फिरौं उदासी।
आसि पासि तुम्ह फिरि फिरि बैसो, एक माउ एक मासी ॥[25]

It is for us to imagine the impact of these stirring words on the women.

United against His Poetry, They Drag Him to Sikandar's Court

The irony of the attempts to humiliate or honeytrap a soul as pure as Kabir fades in comparison to the supreme irony of his own mother leading a delegation to Sikandar Lodhi to file an official complaint about Kabir's activities. When Sikandar, the sultan of Delhi between 1489 and 1517, visits Banaras, Kabir's opponents see it as an opportunity to settle scores. Despite this delegation finding mention in the popular legends around the life of Kabir, court chronicles do not have a record of any complaint. Maybe a military official acted on behalf of the sultan. Maybe the court chroniclers did not think the complaint worth their time. In any case, the Kabir-Sikandar imbroglio is entrenched in cultural memory.

Anantdas's description is cinematic. His account gives us crucial insight into the conflicts over Kabir's ideas and reveals the alliance struck up by regressive forces within both Hindu and Muslim communities in Banaras. The 'pious' Brahmins had no qualms joining hands with the equally 'pious' maulanas against their common enemy—the weaver with the gifts of a poet.

Many modern admirers of Kabir see him as an apostle of Hindu-Muslim unity, but this story suggests that the establishment Hindus and Muslims of his city were united in their disgust for him rather than in their appreciation. His poetry questions organised religion's monopoly on spiritual affairs and rejects the religious identity conferred at birth, in favour of individuality and a credo fashioned through experience, learning and searching for answers to one's questions rather than accepting the received wisdom of priests.

It is a sad irony that Kabir's mother is among the complainants; perhaps, she was led to believe that Sikandar, acting like a family or community elder, would put some sense into her son, persuading him to return to his family and community. Maybe she was told that Sikandar had respect and regard for Sufis and other sadhakas and so no harm would come to Kabir. Whatever her reason, in Anantdas's words, she 'loses her mind' and joins the voices of incrimination.

Sikandar, for his part, is baffled by the urgency of the petitioners. Why are they insistent that Kabir be taught so severe a lesson that his case should serve as a deterrent to others? In what way had this apparently humble weaver harmed the city's high and mighty? 'Had he stolen some land,' asks a bemused Sikandar, 'a village, or even a whole district?'

The answer is blunt: 'He has done something much more serious.

He has dared to tread a new path. He has discarded the ways of Islam and does not care for Hindu traditions. He encourages people to break caste rules, condemns the Vedas and places of pilgrimage, and criticises various deities—Shankar, Ganesha, Shakti. He ignores various planets, rejects the Ekadashi fast and fire sacrifice and even ridicules the universally venerable Brahmins. He ignores family relations and duties, including service to elders. In fact, he just condemns all religious faith systems and does not care for the six schools of philosophy or calendar of holy dates. He has thus corrupted so many people. He is neither a Hindu nor a Muslim.'

At the end of this litany comes the crux of the complaint that united Hindu and Muslim religious 'leaders', the cause for all their anger: 'No one is going to listen to us as long as this wretched weaver continues to live in Kashi.'

कहै सिकंदर क्या है भाई।
गांव-प्रगना लिया छिनाई॥
गांव-प्रगना नहीं लिया।
जुलाहै ऐक अमारग किया॥
मुसलमान की छोड़ी रीती।
अरु हिन्दू की भानैं छीती॥
निंदै तीरथ, निंदै बेदू।
निंदै नवग्रह सूरज चंदू॥
निंदै संकर निंदै माई।
निंदै सारद गणपति राई॥
निंदै ग्यारस होम सराध्य।
निंदै बांभन जग आराध्य॥
निंदै माता-पिता की सेवा।
बहन भांणजी अरु सब देवा॥
निंदै सकल धरम की आसा।
षट दरसन अरु बारह मासा॥
ऐसी बिधि सब लोक बिगारा।
हींदू मुसलमान तैं न्यारा॥
जब लग जुलहा कासी होई।
ता तैं हमैं मानैं न कोई॥[26]

With reference to Islam, Anantdas is content with saying that Kabir has discarded the ways of the religion (मुसलमान की छोड़ी रीती). When it comes to Hinduism, though, Anantdas provides a comprehensive list of Kabir's offences against the tradition. Apart from emphasising that the poet had forsaken the faith into which he was born, the difference in Anantdas's approach indicates the uniformity of Islamic religious practice. Regardless of the cultural and historical varieties and specificities, the foremost requirement of the Islamic faith applies to all Muslims—a belief in and acceptance of the infallibility of 'god's own word' as recorded in the Koran by the Prophet. Hindu tradition, by contrast, has a bewildering number of scriptures, practices and deities around which one can structure one's faith.

Varied and diffused though the practices and texts of Hinduism might be, there is no question in Anantdas's mind, or for that matter Kabir's, that a Hindu community is clearly identifiable. This works as powerful evidence against the theory, popular in some circles, that Hinduism was 'constructed' as a systematic faith and community during the colonial era. Centuries before the British rule, Kabir was castigating both Hindus and 'Turuks' (Muslims) for fighting each other and being ignorant of the essence of Ram and Rahman: 'हिन्दू कहै राम हमारा, तुरक कहै रहमाना। आपस में दोऊ लड़त मरत हैं, मरम न काहू जाना।'[27]

Also, notice the core concern of the Hindu and Muslim establishment—'No one is going to listen to us.' They are, of course, quite correct. Kabir's voice appeals to intelligence and a sense of fair play. He proposes a self-reliant spirituality, cutting out the middle men so prized in organised religions. By questioning the need for an intermediary between the individual worshipper and god, Kabir challenges the vast, multilayered power of organised religions, whether located in the mosque, church or temple. He questions the hold of organised religions on human consciousness. No wonder the Hindu and Muslim clerics were worried. Far from being a negligible, marginalised voice, Kabir was an influential social presence whom the city's mighty could not afford to ignore. In fact, they were so desperate to get rid of him that they begged Sikandar, calling him their 'mother and father' (mai-baap), to banish this thorn in their sides from the city.

Sikandar sends for Kabir. Anantdas takes this opportunity to tell us that the 'dark-complexioned Kabir is as handsome as Kamadeva himself'. This is likely the only reference in any contemporary or near-contemporary source to Kabir's physical appearance. He also notes Kabir's nonchalance:

राम भरोसे गिनैं न काहू। सब मिलि राजा रंक रिसाऊ।
राखनहारा राम है। मारि सकै न कोई।
पातिस्याहू न डरूं। करता करै सो होई।[28]

Due to Ram's support, Anantdas observes, Kabir is self-assured in the company of everyone from a pauper to a plutocrat. What harm could befall him when he is under Ram's protection? 'Having faith in him,' Kabir says, 'I am not scared, even of an emperor.'

When he arrives before Sikandar, Kabir is asked to explain his conduct. The emperor is unimpressed, not so much by the poet's answers but by his 'attitude'. Kabir, the 'child' of Allah and Ram, could not care less for worldly power, the sultan of Delhi being no exception. Moreover, he challenges his detractors about their practices in the very presence of Sikandar, inviting the sultan's wrath for displaying such 'arrogance'. Sikandar orders Kabir's execution, but every method fails, including attempts to drown him, burn him alive and have him trampled by an elephant. Kabir continues to sing praises of his lord, and miracles continue to happen. These and other attempts to torment him were traditionally known as 'kasni'; it is believed that Kabir survived fifty-two kasnis in his lifetime through divine intervention.

The word 'kasni' comes from the goldsmith's way of assessing the purity of precious metals. He rubs a piece of metal on his kasauti, the touchstone, and comes to his conclusion on the basis of the mark left by the gold. This rubbing is 'kasna', from which follows the noun 'kasni', the tests which Kabir was forced to undergo by those envious of his influence. He writes of these trials by fire in two poems, though he does not divulge details, like the names of those who wanted to engineer his death or any particular incident. In one poem, he hints at three attempts to have him trampled by an elephant. He reveals in a different poem how his enemies tried to drown him:

> Though pure, still I, Kabir
> Was chained and thrown in the deep waters of the mighty Ganga
> But when my mind is calm, why would my body tremble?
> I focussed my thoughts on the lotus-feet of the lord
> And lo, here I am
> Sitting unchained on a deerskin on the waters
> Raghunath protects me
> In water, on earth, everywhere

> गंग गुसाइन गहन गंभीर। जंजीर बांधि करि खरे कबीर॥
> मन न डिगै, तन काहे को डराइ। चरन कमल चित्त रह्यौ समाइ॥
> गंगा की लहरि मेरी टूटी जंजीर। मृगछाल पर बैठे कबीर॥
> कहि कबीर कोऊ संग न साथ। जल थल राखन है रघुनाथ॥[29]

Sikandar is astounded by the miracles that keep Kabir alive, and he turns into an ardent admirer of the poet. He apologises profusely for his earlier antagonism, conceding the depth and essence of Kabir's sadhana and the meaning of his Ram bhakti, which the 'mullas and the pandits are incapable of appreciating'. He wants Kabir to accept some royal gifts—insignia, gold, land grants—to seal Sikandar's patronage and support. Kabir has no use for these riches and asks only for the sultan's leave.

Celebrating Kabir's victorious return, Anantdas echoes one of the poet's own utterances, 'Bhakti takes away a multitude of sins, and Hari, the lord himself, follows after the bhakta.' (कोटि पाप हरि भगति नसावै। भगतन पीछैं हरि चलि आवै।) Kabir's expressions of self-confidence are so numerous and sometimes so insistent that some think him to be quite arrogant. But the 'arrogant' poet also shows a touching humility in his verse. In any case, his confidence stems from the purity of his acts, the authenticity of his words, and his moral courage. He did not waver in the face of social castigation or even death. He could both stand up to his own people and speak truth to power—all without any rancour on his part. Kabir's self-belief was a manifestation of the strength of his bhakti:

> Seeing you everywhere, always murmering, 'You, you,'
> None of I is left in me, I have become you.

> तूँ तूँ करता तूँ भया, मुझ में रही न हूँ।
> वारी फेरी बलि गयी, जित देखौं तित तूँ॥[30]

Kabir's relationship with his lord was requited. Such was his devotion, so unblemished was his love that the lord reciprocated. This is in line with Kabir's philosophy of give and take, also evident in his relationship with his guru Ramanand—the idea that a dialogue, a conversation, is infinitely preferable to a monologue.

In Search of Solitude

Why were Kabir's detractors 'forced' to escalate matters up to the sultan? Mostly because they were smarting from having failed so miserably to check his influence themselves. Kabir's fame was sky-rocketing, despite his obvious lack of interest in self-publicity. He still got a lot of 'good press' as news spread of his willingness to confront the most powerful community leaders, his ability to resist temptation and his refusal to back down in the face of threats to his life. He had an aura, and his opponents' obvious frustrations only added to its glow.

Anantdas tells us that, 'Kabir tried to keep away from his fame, like a demure, young woman hides her baby bump.' But people thronged around him day in and day out. He was left with hardly any moments to himself, hardly any of the privacy and solitude he craved to be able to reflect and to be in 'dialogue with his Ram'. Moments of solitude are necessary for us to assess our words, deeds and their impact on others. Seeking such solitude is neither to discard company nor does it mean feeling discarded. The search for solitude is qualitatively different from the desperation and frustration that leads to loneliness. A lonely person feels slighted and is depressed. They want to be part of the crowd and feel sorrow if they perceive themselves to be shunned. Loneliness is an imposition, by others or even oneself; solitude is a choice.

Kabir's is the universal dilemma of creative and reflective souls. He spoke and sang about the bliss and agony of finding a way to connect with and touch people and then the ambivalence he felt about the resulting fame, of the mania of those who desired a connection not just with his words but with him.

One night, he comes up with a trick to rid himself of the baggage of fame. (तब कबीर एक बुधि विचारी। लोक बड़ाई धरूँ उतारी॥) He fills a bottle with water, goes to a sex worker first thing in the morning and convinces her to join him on a walk around the crowded avenues of the city.

His detractors crow. The self-appointed guardians of respectability make their sweeping condemnations:

> This is how
> these disgusting hypocrites from the lowly castes act.
> A few days in supposed bhakti,
> and now, see, there he goes—
> the great bhakta Kabir,
> with a prostitute and a bottle of liquor.

भगति कीया चाहै सब कोई,
नीच जाति तैं कैसे होई।
दिन दस भगति कबीरै कीन्हीं,
अब देखौ गनिका संगि लीन्हीं।[31]

Enjoying the spectacle, Kabir wonders if anyone would bother to see through the 'scene' and take the trouble to search beneath the surface, or would they easily be satisfied by the constructed perception? Most, if not all, fail Kabir's test, including his favourite royal disciple Birsingh Baghel. Kabir makes a point to visit the king, who has already heard about the embarrassing scandal. Seeing Kabir, the king, influenced by the gossip, shows none of his usual respect and warmth, instead turning his face away in contempt.

Unperturbed, Kabir empties his 'liquor' bottle on the floor. Asked to explain this strange act, he says that an admirer in Puri, a panda, or priest, at the famous Jagannath temple in faraway Odisha had burnt his foot and cried out in pain and that this water would soothe him. Having said this, Kabir quietly leaves the palace. He is happy with his trick and thankful to the sex worker. Having shown how easy it is to manipulate perception and earn himself a reputation as a drunkard and lecher, Kabir is finally left alone. He has what he craves—solitude.

But only for a few days.

The king, who wants to believe Kabir, sends his fastest riders to Puri. They return to confirm the veracity of Kabir's claim that a temple priest had indeed burnt his foot and was soothed at the exact time that Kabir had poured the water on the floor of the palace hundreds of miles away. The king is ashamed of doubting the integrity of his guru. His wife advises him to go to Kabir and seek forgiveness, but the king is afraid that his guru might curse him. Gathering his courage, Birsingh Baghel heads out to the poet's home. He is welcomed with Kabir's usual love and hospitality. 'Get rid of your fear and guilt,' he tells the king. 'I am not angry. Why would I be? I nurture no particular affection or enmity for anyone; I make no distinction between prince and pauper.'

डारि डारि माथै का बोझू,
मेरै मन में नहीं किरोधू।
मेरै बैर न मेरै भाऊ,
मेरै रंक न मेरै राऊ।[32]

Kabir's critics had to resign themselves to waiting for some other opportunity (like Sikandar Lodhi's visit in the future) to punish the impudent weaver.

Whatever the lessons Kabir's frustrated critics hoped to teach him, the moral of this parable remains relevant through the ages. An insistence on solitude, for time to think, shows an individual's refusal to be an unquestioning cog in the collective. Such introspection can lead to interrogations of the nature of self and of social relations and mindsets. It is dangerous to give people the time and space to think for themselves. This is why authoritarian regimes, whether nominally on the political left or right, work so hard to make whole populations believe that demands for privacy and solitude are a social offence, a moral vice.

The writer Dave Eggers's novel *The Circle* (2013) paints a horrifying picture of corporate rule, of giant technology companies that want to exercise total control over both employees and consumers. The 'community' (an euphemism for corporate bosses) promotes 'transparency' and 'sharing' as moral virtues and posits that having access to every moment of everyone's life is for the greater common good. 'Privacy is theft' is the company's dictum. Nobody is allowed to opt out on pain of death.

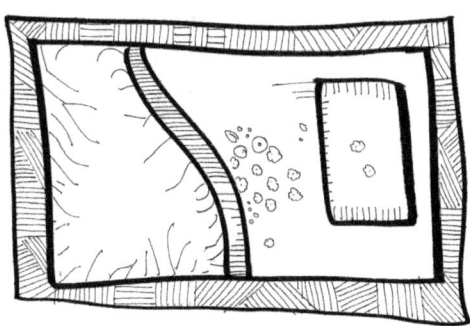

The systematic elimination of privacy is no more just dystopian fantasy. We live in a world in which 'real' lives are manufactured for the purposes of 24x7 'reality' TV, a world in which all of us willingly participate by 'constructing' ourselves on social media, in which our most private moments are compulsively, constantly 'shared'. Worst of all, we embrace social media as if enormous resources aren't being devoted to our manipulation, as if we are vying voluntarily to become lambs for the slaughter.

Kabir's dramatic insistence on privacy, for time away from his followers and admirers, for solitude in which to reflect and seek dialogue with his inner self may have been important in his time. It is nothing short of an imperative in ours.

'Who Is Going to Cry for Me?'

All his life, Kabir searched for authentic answers to questions rooted in spiritual anguish and anger at the structured injustice of social systems. Being a poet, he put in words his moments of bliss, anxiety, faith and doubt. His irony hits hard and his longing moves us to tears. He celebrates life, even as he emphasises its inexorable march towards death.

A great poet, incomparable sadhaka, untiring seeker of the truth, caring teacher and revered miracle worker he may have been, but what Kabir wanted us to recall at all times was that he was human. Only too human. Drained of energy, he once wrote:

> Night over, day too passes
> Hair once as black as a bumblebee
> Turning now as white as a heron
> How can an unbaked vessel contain any water?

The body withers away, the swan is preparing to leave
Having warded off crows all my life
My arm is now aching
Well, my story is over

रैनि गयी मत दिन भी जाइ,
भंवर गये बग बैठे आइ।
काचै करवै रहै न पानी,
हंस चलिआ काया कुमलानी।
काग उड़ावत भुजा पिरानी,
कहि कबीर मेरी कथा सिरानी।[33]

It seems his wife Loi had already passed away and the end was fast approaching. Born and brought up in Banaras, having spent his entire life in the city, Kabir decided to move to Maghar (near Gorakhpur) in his last days.

This choice offers a last example of his congenitally subversive spirit. It was (and still is) believed that dying in Banaras ensured a place in the heavens. Dying in Maghar, on the other hand, ensured rebirth as an ass. Many Hindus from all over the world choose Kashiwas (staying in Banaras) for their final days. But Kabir was scornful:

People lack common sense—
If dying in Kashi was sufficient for liberation
why should Kabir have supplicated Ram all his life?
I have made some 'profit' in my life—
I have progressed a lot since I was born,
undergone a metamorphosis.
I have merged with my Hari
as water merges with water.
This is not incredulous;
anyone sincere in bhakti
can achieve this state of mind.
You only need a guru's grace

and the company of noble souls.
Armed with these, this weaver
has vanquished the whole world.
Listen, my dears, Kabir is telling you,
don't be deluded,
Maghar is no different from Kashi
if your mind is focussed on Ram.

लोका मति के भोरा रे।
जो कासी तन तजै कबीरा, तौ रामहिं कौन निहोरा रे॥
तब हम वैसे, अब हम ऐसे, इहै जनम का लाहा।
ज्यूं जल में पैस न निकसै, यूं हरि मिल्या जुलाहा॥
राम भगति परि जाकौ हित चित्त, ताकौ अचिरज काहा।
गुर प्रसाद साध की संगति, जग जीतें जाइ जुलाहा॥
कहत कबीर सुनहु रे संतौ, भ्रंमि परे जिनि कोई।
जस कासी तस मगहर ऊसर, हिरदै राम मति होई॥[34]

Whether he moved to Maghar alone or with some of his companions and followers, the literature does not say. But in this poem, Kabir takes his standard position—that of a rational

spiritualist. It is consistent with his belief in bhakti, in doing the spiritual work necessary to develop a connection with god, rather than submit to quick fixes and superstition. His confidence in the strength of his faith makes it easy for him to dismiss dying in Kashi as a shortcut to heaven.

Understandably, this poem is very popular with Kabir's rationalist and secularist admirers. But in another poem, Kabir confesses to homesickness in Maghar, to his longing for the familiarity of Kashi. Instead of excoriating others for lacking intelligence, he identifies the same fault in himself and, probably for the first and only time in his poetry, criticises his bhakti as 'mean':

> I did not have enough sadhana in my previous birth
> Thus I am like a fish out of water
> I left Kashi without any thought
> Only Ram knows what is to happen to me
> I spent all my life in the city of Shiva
> Strangely, I have chosen Maghar to die in
> Having done penance for many years in Kashi
> I chose Maghar to wait for death
> How mean is my bhakti
> That I equated Maghar with Kashi
> As the bhaktas, including Shiva himself, know
> Kabir is dying with the name of Ram on his lips

जिउ जल छोड़ बाहर भइयो मीना। पूरब जनम हउ तप का हीना॥
अब कहु राम कवन गति मोरी। तजीले बनारस मति भई थोरी॥
सकल जनम सिवपुरी गवाइआ। मरती बार मगहर उठि आइआ॥
बहुत बरस तप कीआ कासी। मरन भइआ मगहर का बासी॥
कासी मगहर सम बीचारी। ओछी भगति कैसे उतरसि पारी॥
कहु गुर गजि सिव सभु को जानै। मुआ कबीर रमत श्री रामै॥[35]

Shall we argue, then, that this poem is not 'authentic' and has been interpolated into Kabir's works at a later date? That is how some of his 'secular' admirers console themselves. Unfortunately for them, the source of this poem, the Adi Granth, is one of the oldest and most authentic collections of Kabir poems. Or shall we argue that, at the end of his life, the weaver from Kashi finally got it right and repented his condemnation of organised religion? That is how the religious establishment likes to interpret these lines.

But, if you read sensitively and carefully, the poem, far from being any kind of recantation, is a poet's moving tribute to the city of his birth. It is not a paean to Kashi the holy city, dying in which guarantees an ascent to heaven; instead, it's a celebration of his life in the city. Kashi, here, is a living, breathing city rather than a city for the dead, a city in which a thoughtful, curious child grew to find spiritual meaning and in the process became a revered poet, teacher and philosopher. It was in Kashi that Kabir experimented with the Shaktas, explored many systems of sadhana, from Nath panthi to Sufi, before finding in the Vaishnava 'a true friend' who helped him focus his energies entirely on Ram. Kabir died in Maghar, in the throes of nostalgia for Kashi. And, as we heard from Anantdas at the beginning of this chapter, with Kabir's departure, Kashi 'lost its shine'. The city and its illustrious son were entangled in a relationship that went beyond the easy dichotomy of either total acceptance or total rejection.

A sensitive poet, Kabir lived his life in proximity of death. He composed his poems with an eye on posterity: 'The body is transitory, hence Kabir composes poetry.' (छिन महि बितसै यह सरीरा। तिहि कारन पद रचै कबीरा ॥)[36] Malik Muhammad Jayasi was insistent on signing himself into the poem so that 'the reader of this poem, hopefully, will also remember me—the poet'. (जो यह पढ़ै कहानी, हम सँवरे दुइ बोल।) Kabir knows with characteristic self-assurance that readers will mourn his loss:

> I cry for the world
> No one cries for me
> Only he cries for me
> Who can discern the word[37]

मैं रोवूँ या जगत को मोकों रोवे ना कोय।
मोकूं रोवै सो जना जो सबद विवेकी होय।

Indeed. Those who care for the mysteries of the word, for poetry imbued in angst as well as bliss, for the expression of a worldview steeped in intelligent curiosity have always remembered Kabir with gratitude.

III

East and West in Kabir's Time

A Modern Poet in Medieval Times?

Here's a thought experiment I conducted with a young friend. 'What comes to your mind,' I asked him, 'when I say the word "modernity?"' He replied immediately in perfect English, 'Keeping up with the world in terms of style, ideas, etc.' What does he mean by 'the world', I asked. After a moment's pregnant silence, 'Western countries', came the reply.

This young man expressed the prevalent belief that to be modern is to, in some significant sense, imitate the West. It is a shibboleth rooted in the influential knowledge system that tells us that modernity is a Western export to the non-Western world. But, Western export or not, what does modernity mean?

The term 'modern' is etymologically connected to 'mode'. In popular perception, it is associated with anything new, just off the shelves. A thing or an idea in circulation, in fashion. It also carries the connotation of 'improved'. Philosophically, modern indicates a specific orientation of ethics and knowledge leading to the emergence of a new kind of consciousness of the relationship between human being, nature and society. Historically, this new consciousness is related to the spread of commerce and consequent changes in social equations. Many people see modernity as a sort of a violent break from tradition. While modernity may appear like a rupture, if you study its emergence in any society carefully, this 'rupture' can clearly be seen as the qualitative outcome of a series of gradual quantitative changes. No society, simply put, becomes modern overnight.

Until a few decades ago, it was almost universally accepted that the colonisation of non-European countries by European powers was the impetus for modernisation. Writing in the middle of the twentieth century, Muktibodh, an eminent Hindi poet, thought Kabir and 'some Maharashtrian sants' to be much closer to the 'modern mind' than Tulsidas.[1] Linda Hess, translating poems from the *Bijak of Kabir* in 1983, wrote that 'the problems involved in using translations to analyse the style of a medieval Indian poet for a twentieth century Western audience are minimised in the case of Kabir.'[2] Dilip Chitre, an eminent Marathi poet and a fine translator of the seventeenth-century Bhakti poet Tukaram, finds the latter, like Kabir, anticipating the anguish and anxieties of the modern man of 'two centuries later'.[3]

In these observations, 'modern' is indicative of a mind which is sceptical, wary of accepting irrational prejudices and unjust social structures as 'divine' design and judges a human being for their deeds, not their status at birth. Poets like Kabir and Tukaram are described as 'surprisingly' modern for having had such a mindset, the implication being that their society was medieval and stagnant till it came in contact with Europe through colonisation. But what if Kabir and others like him, far from being ahead, were in fact natural products of their time? After all, can people supposed to be ahead of their time be popular and influential among their contemporaries?

While an emphasis on individuality and a rational approach to life are identified as characteristics of an enlightened, modern mindset, industrialisation and urbanisation define the modern social structure. A rational approach and critical thinking cannot become a widespread tendency unless the process of knowledge formation is made truly participatory. In the modern era of the West, knowledge, whether secular or divine, was vernacularised, so that scholarly discourse was conducted in German, English and French, for instance, rather than Latin. Technology and industrialisation helped free individuals from some of the drudgeries of everyday life and enabled them to achieve their full potential. The rapid urbanisation of society also resulted in significant changes to social structures and relationships—joint families gave way to nuclear ones; the political system moulded itself around the individual, so that democracy, in which an individual can have their say via the vote, became acknowledged as the ideal modern form of governance. But for well over half a century now, we have experienced the heat of modernity's flipside too—a soul-deadening spiritual emptiness, the metamorphosis of human beings into robotic consumers, excessive self-centredness and a consequent lack of empathy, and crises in our personal relationships.

As the sociologist Immanuel Wallerstein warned in 1999, 'The modern world-system, as a historical system, has entered into a terminal crisis and is unlikely to exist in fifty years. However, since its outcome is uncertain, we do not know whether the resulting system (or systems) will be better or worse than the one in which we are living, but we do know that the period of transition will be a terrible time of trouble.'[4] We must realise the urgency of taking immediate steps in the right direction. There is no possibility of a return to some quasi-fictional golden past. The undoing of history is a mirage—it makes little sense to condemn modernity and glorify tradition, or vice versa, as there is no straightforward division between the two. Understanding the dynamics of modernity is crucial in order to have a proper sense of the world as we know it; without such an appreciation for historical forces and compulsions, humankind cannot hope to improve its lot and progress.

The traditional fourfold ideal of life, the purushartha chatushtya, is helpful here. It was articulated in the context of personal ethics, but I see it as also providing the basis for a balanced view of the evolution of any society. As in every significant stage of history, the attitudes and inclinations indicating the advent of 'modernity' emerged out of radical shifts in the spheres of kama, desires and needs, and artha, the means and methods to satisfy these desires. Such changes, naturally enough, gave rise to new questions in the sphere of dharma, personal conduct and social order, and moksha, the individual's spiritual quest.

Europe itself was shrouded in medieval darkness until the fifteenth century when it had its Renaissance, a reawakening or rebirth, thanks to the rediscovery of ancient Greek knowledge and a shift of focus from the divine to the human. Alongside the Renaissance and immediately afterwards, between the fifteenth and seventeenth centuries, was a period of what is known as 'early modernity', during which fundamental changes in ideas regarding divinity, humanity and the cosmos were introduced. The process continued vigorously through the 'long eighteenth century' (1685–1815), including the period of Enlightenment. This historical process was rooted in the spread of commerce and the discontent of merchants with the parasitical feudal classes. The church's traditional control of all kinds of knowledge came under increasing scrutiny; the notion that human behaviour was better regulated by rational persuasion than divine sanction took hold and spread fast. These new ideas led to large-scale industrialisation and further massive transformations in social and individual life. In other words, modernity and Enlightenment led to industrialisation, not vice versa. Let us also not forget that it was the ruthless colonial plunder of Asia, Africa and the Americas that also made the European Industrial Revolution possible.

It would be logical to raise the question: how was India doing in the sphere of artha, in the pursuit of material prosperity, and in similar areas before British colonisation? Did Indian society have enabling features of modernity—like the spread of commerce, a growing popularity of individuality and rationality and the vernacularisation of knowledge? If so, then the next logical question would be: did this process lead to industrialisation and subsequent widespread social change? If not, why? What prevented a society experiencing its own early modernity and enlightenment from going onto the next stage by becoming industrialised? Did commerce play a wider role in that society, or was it merely confined to the exchange of luxuries amongst the ruling elite? Was there a real movement towards urbanisation or were Indian cities just centres of pilgrimage and political power with little serious commercial activity taking place? Was India, then, a dynamic society with the potential to become modern, or a stagnant, moribund society waiting for some external power to shake it out of its medieval slumber?

Many people, not least in Britain, continue to believe that but for the British rule, India would not have become modern.

The fact is that India in the sixteenth century had a greater urban population than contemporary Europe, or, indeed, than India had during the British Raj. Far from being a modernising force, the British need to be held accountable for the deliberate deurbanisation and deindustrialisation of India and for the destruction of Indian commerce. We will see in this chapter how the British Raj and its knowledge systems deliberately disrupted India's own early, vernacular modernity. The Raj, of course, was forced to bring in elements of the Western version of modernity but within what the historian Nicholas Dirks calls the 'cultural technologies of rule'. This led to mixed results. One of the disastrous effects was the internalisation of a distorted view of

Indian society and vernacular wisdom and its interaction with the Sanskrit and Persian intellectual world. Any understanding of Indian society without engaging with vernacular sources is bound to be skewed. This caution is important because even well-meaning intellectuals continue to privilege Sanskrit and Persian over vernacular expressions of Indian thought. For instance, Kabir, one of the most argumentative Indians, merits only two or three mentions in Amartya Sen's eponymous volume.

I have been trying to listen carefully to those in history, as well as in my own time, who speak neither the 'language of the gods' (Sanskrit) nor the 'language of the lords' (Persian or English). It has led to exciting results. In this chapter, I will be reflecting on the dynamics of vernacular modernity and the making of the public sphere of Bhakti on the basis of such 'listening'. But let us first hear a very popular leader and effective social influencer from another society.

This man considered Jewish people vile and born liars. Indeed, he authored a book titled *On the Jews and Their Lies*, in which he calls them 'vermin', demands the destruction of their homes and claims he and his people are to blame for having left Jewish people alive. He extolls his followers to make sure 'these people either leave our dear fatherland forever or stay back merely as our slaves'. The writer is not Adolf Hitler, but Martin Luther, a theologist and key figure of the Reformation, and so, effectively, the founder of the Protestant church. Some British scholars in the colonial era have described Kabir as the 'Indian Luther'. But Luther was Kabir's junior and shared none of the latter's openness. Luther's screed against the Jews (needless to say, a seminal influence on Hitler a couple of centuries later) was written not in the heat of youth but just three years before his death.[5] It was only long after the Holocaust that various Lutheran churches in the USA and Europe distanced themselves from the anti-Semitism of their founder.

The ritual of burning books of those they disagreed with was a cherished characteristic of European Christians in those days, and they spread this habit to other parts of the world. Even the word of god, as such, was not spared. Lutheran Protestants in south India accused the Roman Catholic Jesuits (their competitors in the business of soul-saving) of hunting and burning down copies of the Tamil translations of the Bible they had published.[6] Such was the zeal among various Christian sects to burn and destroy, that the sixteenth-century Spanish polymath Michael Servetus, a considerable figure in the history of medicine, fled the Catholics in France only to be executed as a heretic by the Calvinists in Geneva. Servetus had, writes Hans J. Hillenbrand, a professor of Religion at Duke University, the 'dubious honour that Protestants in Geneva burned him and his books in reality, and Catholics in France in effigy'.[7]

If the Koran was spared the flames in Luther's Germany, then in Basel—the Swiss city on the country's border with Germany and France—the local council decided to burn its Latin translation. The order was rescinded only after Luther intervened, arguing that knowledge of the Koran would highlight the 'glory of Christ' to 'the disadvantage of Muslims and the vexation of the devil'.[8] The Koran fared less well in the Spanish Inquisition with fifteenth- and sixteenth-century Catholics burning copies of it as part of efforts to eradicate the substantial influence of Islam on the culture of the Iberian Peninsula. Acknowledging this shameful, grisly European and Christian legacy, the nineteenth-century German poet Heinrich Heine writes in his play *Almansor* that those who 'burn books will in the end burn people too'.

Heine's lines were both a reflection on the past as well as a prophecy. In the spring of 1933, the Nazis launched a campaign to burn books by Heine and other Jewish, hence 'anti-national', writers—a precursor to the Holocaust, the systematic extermination of six million Jews. 'Holocaust' itself is a reference to an ancient sacrificial rite in which the offering is burnt whole. Luther, whose own virulent anti-Semitism was an influence on the Nazis, was a catalyst for the expansion of early modern thought through Europe. His rebellion against the Roman Catholic church was symbolic of a wider rebellion against medievalism, a rejection of supposedly divine ordainment. The early modern attitude, amongst other things, rejected the indulgence of the church and challenged the idea that vast sums of money paid into the coffers of the Catholic church were enough to assure a place in heaven, instead insisting that only a genuinely 'pious' life could earn the grace of god.

Part of Luther's rejection of the Catholic church was to make the Bible available in German, to enable vernacular audiences access the word of god without the need for clerical intermediaries schooled in Latin. Although, what Luther failed to reform was the Christian fondness for burning books, heretics and women who were labelled 'witches'.

This bloodlust, this revelry in death, separated the reformist Luther from the equally, but more progressively iconoclastic Kabir. He may have disliked the Shaktas, just as Tulsidas may have harboured a similar distaste for the Nirgunis, but they were not calling for their ideological opponents to be murdered. Violence had no place in Bhakti, whatever the tenor of the rhetoric or the pitch of the polemic. And to give even imperialists their due, neither the fourteenth-century sultan Firoz Shah Tughlaq nor the fearsome seventeenth-century Mughal Aurangzeb, reviled by Hindus, conceived of so bigoted a project as the persecution, torture and execution of religious and ideological opponents reclassified as heretics. And unlike in early modern Europe, institutionalised witch-burning was not prevalent in 'medieval' India, the land, as British colonialists told us, of sati, a land which could not even think of establishing anything like the Inquisition.

In the previous chapter, we saw that Akbar's grand vizier Abul Fazl, no less, was inspired in his search for a 'non-denominational religiosity' by Kabir—a poet who rose above the binary of Hindu versus Muslim. Akbar's policy of Sulh-e-kul required even the emperor to be above overt religiosity and parochial disputes and to not distinguish between the various faiths contained within the Mughal empire. He tried to rein in, if not entirely eliminate, slavery and the trading of slaves; he also worked to improve the social standing and treatment of both Hindu and Muslim women. These acts imply that Akbar recognised individual agency. He obviously believed that, besides providing protection, it was also the job of the state to encourage people to think and act rationally, to nudge them towards progress in their social attitudes. Akbar had a sure sense of the temper and needs of his time—'mizaj-e-zamana', in Abul Fazl's words. This extremely important phrase tells us that neither Akbar, nor Kabir and Tukaram, nor Abul Fazl, for that matter, were freaks of history. With their own individual geniuses, they and many more were actually representing and responding to the evolving mizaj-e-zamana.[9] It suits a Eurocentric version of history to present Kabir and Tukaram as 'ahead of their time', to portray Akbar as the ruler of a medieval society, static and backwards, while his contemporaries in Europe, burning 'witches' and conducting inquisitions, were to have presided over an enlightened early modern culture.

India was explained away by the Europeans as an area of darkness, a country governed by religious impulse. Too little thought was given to the absence of a church-like institution here. Whereas in Europe, it could appear that you had to seek permission from the church even to breathe, there was no comparable, all-powerful single influence on the lives of the people residing in the subcontinent, where the border between the religious and the secular was porous. And when kings in Europe could not marry without approval from the Vatican, the Mughal emperors of India cared little for the Caliph. Organised religion did not dominate social life in India as it did in Europe; instead, the lack of such an institution as the church coupled with religious and cultural diversity resulted in a uniquely Indian secularism. As the anthropologist Jack Goody reminds his European readers:

> We would have never reached a situation where enlightenment
> in this sense had to take place, had we not been converted to a
> single, dominant, monotheistic faith. In Europe, that religion
> tried to regulate the people's lives in a very radical manner.

In every village, a costly church was erected; a custodian
appointed ... there was little enough space for the secular.[10]

The nineteenth century was one of supreme European self-
confidence in its modernity. The region prided itself on its
rationality and pitied the rest of the world for its lack of intellectual
dynamism and for being largely superstitious. In 1835, Thomas
Macaulay, full of the same European, in particular British, self-
satisfaction, swatted aside the entire body of 'Oriental knowledge'
as superstition; 'a single shelf of a good European library', he writes
in his 'Minute on Education', 'was worth the whole native literature
of India and Arabia'. It was, of course, not at all indicative of any
superstition and intolerance that seven years after Macaulay's
notorious remarks, the British scholar and activist G.J. Holyoke
(credited with coining the term 'secularism') was imprisoned for
six months under the British blasphemy law for suggesting in a
public lecture that god should be retired and given a pension.[11] This
law came under renewed discussion in the late 1980s when some
British Muslims discovered that they couldn't argue in court that
Salman Rushdie had blasphemed in his novel *The Satanic Verses*
as the law protected only the Anglican church against blasphemy.
You enjoyed full freedom of expression in the United Kingdom
so far as other religions were concerned. It took until 2008 for the
British to finally get around to abolishing their blasphemy law.

Britain, so eager to 'modernise' and enlighten the superstitious
Indians, continued to have an 'anti-witchcraft' act in their statute
books until 1951; the last 'witch' incarcerated under this law was
Helen Duncan, just three years before Indian Independence. In
1952, Alan Turing, widely acknowledged as the progenitor of
modern computer science, was charged with 'gross indecency'
and committing a 'crime against nature' and was chemically
castrated because he was gay. It took nearly sixty years for the
British government to apologise for the 'appalling way' Turing
was treated. Britain implemented these cruel and arbitrary laws
as enthusiastically as it conducted its extraordinarily profitable

intercontinental slave trade. Slavery was abolished with much moral preening and fanfare by the British in 1807, only to be replaced by the equally treacherous system of indentured labour. The 'catchment area' for slave labour was Africa; for indentured labour, slavery by another name, it was India.

We can only shake our heads at the ulatbansi—meaning upside-down language, a challenging, wonderfully absurd literary device used by Kabir and other north Indian poets, which I will discuss in the next chapter—that suggests Martin Luther's Jew-hating reformation was a catalyst for the early modern period, while the all-encompassing Bhakti poetry of Kabir, Tukaram and others was a medieval Indian phenomenon.

While trying to upright this ulatbansi, I am not denying the enormous contributions European modernity has made to humanity. All of us, across the world, are forever grateful to individuals, trends, events and systems that contributed to the democratisation of society and the upholding of individual dignity. The point here is to make clear that it is nonsense to contend that colonial rule modernised India, that modern indigenous processes were not already underway. Colonial conquest was a means of economic plunder and, as the victors went about rewriting history, also resulted in the deliberate distortion of knowledge and historical memory.

These distortions opened up fissures, led to a kind of dissociation of sensibility in the minds of the 'native' elite and, indeed, the general populace. We will see in the next chapter how, astonishingly, this dislocation of sensibility continues to affect the treatment of Kabir by modern scholars. Ignoring all evidence of him making a conscious intellectual choice in taking his singular path, these scholars portray Kabir as compulsively following the ways of his predecessors from whatever religious tradition the scholar happens to prefer. These cracks are apparent elsewhere, in scholars' treatment of pre-British India as either a vale of ignorance or paradise on earth. From the latter school are those who attempt to establish the 'science' behind our mythology, who seek to demonstrate some convoluted technological 'fact' that emerges from these stories, rather than to accept and appreciate their poetic beauty and philosophical profundity. This shows nothing other than a deep-seated diffidence among these scholars, an insecurity that feeds a desire, an anxiousness to 'prove' the moral purity of 'our' culture. Such vein, puerile and, frankly, puritan efforts are often made to unabashedly contort erotic poetry into an expression of 'spirituality'. Irritated by such attempts, the doyen of Hindi literary criticism Ramchandra Shukla once remarked, 'Spiritual glasses come too cheap these days. Europeans pronounced Indians to be very spiritual, and people rush to show off their spirituality.' They define us, Shukla seemed to be arguing, and we trip over ourselves to fit into these definitions.

Most distressingly, while the transfer of knowledge and religious and philosophical discourse into vernacular languages is often used as an indication of the movement in Europe from medieval to modern society, in India, such vernacular expression is given short shrift. The young friend of mine we met at the start of this chapter typifies the standard academic and popular position—the use of English and Western mores indicates the arrival of modernity in India, while vernacular voices such as those of Kabir, Tukaram and Mirabai are either merely sentimental or are rehashing Sanskrit wisdom.

Europe's colonial powers thought of and described their colonies as hopelessly backward, if not downright uncivilised, while conveniently failing to own up to or notice their blind spots. The examples of such hypocrisy as cited here represent only the tip of the iceberg. In the interest of comparing apples to apples, we should examine Kabir's early modern India alongside Luther's early modern Europe. And if you insist on continuing this exercise by comparing Indian and European societies between the nineteenth and twenty-first centuries, then you cannot forget the destruction and havoc wreaked by colonialism.

It took the West centuries of hideously violent upheaval to democratise itself from within, to learn to live with religious, cultural, racial and even gender diversity. The Magna Carta, that 'great charter of freedom', for example, was signed in 1215, but it took until 1928 for British women to get the vote. In the United States, women won that right just eight years before. And despite the Enlightenment separation of church and state, the cultural and symbolic dominance of Christianity continues. Almost every US president, for instance, has sworn on the Bible to uphold his constitutional office; and as recently as 1956, the US chose to make 'In God We Trust' its official motto, printing the legend on its paper currency, rather than 'E Pluribus Unum'—Out of Many, One—its celebration of unity in diversity. The British monarch, incidentally, the titular head of a modern, multiracial, multifaith country, is still the 'defender of the faith', the 'supreme governor' of the Anglican church. Nobody disputes that modernity is a process rather than a one-time event like the Big Bang. This is accepted of the West. Why not of India?

Is Europe the Sole Inventor and Exporter of Modernity?

The philosophical crux of modernity is best defined as 'disenchantment', a term borrowed from Friedrich Schiller by the sociologist Max Weber in order to describe a fundamental shift in human attitude. Disenchantment summed up the growing dissatisfaction people felt with the available ideas about the place of humans in the universe. With disenchantment came the process of 'desacralisation', the interrogation and gradual rejection of the narrative of cosmos, divinity and humanity imposed by the church. Questioning the geocentric model of cosmos was one aspect of disenchantment, protesting against the religious authority of the Catholic church was another. Desacralisation also led to the separation of church and state power and a strictly delineated border between religious, mostly private, life and the secular, mostly public, life. The defining characteristics in Europe of the modern mindset gradually replacing the medieval one are as follows:

The philosophical insistence on rationalism, as opposed to surrendering to the dictates of the church. This rationalism is not the same as crude pragmatism or indifference to the human exploration of the spiritual. What the modern mindset prized above all else was individual experience. The individual should be untethered to a social identity fixed at birth and should be able to make a life for themselves according to their abilities. The emphasis on the individual meant that knowledge was the product of individual experience and enquiry, that what was known could change depending on the proof and evidence provided in favour of the new hypothesis. This was radically different from knowledge based on divine provenance, knowledge that was by definition beyond argument and question. Naturally, this led to the vernacularisation of knowledge since the individual was responsible for his own enlightenment. For the modern, 'Man' was the master of his own destiny, rather than a slave to divine design.

Disenchantment, desacralisation, vernacularisation, indivi-duality and rationality—these essential features of modernity were catalysed by the spread of commerce and resultant urbanisation. Industrialisation and the formation of nation states followed if the historical process of modernisation in a society was not interrupted. The key was commerce, as Weber recognised. Looking at the size of the Chinese and Indian economies, he proposed that 'if Europe [had] not been the region most prepared to carry out the Industrial Revolution, it would have been China or Hindustan'. But, against his own better judgement, Weber argued that the Industrial Revolution could not have happened in China or India because both societies lacked something akin to the Protestant work ethic.

Weber should have trusted his instinct. His later argument about Protestant ethics as opposed to, say, an Indian system, is untenable, rooted in a mistaken, otherworldly reading of karma and a distorted understanding of Indian society informed by colonial scholarship. In Weber's understanding of Hinduism, 'every change of occupation, every change in work technique, may result in ritual degradation'. Such a system, he concludes, 'is certainly not capable of giving birth to economic and technical revolutions from within itself'.[12] For Weber, the Protestant edge over both India and China was a tradition, going back to the prophets of Israel, that considered wealth 'a divine blessing'. The Argentine-Mexican historian Enrique Dussel explains that in 'Weber's understanding, such respect for wealth was missing in "otherworldly and static" India'.[13] Such a reading of Hinduism is quite amusing, and the fact that it was taken seriously is indicative of the power of colonial knowledge system. It is, indeed, surprising to see a culture that respects artha as much as it does moksha described as otherworldly.

The Protestant ethic considered wealth a 'divine blessing'? Fair enough, but did Hindus treat wealth as demonic? How did it escape this estimable scholar's attention that Hindus worship Lakshmi, the goddess of wealth? Worshipping Lakshmi is symbolic both of the Hindu respect for wealth and the Hindu understanding of the crucial role commerce plays in the life of a community. Commerce, here, is an exchange not only of goods but also, indirectly, of ideas, habits and attitudes. Exchange, by definition, is a two-way affair. Every civilisation learns from others; those who do not, perish. Alongside Western, the Arabic, Turkish and Persian influences on India's languages, ideas and everyday life are quite visible; English is the lingua franca of Indian intellectual discourse. To claim a one-way vishva-guru, teacher-of-the-world, status, as many Indian politicians and their supporters claim these days about the country, is in fact to admit an incapacity to learn, not a good trait for any guru.

Europe 'reawakened' to the wisdom it had lost in medieval times because that wisdom was preserved in Arabic translations.

It was rediscovered due to the rising volume of Europe's trade with the Arab world and other parts of Asia. The continent learnt how to use the zero and the decimal system from the Arabs, who themselves called these numbers 'Hindsa', or from India. Double entry bookkeeping, with debit and credit, came from India, while the Chinese art of block printing was the catalyst for the development of the printing press in Europe. As Europe's appetite for commerce grew in the twelfth and thirteenth centuries, India, due to the quality of its goods and high volume of production, became a lodestar of global trade. The voyages of 'discovery' by the likes of Vasco da Gama and Christopher Columbus were sponsored respectively by the Portuguese and Spanish monarchs in order to find better sea routes to India. Everyone knows that Columbus described the indigenous tribes of the American continent as 'Indians' because he thought he could find a shorter route to the riches of India by sailing west from Spain. But what about Indians in India? Did they venture out overseas for commerce? The British believed that while Muslims did sail abroad from India, few of them were involved in commerce and that Hindus considered crossing the seas a sin.

This supposed Hindu 'taboo' is another example of how colonial half-truths and misunderstandings are given the veneer of scholarship and later become received wisdom. Brahmin communities in Bengal and the eastern parts of Hindi-speaking areas did avoid seafaring. The British noticed and extrapolated from this regional and community-specific practice to identify an eternal and universal Hindu proscription. It mattered little that merchants from southern parts of the country and from Odisha, say, travelled far and wide in southeast Asia by sea, right up to the eighteenth century. The thriving Hindu community in Bali and evidence of Hindu presence in Vietnam and Cambodia, in the form of the spectacular Angkor Wat, the largest Hindu temple complex in the world, bear witness to mercantile and political expeditions by Hindus. In Gujarat, Multan (now in Pakistan) and (present-day) Rajasthan, merchants (and not all of them were either Muslim by religion or Baniya by caste) took unhesitatingly to the sea, dominating trade in cities as far afield as the Egyptian capital Cairo and Astrakhan in southern Russia.

The historian Ashin Das Gupta informs us, on the basis of contemporary Arab chronicles, that Gujarati Baniyas had settled in Arab lands by the fifteenth century; in Cairo, local Jewish merchants described Hindu merchants as 'brothers' and Muslim ones as 'friends'. The phrase 'Hindu brothers' used in the records of the time sharply cuts through the British-fuelled stereotype of the hyper-conservative and insular Hindu.[14] Jawaharlal Nehru writes in *The Discovery of India*, on the basis of 'documents brought to [his] notice by a friend', that 'in 1625 the governor of Astrakhan got a "Hindi Serai" built for the Indian traders to his city'. Nehru adds that in 1722, the tsar Peter the Great visited Astrakhan and directly addressed problems faced by Indian traders. The documents that Nehru accessed also mentioned the arrival in Astrakhan in 1745 of a group of sadhus.[15]

Surendra Gopal, of Patna University, was the 'first non-Russian historian to recognise the worth of the Astrakhan archives', writes the academic Stephen Dale, who lectured at the Banaras Hindu University in the 1960s. I was fortunate enough to visit Astrakhan in 2012 and consult the city archives, albeit briefly. (I wrote in detail about this visit in my 2013 travelogue *Hindi Serai: Astrakhan via Yerevan* published in Hindi by Rajkamal Prakashan.) It is abundantly clear from the city's archives and descriptions of travellers that from the seventeenth century through the nineteenth century, Indian traders exercised a significant influence not just in Astrakhan but also in the imperial court in Moscow. There were hardly any Muslims amongst these traders and, in December 1744, the Astrakhan governor issued a decree (duly endorsed by Moscow) 'strictly forbidding' the imposition of Christianity on these 'cow-worshippers'. These largely Hindu traders repaid the favour by providing financial assistance to the tsar Alexander I during the Napoleonic wars of the early nineteenth century.

A member of the Russian imperial academy of sciences, P.S. Pallas, published a description in 1799 of a 'Takur Duara' (the temple Thakur Dwara) and the Vaishnava form of worship he witnessed. Pallas noted that the prayers he attended were not led by a Brahmin pujari but by a 'dervish' (he likely means a sadhu of indeterminate caste). Contemporary writers also observed that the 'cow-worshippers' of Astrakhan, to fulfil the requirements of their rituals, would empty a potful of Ganga water into the Volga, thus turning 'Volga-jal' into Ganga-jal.

These accounts put a spoke in the colonial narrative of the insular Hindu completely lacking in enterprise. Hindu merchants may not have kept many journals of their travels, but it is plain that their religious beliefs did not prevent them from going overseas to do business. It is a measure of how successfully British colonialists were able to shape Indians' own understanding of themselves and their history that most believed tall tales such as a Hindu taboo on seafaring in early modern India and so, defensively, began to reach further and further into the past for the comfort of prelapsarian glory.

Perhaps, Indian scholars should now lead a conscious effort to re-theorise the very idea of modernity in the light of our knowledge of evolving ideas and customs in Indian and other non-Western societies. Scholars such as Sanjay Subrahmanyam, Velchuri Narayana Rao, Sheldon Pollock, David Lorenzen, Sudipta

Kaviraj, David Shulman, Hetukar Jha, John Stratton Hawley, Satya P. Mohanty, Allison Busch and Christian Novetzke have produced exciting explorations of the process of vernacularisation and the emergence of early modernity in India. Earlier, the eminent Hindi critic and historian of literature Ramvilas Sharma made path-breaking contributions in this area. Thanks to the work of these scholars, it is now difficult to ignore Sanjay Subrahmanyam's telling observation:

> Modernity is historically a global and conjectural phenomenon, not a virus that spreads from one place to another. It is located in a series of historical processes that brought hitherto relatively isolated societies into contact, and we must seek its roots in a set of diverse phenomena—the Mongol dream of world conquest, European voyages of exploration, activities of Indian textile traders in the diaspora ...[16]

British Rule: The Destruction of Artha and Distortion of Shastra

In order to assess the effect of British rule in India, we must ask if pre-British India possessed the following in some measure: enough commerce to have led to industrialisation; some momentum of change in attitudes, ideas and practices; and enough empirical rationality to suggest the potential of systematic, scientific rationality. Was there a sustained interrogation of organised religion? Could an individual aspire to escape the circumstances of their birth to move up or down the social hierarchy? Was knowledge and discourse being vernacularised?

Let us begin with the Indian economy. Edmund Burke
(eighteenth century), William Digby and Dadabhai Naoroji
(eighteenth and early nineteenth centuries), followed later by the
likes of Andre Gunder Frank, Jack Goody, Angus Maddison, Mike
Davis, Utsa Patnaik and Abraham Eraly have all written in forensic
detail about the disastrous economic impact of British rule in
India. In response some have argued that as there was no 'India',
in the sense of a single nation, or even a single political unit before
the British Raj, how could data from various sources be aggregated
as if to provide a national picture of an Indian economy?

Aurangzeb, the last Mughal emperor worthy of the title, ruled
over almost the entire Indian subcontinent. Mughal records are
well preserved, and estimates of the state of the Indian economy,
both before and after the Raj, are based on these and the archives
of British rule in India. There is simply no denying that the British
drained Indian wealth, that they hugely enriched Britain at India's
expense. I wrote about this in some detail over a decade ago in
my book *Akath Kahani Prem ki: Kabir ki Kavita aur Unka Samay*;
more recently, Shashi Tharoor has aggregated most of the relevant
research in his compellingly damning account of the Raj, *An Era
of Darkness: The British Empire in India*. The interested reader can
consult these works for fully referenced details. For the moment,
though, let us linger on just some of the most relevant facts.

Only recently have scholars and researchers been telling British
people the uncomfortable truth that their beautiful cities, indeed
their welfare state itself, were funded by colonial loot. In the colonial
period, more than half of Britain's domestic budget was extracted
from its colonies. India paid the lion's share. In 1700, most credible
estimates put India's share of the global GDP at 24.43 per cent;
by 1950, three years after India won its independence from the
'benevolent' British Raj, that share had come down to less than 5
per cent. This wholesale plunder was camouflaged in the history
textbooks of British India by a pronounced focus on the cruelties
of medieval Indian rulers, all the while failing to detail the often
greater cruelties of medieval British and European rulers. The

Crusades, of course, were the wars fought between Christians and Muslims from the eleventh to the thirteenth centuries to secure control of sites considered sacred by both groups. In ruthlessness and depravity, these 'holy wars' are arguably unparalleled in world history. It was during these wars that the Christians raised the world's first army made up of child soldiers.

Before the Raj, 15 per cent of the Indian population lived in cities and towns, a higher proportion than that in Europe at the time and, for that matter, a higher proportion than in cities in British India in the nineteenth century. Many Indian cities had populations ranging from a quarter of a million to one million. European travellers were awestruck by the size and dynamism of Indian cities like Agra, Delhi, Dhaka, Vijayanagara and Murshidabad. These travellers would find incomprehensible the claims made by latter-day historians that Indian cities were not cities so much as court towns and centres where pilgrims gathered. These travellers would have known from their experiences that Delhi, for instance, did not become a 'deserted village' even when Akbar chose Agra as his capital. And Agra, in its turn, continued to be a major city after Shah Jahan moved the Mughal durbar back to Delhi. While Mathura, situated between Delhi and Agra, was a centre for pilgrimage alone, Varanasi maintained its traditional status as a religious, cultural and commercial centre and surely could not have been described as anything but a great city.

The deurbanisation of the Indian landscape and consequent increase in the rural population was a result of colonial policies. Britain became magnificently urbanised while India retreated towards its impoverished, albeit conveniently romanticised villages. India was systematically drained of wealth and resources. So-called medieval Indian rulers taxed peasants on their produce, on the yield in a given year; the enlightened British based their taxes on the land, regardless of the yield in a particular year. It is like taxing a middle-class professional on the possible package they might command in the market rather than their actual earnings over the year.

Writing in the *Boston Review*, the sociologist Vivek Chibber claims that Niall Ferguson, a well-known apologist for the British Raj, 'bases his defence of colonialism principally on the Indian experience'. Borrowing from Mike Davis's 'stunning book *Late Victorian Holocausts*', Chibber excoriates the indifference of colonial authorities that exacerbated the ruinous effects of famine. It is worth quoting at length:

> According to the most reliable estimates, the deaths from the 1876–1878 famine were in the range of *six to eight million*, and in the double-barreled famine of 1896–1897 and 1899–1900, they probably totalled somewhere in the range of *17 to 20 million*. So in the quarter century that marks the pinnacle of colonial good governance, famine deaths average at least a million per year. … The Report of the Famine Commission of 1878 [said]: 'The doctrine that in time of famine the poor are entitled to demand relief … would probably lead to the doctrine that they are entitled to such relief at all times … which we cannot contemplate without serious apprehension.' So Viceroy Lytton sent a stern warning that administrators should stoutly resist what he called 'humanitarian hysterics' and ordered that there be 'no interference of any kind on the part of Government with the object of reducing the price of food'. … Curzon, who oversaw the decimation wrought by the 1899 famine, warned that 'any government which imperiled the financial position of India in the interests of prodigal philanthropy would be open to serious criticism; but any Government which by indiscriminate alms-giving weakened the fibre and demoralized the self-reliance of the population, would be guilty of a public crime'.
>
> To help Indians internalize this Spartan ethic, Lytton, Elgin and Curzon shut down all but the most anaemic relief efforts across the country. Grain surpluses in states where rainfall was adequate were not used for famine relief but were shipped instead to England, which apparently could relinquish its

own self-reliance in agriculture without descending into moral turpitude. To further help the Indian peasant pursue his virtuous path, all pleas for tax relief were rebuffed and collection efforts were redoubled: not a rupee of revenue was to be left on the parched plains. And in case peasants didn't get the point that they were supposed to pay the government and not the other way around, relief camps were closed down in areas where tax collection threatened to fall short of normal receipts.[17]

In 1900, the population of the Indian subcontinent was around 238 million people. Some 25 to 30 million of them died in famines in the Victorian era. Any aid proffered to the dying was considered 'humanitarian hysterics', a 'public crime' that would have 'weakened the fibre and demoralised the self-reliance of the population'. Can this faux concern for the moral fibre of Indians be described as anything other than evil design? The same, horrifying story was repeated during World War II under Winston Churchill, so celebrated for delivering Europe from the evils of Nazism, yet so willing to visit the evils and depredations of the British Raj on Bengalis. But British-enabled famines, directly responsible for the deaths of millions, apparently do not count on any global register of holocausts. On the contrary, many believe that the Raj was benevolent, particularly for the Dalit and other 'backward' castes. It would be a good idea to investigate how many of those who perished in the famines belonged to the upper castes.

A static, insular society could probably not have controlled a quarter of the world's trade, a share of the global economy that was deliberately sabotaged as forced deindustrialisation led to enormous transfers of wealth from India to Britain. Perhaps, had India lost its share of the world's GDP due to 'free market' competition or had early modernity in the subcontinent not been disrupted by colonialism and its people had still not laid down railway tracks or the region not become industrialised, then one might have been on firmer ground when describing Indian society as lacking dynamism and momentum. The establishment of British rule certainly indicated major cracks in the final years of a weakening Mughal empire and the inability of regional powers to step into the breach, but it did not suggest that the Indian economy or society was moribund and backward.

In fact, the opposite could plausibly be argued—that the spread of commerce and urbanisation in pre-British India had created the basis for opposition to caste-based hierarchy to be quite widely accepted. Cosmopolitan Indian cities had also brought Hindus, Muslims and people of other faiths closer together, ensconced in mutually profitable relationships. Artisans and merchants in early modern India grew not only in numbers but also in social and cultural influence. Many leading Bhakti poets, including Namdev and Kabir, came from the artisan class. Guru Nanak hailed from a family of merchants, while Banarasidas Jain, a Braj Bhasha poet, was a prosperous businessman in the seventeenth century who founded an autonomous and radical panth that rejected the control exerted by Jain priests over religious practice. The poet Tukaram sought to delink caste and inherited occupation by describing himself as a Shudra by caste and Vaishya by profession.

Early modern economic dynamism led to significant changes in popular attitudes, social practices and theoretical discourse. Bhakti voices contributed to these changes and also drew strength from them. A picture of a society in flux emerges from contemporary vernacular sources and popular legends. Tapan Raychaudhuri, surveying the eighteenth-century Indian economic scene, notes that Indian technology in agriculture as well as in manufacture, 'had largely been stagnant for centuries'. At the same time, he also notes 'a large commercial sector with a highly sophisticated market and credit structure, an extensive domestic and overseas market, the competitive power of the Indian textile trade, signs of market integration, increasing involvement of agricultural and rural manufacturers with the money economy, wage labour, centralised control, adoption of joint stock principles by sections of the commercial class and the entrepreneurial spirit manifested in

European-style shipping'. But, the fact remained, he writes, that 'no scientific or geographical revolution formed part of the eighteenth-century Indian's historical experience'. And so, Raychaudhuri concludes, 'In terms of ideas and attitudes, mid-eighteenth-century India was not all that different from the country described by Marco Polo. Spontaneous movement towards industrialisation was unlikely in such a situation.'[18]

Marco Polo visited Tamil Nadu and Kerala at the end of the thirteenth century. He found the locals wandering about 'virtually naked, only wearing a scrap of cloth'. The king, though, covered his upper body 'with a fine cloth and a lot of precious stones'. Could the same be said about the dress of commoners and kings in late-thirteenth-century north India? The question is pertinent to all everyday practices and even subtler expressions of ideas and attitudes. While some of Marco Polo's descriptions (Hindus bathing twice a day, for instance) might have been true of other parts of the country, others may not be. Readers have to be careful about the inferences they draw and assumptions they make about the whole of 'Indian' society based on information about a part.

There is evidence in vernacular sources as well as more formal Sanskrit texts of a kind of societal churn. In the period under study, we find a huge body of such scholarship in the form of commentaries ('tikas' and 'bhashyas') on the Dharmashastra.

Ashutosh Dayal Mathur, who has studied early modern interpretations of the Dharmashastra, detects a distinct shift towards what might, somewhat cumbersomely, be called the 'arthashastrasisation of the Dharmashastra'. Kautilya's Arthashastra is a famous practical volume, concerned with matters of statecraft and revenue management. Mathur invokes it to indicate a growing 'secularisation' of the Dharmashastra among the interpreters and scholars of the age. Encouraging commerce appeared to be the main concern of both kings and scholars; inevitably, thoughts on the sanctity of trade agreements and best business practices made their way even into treatises on the Dharmashastra. In the twelfth century, Acharya Devan, a scholar and expert of the text, stated unequivocally that 'so far as commerce is concerned, real practices and conventions of trade are to be given precedence over the hundreds of scriptural instructions, even if the instructions are from Manu himself'.[19]

According to Manu, under no circumstances was a Brahmin convict to be sentenced to death. But already in medieval India, the scholar Haradatta, in a commentary on the *Gautama Dharmasutra*, opined that only a Brahmin who perfectly observed all the rules and rituals could be given some concessions. Not every Brahmin deserved such leeway as a birthright. Chandesvara, the author of the *Vivada-Ratnakara*, a treatise on Hindu law, imposed such stringent conditions on the granting of clemency to Brahmins that special treatment was virtually impossible. He restricted exemption from capital punishment only to a Brahmin who was 'well-versed in Vedas, Vedanga, logic and history [and] regularly and diligently performs the six daily rituals'. Even such a pious and scholarly Brahmin could be spared the death sentence only if his offence was unintended. This reading of Hindu law is vital because the harshest punishment prescribed by Manu for even an illiterate Brahmin was banishment, that too without the confiscation of his property.[20]

When conservative medieval religious scholars writing in Sanskrit about ancient texts do not resist new ideas and changing mores, it's hard to accept Raychaudhuri's view that India remained unchanged and unchangeable in the centuries between Marco Polo's visit and the arrival of European colonialists. And if Sanskrit scholars were open to what was happening around them, imagine the leaps made by vernacular thinkers and writers. For them, the very idea of the authority of the *Dharmashastra* was open to question. The pettifogging niceties of Sanskrit scholarly disputation was of little interest to these crucial voices invigorated by the possibilities of the present.

The Turks and the Mughals, like the later European colonists, also faced the problem of knowing India in order to rule it. But they did not suffer from the white man's burden; they did not take upon

themselves the task of civilising the 'savage', and so they sought to learn about India from the everyday practices of the people rather than from ancient texts. They too extracted surpluses and lived off the fat of the (Indian) land but, in the ultimate analysis, wealth was pumped back into the economy instead of being exported. The decline of the Mughals, in fact, led to Indian commerce losing its protection and support structure in the domestic and world markets. The result, we already know, was a precipitous fall in India's share of the global GDP.

Muslim rulers learnt the local ways from caste and community chiefs, mendicant sadhus and feudal lords and incorporated this learning into their administration. They also brought new foods, habits of dress and technologies with them that were introduced into the Indian way of life. Some rulers insisted, theoretically, on Sharia, the Muslim law, but in practice they took the jahandari, or pragmatic/worldly, path. There were, no doubt, instances of temple destruction, massacres, forced conversions and other atrocities, but there was also great respect and cultural crossover. Muslim rulers were patrons of scholars, including Sanskrit ones, poets and artists; they took a keen interest in classical Hindu wisdom, but realised the importance of local custom in the religious, cultural and 'legal' life of Hindus. The Mughal emperor Akbar, for example, commissioned a translation of the *Mahabharata*, but not of the

ordinances of Manu, even though his intellectual friend Abul Fazl
was obviously aware of Hindu law as expounded by Manu.

The British, though, were in India to loot rather than to 'rule'.
Due to their shared Semitic religious background, the British
understood Muslims as also people of the book. Hindus, though,
were an enigma with their mind-boggling diversity of customs,
rituals and practices. They had a complex social structure, rich
cultural heritage and intellectual achievements. How to make
sense of them? Steeped in Protestant monotheism, theologically,
and in puritanism, ethically, the British could see the world only
in terms of this *or* that. This *and* that was unimaginable. They
could not understand how a Hindu could revere Muslim saints.
Or how one could be Muslim but still follow the rhythms and
customs of Hindu life. How a Muslim (Kabir) could take a Hindu
(Ramanand) as his spiritual teacher and guide. How 'idols' could
be worshipped if one believed in the high philosophy of monism
(very different from monotheism). How one person could be
vegetarian with a religious fervour and another enthusiastically eat
meat, yet both identify themselves as Hindu and recognise each
other also as Hindu. How segments of a large community could
follow such diverse, even contradictory, practices and yet belong
to one religious tradition—Hinduism.

Confused, yet arrogant, the British did not cut the cloth to fit the
body, choosing instead to cut the body to fit the cloth. They looked
for one sacred language, one holy book and one book of Hindu
laws, settling on Sanskrit, the Bhagavad Gita and *Manusmriti*
respectively. They relied on Brahmins, albeit selectively, to come
to these conclusions. Recall the nineteenth-century English
orientalist H.H. Wilson's assertion that the 'Hindu population
of these extensive realms' could be fathomed '*only* through the
medium of *Sanscrit*'. This, though Wilson himself was aware of
Kabir panthis and translated a hundred Kabir saakhis into English
for his book *A Sketch of the Religious Sects of the Hindus*, first
published in 1828 and then again in 1846 in an expanded edition.
It is a testimony to this sort of prejudiced scholarship that Wilson

did not bother to ponder the 'curious' fact that Kabir panthis were Hindus but the *Bijak* that they revered as scripture was not written in Sanskrit. Similarly, while *Manusmriti* was an important source for the Hindu law, it was by no means the only one.

Some scholars were switched on, but their efforts were in vain. Towards the end of the nineteenth century, George Grierson, an Irish linguist who worked in the Indian Civil Services, had already described Tulsidas's *Ramcharitmanas* as 'the bible of north India'. Not only did Tulsidas deliberately write his epic poem in Awadhi to make it accessible to a wide swathe of society but also, rather than translating the Sanskrit *Ramayana*, incorporated many sources and stories.

Just as most British scholars could not be persuaded to treat vernacular sources on par with Sanskrit ones, they could also not be persuaded that the harsh penal recommendations of Manu did not necessarily reflect either past or present practices. If that is the way to read a normative text like Manu's, then we ought to believe that with the US Declaration of Independence in 1776, all humans, 'created equal', instantly enjoyed equality *in practice*. In reality, there were 'lynching carnivals' in the US well into the twentieth century, with white people turning out in droves to watch black men being hung from their necks. Between 1877 and 1950, as many as 4,000 black people were lynched, many in public spectacles, with those in the crowd vying to take home such keepsakes as the victims' fingers.[21] Despite the introspection and social change forced by powerful civil rights movements, racism persists in the US, as does the resistance to racism, as we saw in the extraordinary scenes after George Floyd was effectively murdered by the police in Minneapolis in May 2020.

No society ought to be expected to transform overnight and normative texts must *not* be read as reporting real, everyday practices. Such texts can be 'read' properly only when assessed in the context of everyday reality. That would be the way to form a reliable idea of the role and relevance of the *Manusmriti* or any other text. How else do we read European texts, other than to assess them in the context of events and lived experiences?

But Europe is historically vital, of course, while India is frozen in time, or eternal, if you please.

The compilation and codification of laws in itself was not wrong; the problem was the total neglect of everyday practices and the exclusion of non-brahminical voices. This turned the Hindu laws that the British had so carefully compiled into an alien presence in the Indian context, in the very society from which these texts had emerged. The detachment of text from the context had far-reaching consequences. It became received wisdom across academic approaches and disciplines, from history to politics, to believe, as the American academic Nicholas Dirks puts it, that 'caste, specifically caste forms of hierarchy—whether valorised or despised—is somehow fundamental to Indian civilisation, Indian culture and Indian tradition'. On the contrary, Dirks points out, 'Caste, *as we know it today*, is a historical phenomenon ... specifically a result of a historical encounter and Western colonial rule.' This has led to a lot of controversy in academic, even political, discourse, despite Dirks's disclaimer: 'By this I do not mean to imply that it was simply invented by the too clever British. ... But I am suggesting that it was under the British that "caste" became a single term capable of expressing, organizing and above all "systematizing" India's diverse forms of social identity, community and organization.'[22]

To cut a very long story short, caste was made into shorthand for Indian social organisation by the British, ignoring or refusing to understand the complex economic and political power equations between and within caste groups. The four varnas became understood as the classification of existing, stable social groups formed on the basis of descending racial purity. The dominant colonial scholarship was bent upon proving that the status of innumerable caste groups throughout India was decided on the basis of purity of blood or, in terms of racial hierarchy, from fair to dark. Not incidentally, this tallied with the eugenics and scientific racism that had become voguish in Europe during the Enlightenment and extended its tentacles well into the twentieth century.

But it was a disastrous, even tragic, misreading of the Indian social order.

The fourfold varna hierarchy of Brahmin, Kshatriya, Vaishya and Shudra was an abstract model, while the caste system on the ground was a variegated, shifting reality. The varnas were not racially determined, stable categories. They were available slots in which castes could be placed depending upon the power and influence they wielded in a particular area, at a particular point in time. Purity of blood had nothing to do with it. The slots in which particular castes fit or were placed were neither eternal nor universal; colonial insistence on varnas as fixed reality was to shy away from real and necessary questions pertaining to the dynamics of caste.

Let us look at the lists of Other Backward Classes (OBCs, as classified) in our own times, as these are drawn up on the basis of disadvantages experienced by the castes in question. These lists comprise castes that would be classified as 'Shudras' in varna terms, but included as OBC in the Manipur list, for instance, are Maiti Brahmins. The Koris are considered OBCs in Uttar Pradesh and Bihar, but in Madhya Pradesh they belong to the Scheduled Castes. Baniyas (Vaishyas in varna terms) are forward castes in Rajasthan and Haryana but OBCs in Bihar. Such famous Kshatryia kings of ancient India as Ashoka and Chandragupta Maurya are nowadays being rediscovered as OBC icons. Alauddin Khalji defeated the reigning Yadav king of Devgiri, and Lord Krishna, an avatar of Vishnu, is a Yadav, so how do we describe such Yadavs in varna terms? None of them was born as Kshatriya, but their dynasties and caste groups were placed in that varna due to the power and status these rulers earned, without reference to race or birth. Quite naturally, because varna classifications of high or low status were never static, depending instead on the material and real-world circumstances in which a given caste found itself in a given historical moment. Both Lord Krishna and Ram are thought of in the popular imagination as dark-complexioned (so black that they were blue, as has been said of so many Africans and African-Americans); did they belong to the fair-skinned 'Aryan race'?

The colonial obsession with the text detached from context led to far-reaching misinterpretations of the nature of power in Indian society. We can only briefly discuss the fallouts of these misapprehensions here, but it can be stated safely that there is ample historical and empirical evidence to prove that the dynamics of political power and commerce decisively impacted caste hierarchies.[23]

By ignoring socioeconomic dynamics and their impact on caste, colonial scholars imposed ideas of race on the varna order. H.H. Risley, an Indian Civil Service officer and ethnographer, was arguably the most active and influential proponent of treating caste as race. In the nineteenth century and even up to the fourth decade of the twentieth century, race was a respectable area of study and research in Europe. It carried the imprimatur of science, and its prejudices were taken as 'scientific' truths. Risley's insistence on the racialisation of caste perfectly suited the larger designs of the Raj. After the 1857 rebellion, the British authorities were very keen to 'understand' Indian society, not in an academic and objective way but as an aid to control.

Risley's *The Tribes and Castes of Bengal*, published in 1891, was such a document, a testament to prejudiced colonial 'scholarship'. According to Risley, 'Indian society has sacrificed everything in order to organise itself according to purity of blood and social purity; caste was invented precisely for this purpose.' He laments that 'in Europe, anthropometry finds itself blinded due to constant intermixture of races', while in India it can still find plenty of 'pure' samples of various races because 'such intermixture is to a large extent eliminated'. Caste hierarchy, in this view, is about purity, and Brahmins, at the top, due to their endogamous efforts to preserve their purity, are marked out by such attributes of racial superiority as fair skin and sharp features.

Setting aside the ethics of scientific racism, Risley's

observations, in an empirical sense, are false. His most vocal opponent was William Crooke, an Irishman and a civil servant himself, whose own voluminous study, *Tribes and Castes of the North Western Provinces* (1896), showed that caste had little to do with racial determination and was more likely to be arranged by occupation.

In his study of castes in northern India, Crooke found that both among high-caste Brahmins and lower-caste Julahas/Koris (weavers), there were gotras, or clans, which indicated descents from other castes. Amongst Brahmins he found gotras suggesting origins in 'lower' castes such as Chauhans and Sunars (goldsmiths). Amongst Julahas he found gotras indicating 'descents' from such higher-caste groups as Brahmins, Thakurs, Baniyas, Kayashtas and Sheikhs. He also found in family records and other documents, not to mention popular legends, instances of a king or a local chief bestowing Brahmin status on a lower-caste person or group as a reward for a service or to meet some ritualistic exigency. No wonder, Crooke concluded: '... the theory of the ethnological basis of caste must be to a great extent abandoned. We have then to search for some other solution of the question of the origin of our present castes. This can only be found in community of function or occupation.'[24]

Apart from Crooke, other officers too wanted the 'theory of the ethnological basis of caste' to be abandoned. They told the higher-ups in the administration that the racial basis of caste projected by Risley to be hoary Indian tradition was, simply put, not traditional at all. Every caste comprised a variety of 'racial stock' and the rules amongst so-called occupational castes and professional guilds regarding social conduct were marked by a pragmatic flexibility. For instance, as Crooke noted with reference to widow marriage:

> The castes that do not permit widow marriage are roughly one-fourth of the whole, so that Hindus as regards female re-marriage occupy a position between Muhammedans and Jains, but nearer the former than the latter. The latter are

practically, as regards such matters, Hindus of high caste and permit no widow re-marriage ...[25]

He summed up the results of his research pointwise, including the following:

- The first trace of modern caste is found in the 'Institutes' of Manu: but here the rules of food, connubium and intercourse between the various castes are very different from what we find at present.
- Caste so far from being eternal and changeless is constantly subject to modification, and this has been the case through the whole range of Hindu myth and history.
- Caste is in its nature rather a matter of sociology than of religion.
- The primitive so-called division of the people into Brâhmans, Kshatriyas, Vaisyas and Sûdras does not agree with existing facts, and these terms do not now denote definite ethnological groups.[26]

But the Raj preferred Risley's racially charged approach and endorsed it enthusiastically. He was appointed commissioner of the census in 1899 and then director of ethnography. Back in England after retirement, he also served as a permanent secretary of the judicial department of the India Office. The Indian Civil Services career of Crooke, on the other hand, came to a premature end because of what was described by later scholars as personality clashes with his superiors; he ended up seeking voluntary retirement from the services due to personal reasons. What Crooke and those who supported his position were arguing was simple— in India too, like everywhere else, the society was fluid, evolved through its history and was not frozen in some prelapsarian past.

Interestingly, or rather expectedly, while the people trained in colonial thinking started looking at the fourfold varna order as having been the historically *real* thing, instead of just a theoretical model, and the on-the-ground caste system as its *corruption*, the scholars and administrators steeped in the legacy of early modernity of India would find nothing surprising in Crooke's observation—caste, 'is constantly subject to modification and this has been the case through the whole range of Hindu myth and history'.[27]

Pandit Jwala Prasad Mishra of Muradabad in Uttar Pradesh was a very conservative Brahmin scholar. A staunch critic of the Arya Samaj, Mishra published his *Jati Bhaskar* in Hindi about twenty years after Crooke's study, but there was no question of him being aware of Crooke or Risley, or other contemporary scholars, because he had no English. At the outset, he made clear his dislike of those defending caste based on karma, and he argued forcefully instead for birth-based caste. Mishra's academic integrity makes his work important. Instead of bending facts to suit his theories, he described things as he saw them. He, quite nonchalantly, accepted the 'duality' of any given individual's caste identity—one assigned at birth and another as a function of one's work. So, a betel-leaf seller, for example, effectively belongs to the Tamboli caste, whatever his caste by birth.

Mishra believed, in theory, that only Kshatriyas deserved to be kings, but he was honest enough to acknowledge that the seventh-century king Harshavardhana of Kanyakubja (modern-day Kannauj in Uttar Pradesh) and the sixteenth-century king Hemu Vikramaditya (known as the last Hindu king of Delhi, defeated by Akbar) were Baniyas by birth. He also noted that both men were respected for their valour and other 'kingly' qualities. There are also accounts of Gond and Bhil kings being praised and followed by Brahmins in early modern India. Conservative or not, Mishra was aware, in his own way, that caste, as Crooke asserted, 'is rather a matter of sociology [and history] than of religion'. Armed with knowledge both of his 'hoary' tradition and his own time, Mishra would have been surprised by the scholarship of the likes of Risley that 'proved' that caste was a racial hierarchy immune to historical change. Instead, Mishra tells us that amongst Brahmins too, there were Bhil tribals and Abhirs (Yadavs) who had been given their status by Lord Ram himself as a reward for their help. Mishra even offered up an exact year for the 'creation' of Devrukhe Brahmins—1419 in the Saka calendar, or 1497 in the Gregorian. Needless to say, Devrukhes were created by a much lesser figure than Lord Ram.[28]

Varnashrama was not a social fact or a once 'pure' system in the long-distant past that had become corrupted. It was a model used, post facto, to justify the ascendance of powerful caste groups at a given period in history. In India too, for all its supposed otherworldliness, the sword mattered and money talked.

The 1891 census conducted on the 2.5 million residents of Marwar state (present-day Jodhpur) was a vernacular attempt to follow new colonial knowledge-gathering practices, but the report, published five years later, steers clear of making false colonial assumptions. 'Munshi' Hardiyal Singh, the 'superdent', as in superintendent of the census, wrote in the preface to the report:

> Shri Darbar (i.e His Highness) desired that the everyday practices ['reet-bhant, chaal-chalgat' in Hindi, meaning customs and manners]—of the twenty-five lakh people counted in Marwar must also be researched into and published for the benefit of state as well as that of the people; because with reference to everything, *it is better to know than not to know*.[29]

The census report documents a fact often missed in the academic discourse on caste. The reverence shown to the Brahmin is not necessarily evidence of any superiority accorded him in everyday practice. Superiority for the purposes of ritual must not be taken as evidence of a hierarchy independent of power, in which the Brahmin retains his seat at the head of the table as a matter of course regardless of material circumstance.

Recording the practices of people, rather than accepting caste hierarchies on paper, the census report puts the 'warriors and rulers' ('qaum' is the word used for social group here) in class A, at the very top. Included in this class are, naturally, the Rajputs, but also, instructively, Mughals and Pathans. Caste is, after all, a matter of sociology than religion. Brahmins are also at the top of the social order, but in class B reserved for priests, entertainers and professionals. Other groups sharing this space with Brahmins include sanyasis, Vairagis, Sayyids and even acrobats, dancers, sex workers and hijras. Just like Crooke's survey, this report notes the prevalence of widow remarriage and divorce amongst many castes.

The writers of this report were not heretics or disrespectful to tradition. On the contrary, they showed due reverence to Brahmins and Sayyids in everyday life and in moments of religious and ritual observance. They were also conscientious in their observations of society and understood the power structure and its logic—the group with political and military muscle sat at the top of the social pyramid, never mind what the books said.

There are numerous other examples that indicate how caste hierarchies were in practice changing because of the growth of trade and commerce. So much was lost on those colonial scholars who insisted on their theories of racial purity. They not only missed Baniya, Gond and Bhil kings but also Brahmins who made their living with their hands. Though Brahmins were supposedly prohibited, like many priestly castes in societies across the world, from labouring, given that their lives were intended to be devoted to religious study, in eighteenth-century Mithila, a stronghold of brahminical traditionalism, 68 per cent of Brahmins worked in agriculture. Across the country in Surat, Gujarat, a large number of Brahmins were not teachers or students but labourers. Citing these and other facts, the historian K.N. Panikkar correctly advises scholars to rid themselves of the habit of assuming Indian 'enlightenment' as a result of the British presence and to look instead at the 'changes in attitudes and ideas' in the context of India's own particular socioeconomic and cultural dynamics.[30]

We need to confront the effect of colonial scholars and orientalists choosing to propagate the Brahmin way as set out in Sanskrit texts as the only authentic model of Hindu life. It was a falsehood enthusiastically supported by conservative Brahmins eager to retain their hierarchical status and privileges. As a result, at the beginning of the twentieth century, many 'lower'- and 'middle'-caste groups began to drift away from their socially liberal practices (widows marrying again, for example) to become 'better' Hindus in brahminical terms and clamoured for entry into a higher varna. Still, the good practice of widow remarriage continued in many castes across north India, ironically alongside the patently false 'scholarly' assessment that Hindus as a whole disapproved of it.

And as far as the racial purity theory superimposed by Risley on the varna system is concerned, B.R. Ambedkar hit the nail on the head. In his 1946 book *Who Were the Shudras?* he categorically rejects the Aryan race theory and the idea of an Aryan invasion of India. In response to those who claimed the varna system reflected the Aryans' insistence on purity of race, Ambedkar writes:

> Again, to say that the institution of Chaturvarnya is a reflection of the innate colour prejudice of the Aryans is really to assert too much. If colour is the origin of class distinction, there must be four different colours to account for the different classes which comprise Chaturvarnya. Nobody has said what those four colours are and who were the four coloured races who were welded together in Chaturvarnya. As it is, the theory starts with only two opposing people, Aryas and Dasas—one assumed to be white and the other assumed to be dark.[31]

Every historian would agree with Tapan Raychaudhuri's description of the Indian economy just before the British rule, that it was varied and complex, that it was not as stagnated or backward as some British apologists for colonialism have argued. Commerce was conducted through promissory notes, commission agents, a putting-out system (merchants giving out advances to artisans in exchange for exclusivity commitments), 'rationally' written agreements and account books, and the mechanisms to ensure compliance with agreements and promises. He also notes the existence of long-term investments and the notion of a businessman's ethics, which, unlike the feudal idea of 'honour', gave precedence to prudence over ostentation. So, contrary to what Weber believed, even if merchants weren't Protestant, they could have an ethical system around business and material concerns. Certainly, many Hindus were careful with the 'divine blessings' of artha and kama and considered them to be equal to dharma and moksha. The ethical concerns of merchants and businessmen were a catalyst for change. Kabir's was not a society based on the jajmani system, in which services, often provided by lower castes, were exchanged for goods. There was, of course, brahminical hegemony, but there was also resistance, merchants and artisans constituting its social base. By Kabir's era, they had grown influential enough to challenge brahminical supremacy. Going by evidence from real-world practices, rather than millennia-old texts, one would have to agree with Jack Goody's conclusion about early modern India: 'of their [Banias and traders] importance there can be no doubt, whatever the Brahmin ideology had to say'.[32]

'Brahmin ideology' was given a wonderful opportunity by British colonialists to reverse the tide and reinforce its increasingly precarious position at the top of the social hierarchy. British rule, with willing cooperation from 'official Brahmins', disrupted the dynamism of Indian vernacular modernity; as a result, what was 'invented' in the eighteenth and nineteenth centuries was not Hinduism, as some people believe, but 'Brahminism—suitable for export', as the French scholar Raymond Schwab tellingly put it.[33]

Public Sphere of Bhakti

The 'public sphere' has attracted a lot of attention since Jürgen Habermas published his path-breaking study *The Structural Transformation of the Public Sphere* in German in 1962, translated into English some twenty-seven years later.[34] For Habermas, the public sphere was a space for conversations about social, political and cultural concerns. Traditionally, this sort of gathering place might be a cafe in a public square or in the letters pages of newspapers and magazines. Nowadays, of course, it is on social media, where this kind of conversation is conducted, alongside the media. The public sphere is a liminal space, distinct from the private space of home and family and the political space dominated by state institutions and officialdom with the distinct and deadening language of bureaucrats and functionaries.

Conversations confined to your dining table do not form or impact public opinion, and conversations in coffee houses or in the media per se do not translate into government policies or state actions. But conversations that crystallise into broad public opinion do affect government policies in a democracy. With the increasing reach of mass media, public-image management is essential not just for politicians but all public figures. Similarly, conversation in the public sphere is about more than the effect on government policy; it is about setting the tone for the zeitgeist, about developing a society's cultural and moral positions. The growing disapproval of racism, casteism, religious hatred, misogyny and homophobia, for example, is testimony to the impact of opinion developed and hardened in the public sphere. Unfortunately, so is the strengthening of reactionary attitudes and the emergence of a 'post-truth world'.

In a similar way, the Nirgun critique of the brahminical worldview, coupled with the spread of commerce, prepared the ground for the turning of public opinion against what had been the prevailing social order. Nirgunis called for a rational reassessment of dharma and moksha and also argued for the validity of kama and artha, as almost all of them were regular householders. Their impact was felt throughout society, as communities of admirers and supporters, the panths, gathered regularly to exchange ideas in satsangs in a public sphere that included maths, institutions for spiritual and philosophical study, as well as for an enquiry in a variety of other fields.

Spaces were created to debate everyday pragmatic and social concerns. This was a wider, more inclusive space for public discussion than what was made available by caste panchayats and professional guilds. Such public conversation enabled the spread of Bhakti ideas beyond the followers of a particular panth or worshippers at a particular math. It was through the public sphere that the terminology and mythology of Bhakti became the idiom of public discourse in early modern India. Its lingering effects are still present today, even if occasionally used in a sarcastic fashion. Take, for instance, the contemporary connotation of the word 'bhakt' in India's political discourse.

There is no denying that bhakti in this era was not merely a mode of worship—it was an entire worldview, a public, not personal, commitment. When thanking Kabir for saving bhakti from the joint onslaught of lok, veda and Kali yuga, Pipa was referring to the oppressions of the prevailing social norms. The resistance and, indeed, overturning of such ideas had to be perforce a public activity. If for the Nirgunis resistance was necessary, for Tulsidas—arch critic of the Nirgunis—vernacular expression was a choice. He could very well have composed his verses in Sanskrit; his command over Sanskrit prosody and poetic conventions shines brilliantly in *Ramcharitmanas* and other works. He chose the vernacular to reach the broadest possible audience to warn them of the 'evil' of the Nirgun sensibility. For their own reasons, Jnaneshwar, Sankardev, Eknath and Vishnudas also chose to write in vernacular languages, though they knew they would

get more recognition in the elite literary and intellectual circles
of the time if they had composed their poems in Sanskrit.

These poets did want access to larger audiences but, more
importantly, it was the very nature of their poetic sensibility
that made them turn away from Sanskrit and towards their
own languages. Each and every Bhakti poet, regardless of their
position on the central question of caste, saw social concerns
and spiritual angst as part of an integrated whole, not as neatly
compartmentalised entities. This integrated approach set them
apart from the sawdust-dry intellectual musings of their Sanskrit-
writing counterparts.

Along with their Nirgun counterparts, the Sagunis, like
Tulsidas, were contributing to the evolution of a Hinduism that
although did not shun Sanskrit, was not dependent on it or
beholden to it. Instead, the public sphere of Bhakti was a space of
philosophical and pragmatic conversation, autonomous from the
hegemony of Sanskrit.

There was anger within the dominant sections of society
at the challenge from the Nirgun poets and the support they
were getting from people, including some sections of the
elite. Because the Nirgunis were redrawing the contours of
philosophical and social discourse, the dominant sections were
furious, and their fury found eloquent expression, again through
the pen of Tulsidas: 'These days, nobody talks of anything but
the knowledge of the Brahman. But Brahmins even murder the
guru for a pittance. Shudras challenge Brahmins and chastise
them, saying that they are their equals, that a true Brahmin is
one who knows the Brahman, irrespective of his caste. Such
people talk in saakhis, dohas and anecdotes. In this Kali yuga,
the so-called bhagats go on denouncing the Vedas and the
Puranas.'

ब्रह्मग्यान बिनु नारि नर कहहिं न दूसरि बात।
कौड़ी लागि लोभ बस करहिं बिप्र गुर घात॥

बादहिं सूद द्विजन्ह सन हम तुम्ह ते कछु घाटि।
जानइ ब्रह्म सो बिप्रबर आँखि देखावहिं डाटि॥

साखी सबदी दोहरा कहि कहनी उपखान।
भगति निरूपहिं भगत कलि निंदहिं बेद पुरान॥[35]

Here, Tulsidas is quoting Kabir verbatim—'We call only him
a Brahmin who actually knows the Brahman.' (कहू कबीर जो ब्रह्म
बिचारे। सो ब्राह्मणु कही अतु हमारे॥) Of course, Tulsidas didn't need to
identify the target of his barb by name; it would have been obvious
to everyone.

As stated in the first chapter, Nirgunis and Sagunis were both
persistent in their efforts to win friends and influence people
by presenting their respective arguments and polemics in the
public sphere.

I introduced the specific category of the 'public sphere of
Bhakti' in my study of Kabir just over a decade ago. There have
been historians who have acknowledged the existence of a public
sphere, as such, in India, before British rule. Christopher A. Bayly,
for instance, observed:

> Recent polemics against the 'derivative' character of modern
> Indian political ideology have not even begun to characterise
> indigenous political theory and practice … political theory,
> individuality, rationality and social communication in the
> Indian context. These, of course, are all essential elements in
> the concept of critical politics which developed in the West
> and they all find a place in Jurgen Habermas's influential
> discussion of the 'public sphere'. All had analogues within the
> north Indian *ecumene*.[36]

Let us be clear: to talk of the public sphere of Bhakti is not to talk
of the strictly European or even 'bourgeoise' variety, the historical
phenomenon which is the subject of Habermas's enquiry. That
said, Habermas gives a very basic, broad definition of 'public'—

'We call events and occasions "public" when they are open to all, in contrast to closed or exclusive affairs.' He explains further:

> But as in the expression, 'public building', the term need not refer to general accessibility; the building does not even have to be open to public traffic. 'Public buildings' simply house state institutions and as such are 'public'. The state is the 'public authority'... The public sphere itself appears as a specific domain—the public domain versus the private. Sometimes the public appears simply as that sector of public opinion that happens to be opposed to the authorities.[37]

As already noted, for Habermas, secularity is an inevitable ingredient of the public sphere. Maybe this makes the idea of an Indian public sphere, especially one catalysed by Bhakti, appear incongruous to some. But if we go by the usual binary of secular versus religious, then the 'totally' secular picture of even European modernity is a myth for the simple reason that 'religion' is not merely structured faith but an integral part of culture. Moreover, India did not, and could not, have a European-style rupture between the 'religious' and the 'secular' (state), as no religious institution dominated every aspect of Indian life and society as the church did in Europe. Even today, after the formal separation of church and state in societies like the United States, religion still exercises great influence over both private lives and the public sphere.

Philosophically, 'secular' implies 'worldly', concerned with matters of this world; theoretically, the public sphere too is worldly, consumed by the social and political, rather than spiritual affairs. But the erasure of the cultural aspect of religion is not so easy. While you might be able to avoid discussing the 'word of god', say, in the public sphere, can you ignore the impact of Christian fundamentalism on society and politics?

The Bhakti sensibility, particularly Nirgun, is unique in its combination of worldly and otherworldly concerns. A public sphere in which secular issues can be threshed out and spiritual questions are not entirely neglected is surely an improvement on the bourgeois public sphere envisioned by Habermas. Moreover, Namdev, Jnaneshwar, Sarala Dasa, Kabir, Pipa and Mirabai did not vernacularise the word of god; they turned the vernacular into the language of god. Their poetry is a scripture for their followers. *Ramcharitmanas* is the 'holy book' for many in north India, as is the *Jnaneshawari* in Maharashtra. And Sikhism gradually evolved into a totally autonomous religion with an anthology of vernacular poetry worshipped as its most venerable text. Perhaps the most perceptive observation on both the public nature of Bhakti and its social impact on north India was made by Crooke (yes, him again) who had this to say:

> We can stand and watch the creation of new so-called castes before our eyes. And the process is facilitated by the creation of new religious groups, which base their association on the common belief in the teaching of some saint or reformer. Most of these sects are connected with the Vaishnava side of Hinduism, and are devoted to the solution of much the same religious questions which beset the searcher after truth in western lands. All naturally aim at the abolition of the privileges and pretensions of the dominant Brahmin Levite, and the establishment of a purer and more intellectual form of public worship.[38]

The point is, whatever be the direction of the ideas and attitudes of a particular bhakta, sampradaya or lay follower, the public sphere of Bhakti provided an arena of contest as well as a space for rhetoric, not directly involved with the political powers, but not entirely indifferent to political patronage either. The Bengali Vaishnavas and the Pushtimarg of Vallabhacharya were well known for their systematic lobbying for the support of influential political figures. But even if there were no conscious attempts to force a change in the power structure, in the case of the rise of Sikhism in Punjab or the Satnamis in central India, the ideas and practices circulating in the public sphere of Bhakti led inexorably to political upheaval. The 'ecumene' described by Bayly consisted of the 'most enlightened intelligentsia' belonging to the elite classes, but possessed 'a deep historical lineage in the popular critique of Brahmin pretensions in the earlier centuries'. [39]

These critiques took many forms in early modern India. Not only were traditionally available 'names' like Ram being given a new meaning, but also new, more interrogative versions of available Puranic narratives were being created and propagated. The various Puranas were usually supposed to have appropriated subaltern voices into the brahminical hegemony, but the *Lakshmi Purana* composed by the sixteenth-century Odia poet Balramdasa, for instance, is clearly a counter-hegemonic text. The Bhaktas and their sampradayas did not have a well-defined common goal, but they shared a common idiom, practices and institutions in which they sought to validate their respective ideas and positions. As late as in the eighteenth century, Dariya Sahib (of Bihar), who was a Muslim tailor, wrote his own version of the Nirgun Ramayana under the title *Gyan-Ratan*, following the forms and style of Tulsidas's *Ramcharitmanas*. The Jain merchant Banarasidas founded the Adhyatma movement within Jainism and wrote his autobiography, *Ardhakathanaka* (Half a Tale), in Braj Bhasha. It seems like a distinctly modern, even contemporary thing to do; how many memoirs and autobiographies are published in a given year in the English-speaking world alone? His conviction in writing the book, in confronting his life, failures et al, shows that individual self-consciousness was not necessarily an idea imported from Europe. [40]

But the British rule sounded the death knell for the development of a distinctly Indian modernity. Dismissing the serious misgivings of many of its own officers, the Raj upheld Risley's racist reconstruction of caste as an accurate description of the 'framework of native life' and decided to administer the country accordingly. [41] It was only to be expected then that in the early twentieth century, many castes launched campaigns to prove their 'purity' so that they could be entered in the census as belonging to the higher echelons of the race hierarchy. Yes, under British rule, India came into contact with ideas of the European Enlightenment that played a crucial role in the making of Indian modernity as we know it today. However, as far as the dynamics of the Indian economy and tradition itself is concerned, the impact of British rule can be summed up this way: artha was taken away, kama was denied and stigmatised. Indians were expected to sit back, relax and follow dharma and teach moksha to each other, but only in the distorted way—'brahminism suitable for export'— constructed by the British and their Brahmin collaborators.

A depressing result of the internalisation of colonial 'knowledge' about India has been the general public's acceptance of a peculiar idea of Indian tradition—that a country as varied as India could be so deeply asleep until the British stirred it awake. Only in such a version of Indian history could the entire intellectual churning of the period of vernacular modernity be so completely ignored. Such a flat idea of Indian tradition is then used as a magic wand to ward off any progressive and liberating change in attitudes and ideas. The facts of centuries of composite culture are denied, and arguments for nationhood defined in terms of religious identities (Hindu and Muslim) are made. While social evils like polygyny, widow burning, untouchability and homophobia may have been supported in the name of tradition, it is forgotten that resistance to such practices was also tradition.

Curiously, the most vocal votaries of Indian tradition flaunt this stagnation, this illusion of an unchanging, unchallenged tradition (which is nothing but a colonial construct) with enviable smugness, all the while condemning individuality, rationality and interrogation as evil 'foreign' influences. If you choose to forget that modernity everywhere emerges from tradition and that tradition everywhere has the potential to modernise, and if you exclude the history of vernacular modernity from your idea of tradition, then any dynamism, even indigenous, would seem alien.

In any case, foreign influences on any tradition per se can hardly be described as evil; in fact, absorbing them with discretion, with vivek, indicates the self-confidence of the tradition in question.

Let us now turn to the ways in which the poet, who insisted throughout his life on the need for vivek, has remained alive over the centuries since his physical departure from our world.

IV

'Life Is Momentary, Kabir Composes Poetry': Many Avatars of the Poet

'Who Was Mr Kabir?'

Shabnam Virmani made four films that document the traditions and devotions that have grown around the legends and songs of Kabir. She recorded performances of Kabir bhajans in Malwa in Madhya Pradesh, in Rajasthan and Sindh and interviewed such eminent singers as Prahlad Singh Tipanya, Farid Ayaz and Mukhtiyar Ali, among others. Virmani's 'The Kabir Project' grew out of the angst and despondency she felt in the wake of the Gujarat riots; she went on a personal quest for 'Kabir's Ram' as an antidote to sectarian tension and violence in contemporary India.

In one of these documentaries, *Had Anhad (Bounded-Boundless): Journeys with Ram and Kabir*, Virmani speaks to some well-to-do traders of the Ansari community of Muslim weavers in Banaras. The filmmaker appears to take it for granted that her interlocutors would enthusiastically endorse Kabir as one of their own. He was, after all, born to a Muslim weaver couple, right? But the men are ambivalent. One of them—also named Kabir, which happens to be one of Allah's names in the Koran—captures this ambivalence succinctly: 'Some people say he was a Muslim; some say he was a non-Muslim; but it has not yet been decided to which religion Mr Kabir belonged.' Everyone in the shop agrees. 'Kabir was a nice man,' they say. 'He wanted to take everybody along, but he was not a Muslim, could not have been, as he went beyond the "boundaries" of Islam.' At a philosophical level, the poet himself would have happily agreed with the men and might have answered the question about the religion of 'Mr Kabir' in the following words:

A Hindu utters the name of Ram,
a yogi that of Gorakh.
A Muslim believes in monotheism,
Kabir's lord permeates all existence.

जोगी गोरख गोरख करै, हिन्दू राम नाम उच्चरै।
मुसलमान का एक खुदाइ, कबीर का स्वामी रह्या समाई।[1]

The Hindi writer and scholar Hazari Prasad Dwivedi reads the above saakhi not as a philosophical self-description but as social fact. He interprets Kabir as saying not only that he is 'neither Hindu nor Muslim' (ना हिन्दू ना मुसलमान, as paraphrased by Dwivedi, not Kabir's own words) but also that he is genetically influenced by the Nath panth because his ancestors from just a couple of generations ago were followers of this sect. In Dwivedi's famous book *Kabir* (first published in 1942), the first six chapters are devoted to the metaphysics of Nath-panthi yogis. The point Dwivedi makes with such insistence is that the metaphysics underlying Kabir's poetry can be directly linked to the Nath panth. Followers of Guru Gorakhnath, the metaphysics of the Nath panthis draws from Shaiva and Buddhist traditions. They insisted on renunciation and yogic practices, were quite influential in early modern India and were respected and even feared for their 'miraculous' powers. Dwivedi calls this metaphysics 'dwaitadwaitvilakshanwad' (distinct from both monism and dualism).[2] Again, this is Dwivedi's own coinage, not nomenclature borrowed from any school of philosophy. Kabir's unique theological perspective was the outcome of his being brought up (notice, Dwivedi says brought up, not born) in a Muslim weaver's family that had the Nath-panthi yoga imprinted in its religious DNA—or so goes Dwivedi's argument.

Pitambar Dutt Barthwal was the first scholar to place Kabir in the Nath lineage. While tracing the yoga-pravaha, or stream of yoga, in Hindi literature, he describes the Nirgun panth as a 'metamorphosis of yoga'. Why was there so much yoga in Kabir, Barthwal wonders, and so little Islam? The answer he comes up with is: 'Kabir was born in a lineage of recent converts to Islam.'[3] This argument was adopted lock, stock and barrel by Dwivedi, who made it much more insistently, and later by the French Kabir scholar Charlotte Vaudeville.

Many accuse Dwivedi of 'brahminising' Kabir, but it would be more accurate to say that by making the Nath panth so central to Kabir's worldview, he was positioning the poet as more of a Buddhist, a popular form of which the Nath panth is supposed to have evolved from. Dwivedi attributes the Nath element in Kabir not to any personal choice or learning but to his DNA structure. Essentially, had Kabir not been born into a family of recent converts, we would not find so much of the Nath element in him. Barthwal, even while describing the Nirgun panth as a 'metamorphosis of yoga', recognises that Kabir was born to Muslim weaver parents. Not Dwivedi, though, who could barely bring himself to acknowledge that Kabir was merely brought up by Muslims.

Kabir distanced himself from religious traditions and practices—'the weaver from Kashi' is how he identified himself—but nowhere in his verse does he deny being born in a Muslim household. The saakhi cited above cannot be said to indicate any 'social fact'; it simply makes a point about metaphysics and leaves no space for any speculative 'reading'. Kabir is distancing himself from Puranic Hindu, Nath-yogi and Muslim positions by mentioning Ram, Gorakh and Khuda respectively. He is emphasising that his own notion of Ram is distinct from Puranic Hinduism's. The nature of his yoga sadhana is sahaj, an enlightenment and practice that is so rehearsed it appears to come naturally, unlike the almost deliberately complicated and esoteric practices associated with Nath-panthi yogis. And while Khuda in the Islamic tradition is a distant, even fearsome, creator, Kabir's god permeates the entire universe, is found everywhere and in everything.

So far as Kabir's identity as a 'social fact' is concerned, not even once does he call himself a yogi or a Sufi. And as we already know, he expresses derision for Shaktas and an affinity with Vaishnavas.

He unhesitatingly borrows words, terms and metaphors from all available spiritual lexicons but creates his own grammar. Oddly, Kabir scholars, Indian and foreign alike, are in agreement when it comes to denying him what he always insisted he had—individual choice and moral agency. These scholars appear to find it so inconceivable that making individual choices and exercising moral agency—such typically modern privileges—could be possible in 'medieval' India that they feel compelled to forage through Kabir's 'lineage' to locate antecedents that might explain his worldview. Parshuram Chaturvedi and Mata Prasad Gupta are exceptions to this strange scholarly consensus. They argue that the evidence suggests Kabir chose his path after careful study and having assessed various traditions. Gupta also categorically rejects the idea that Kabir might have been illiterate, writing, 'There cannot be a more baseless statement.'[4]

Reverend G.H. Westcott, a missionary posted in Kanpur, wrote *Kabir and the Kabir Panth* (1907), perhaps the first full-length study, certainly in English, of Kabir. That, Westcott observes wryly, 'a Muhammadan should have been the father of Hindi literature may indeed be a cause of surprise'. But he reminds his readers that many Hindus have composed poetry in Persian. Westcott is quite convinced that Kabir was a Sufi Muslim, who was speaking in Hindi, 'to get his message accepted by those who were best reached through the Hindi language'.[5] Here, Westcott is projecting onto Kabir the traits and behaviours of a nineteenth-century Christian missionary, many of whom adopted the cultural idiom of the Hindus in order to proselytise them (some of them went to the extent of putting on the janeu, the sacred thread worn by Brahmins). It is hard for Westcott to imagine Kabir's life outside this paradigm. Being a Muslim, surely Persian was Kabir's natural tongue, not Hindi. And how could a Muslim be a Bhakta? He was bound to be Sufi and chose to speak the language of Bhakti only to convert Hindus. So, even if Kabir was exercising a personal choice, it was not at the deeper level of conscience but only superficially, as a public-relations stunt.

Kshitimohan Sen, a close associate of Rabindranath Tagore and a professor at Shantiniketan, published a volume of Kabir's poems, collected from various sources, out of which one hundred were translated in 1915 into English by Tagore himself. The influence of Tagore and Sen is apparent in Dwivedi's reading of Kabir. Before Dwivedi, Ramchandra Shukla, the doyen of Hindi literary criticism, expressed his enjoyment of Kabir's wit and his castigation of Hindu and Muslim fanaticism but was extremely uncomfortable with the poet's critique of caste hierarchy and wrote of the 'futility of trying to find any philosophical system in Kabir'. It was in response to Shukla that Dwivedi declared Kabir to be a Nath panthi. But Shukla has a point. Kabir's worldview does not fit neatly into any of the traditional six systems of philosophy, not even with Buddhism, Jainism or what Dwivedi calls the 'dwaitadwaitvilakshanwad' of the Nath panthis.

The critic Namvar Singh's description of the Nirgunis as 'empirical rationalists' is much better, as we will see in the next chapter. For now, though, let us continue to consider the

astonishment with which even followers and admirers of Kabir regard his ecumenism. Shyam Sundar Das, the editor of *Kabir Granthavali*, for instance, believes 'Kabir had Hindu, if not Brahmin, blood in his veins'—how else could he be so knowledgeable about things Hindu? The Hindi scholar Chandrabali Pandey points out that Kabir also knew much about and had great insight into Islamic thought. In one essay, Pandey writes that in Kabir's era, 'many Hindus had started describing themselves as Sufis and many Muslims had turned Vaishnavas in spirit'.[6] Kabir, though, was different, Pandey concludes—Kabir was a 'Zind', a Sufi of subtle practice and high distinction. Remember the question the young Muslim weavers express in Virmani's documentary, *Had Anhad*: to which religion did Kabir belong? Most Kabir scholarship in the colonial period, and later for that matter, responded to this based on finding the answer to an even more 'essential' question: who, by birth, was Kabir?

Was he a Nath panthi, because his ancestors were recent converts from that tradition, even if they later described themselves as Muslims? And since he is supposed to have had Hindu blood in his veins, could Hindus claim Kabir? Well, others argue, he must have been Sufi because he was born Muslim. What apparently can not be considered is that Kabir did not want to be straitjacketed by arbitrary labels and had decided to follow his own path.

None of the scholars mentioned above could have been ignorant of the fluidity of such categories in Indian life. Pandey even notes the 'many' Hindus who described themselves as Sufi and their Muslim-Vaishnava counterparts. Despite this knowledge, perhaps scholars still leaned on received wisdom like a crutch, and everyone 'knew' that the modern individual did not exist in pre-British 'medieval' India.

It has almost become an article of faith that in Kabir's India, one's caste predetermined one's vocation, and the family background not only shaped but also set one's ideas and attitudes in stone. Any deviation from the path supposedly fixed at birth meant that something outrageous and inexplicable was afoot. This problem is not confined to India. The conscious or unconscious internalisation of the prejudice that Europe is the sole inventor of modernity and its core idea—individuality—affects the study of all non-European societies. As the Cameroonian political scientist Achille Mbembe writes:

> On key matters, the Hegelian, post-Hegelian and Weberian traditions, philosophies of action and philosophies of de-construction derived from Nietzsche or Heidegger, share the representation of distinction between the West and other historical human forms as, largely, the way the individual in the West has gradually freed her/himself from the sway of traditions and attained an autonomous capacity to conceive, in the here and now, the definition of norms and their free formulation by individual wills. These traditions also share, to varying degrees, the assumption that, compared to the West, other societies are primitive, simple, or traditional in that, in them, the weight of past predetermines individual behaviour and limits the areas of choice—as it were a priori. The formulation of norms in these latter societies has nothing to do with reasoned public deliberation, since the setting of norms by a process of argument is a specific invention of modern Europe.[7]

Due to such prejudiced notions, the historical significance of not only Muslim Vaishnavas, mentioned by the traveller Mahmud Balkhi and scholar Mowbad Shah, but also of prominent literary figures has eluded the radar of most 'modern' scholars. Rahim, a minister in Akbar's court, and Raskhan, a nobleman, were famous poets writing in Braj Bhasha and had imbibed aspects of the Bhakti sensibility. A rather less-noticed poet, Taj, a royal lady, composed moving poems of love for Krishna. None of these Muslims who turned devotees of Krishna suffered either a fatwa from Muslim clerics or a boycott by Hindus. The Sufi poet Malik Muhammad Jayasi, who, unlike Kabir, was a believing and practising Muslim, demonstrated in his works an abiding knowledge of and affection for Puranic Hindu and Nath-panthi mythology, traditions and practices. Even Tulsidas had little hesitation in using the rather unusual Arabic word 'haboob' to describe an intense wave of emotion because it fit his rhyme scheme better than the Sanskrit 'tarang'.

These individuals were by no means rare or exceptions to the rule. They were only too well known in their own time. Such examples can be multiplied many times over. Whatever the particular views of these early modern Indian poets and non-poets, one thing they have in common is that they were not mere ciphers of their birth, caste and religion. They were all self-aware moral agents making conscious intellectual, aesthetic and vocational choices. Kabir was not a slave to family tradition, as too many of his modern interpreters would like him to be. He made his own choices and paid the price, from having his mother grieve publicly about his 'waywardness' to his poetry uniting both pandits and maulanas in their contempt.

All this is not to say early modern India was some oasis of tolerance. Apart from the likes of Jayasi, Sufis like Baba Farid and Abdul Quddus Gangohi were also famous for their knowledge and practice of yoga. Gangohi, in fact, composed a famous yoga treatise called *Alakh Bani* (The Voice of the Invisible). At the same time, though, Gangohi wrote letters to Babur asking him to put the 'kafirs' in their place by keeping them in a state of poverty, far from the responsibilities and privileges of administration, and even to ban their right to worship.[8] The point is that one could do 'yoga sadhana' while remaining an extremist or fundamentalist. But one could also make one's philosophical practice integral to everyday life and reject the religious divide. It was upto the individual. Inevitably, some allied themselves to Gangohi's militant position, while many others chose Kabir's inclusive stance. Is it not true, even today, that practising yoga does not turn one into a Hindu, Buddhist or Jain?

These porous boundaries are not merely a historical oddity. I have visited the shrine of Baba Badam Shah in Solampur, a village near Ajmer, where the chief khadim—literally meaning servant, the spiritual and administrative head of the shrine—happened to be a Mishra Brahmin by ancestry. My driver on this trip, Mumtaz Ali, a believing, orthodox Muslim, was a devotee of the local Radha-Krishna temple belonging to the Nimbarka sampradaya, one of the four Vaishnava religious systems. He insisted on taking me to the temple to meet the mahant, his spiritual guru. I have also met other Muslims (and you probably have too) who, while being true to the Islamic faith, have Hindu or other non-Muslim spiritual advisors in 'secular' matters.

The famed 'composite culture' of India is neither an empty slogan nor did it drop from the sky. It was created by individuals exercising moral agency, making choices and opening themselves up to possibilities. It is only natural that ground zero for India's uniquely melded culture would be from about the fourteenth century on when vernacular poets flourished. People felt empowered to participate in religious exploration because they could establish an individual relationship with the godhead; they weren't cut off by clerical intermediaries (Brahmins) or language (Sanskrit). The vernacularistion of discourse was an essential, universal feature of early modernity, which expressed itself in India through specific characteristics.

Colonial 'documentation' of Indian social life pigeonholed people into mutually exclusive religious slots. British scholars and administrators came from a context where relations amongst the various sects of Christianity were strained and often violent. In Europe, it was impossible to imagine a person being both Catholic and Protestant, never mind sharing the practices of another faith without formally converting to it. It beggars belief that the parochial and rather literate British thought that part of their role was to civilise the Muslim Vaishnavas and Hindu Sufis of stagnant, sleeping India. The vibrancy of multifaith, multicultural early modern India was erased, particularly in the imaginations of those who wished to use history for their personal and political agendas.

In order to convert Kabir into a militantly exclusionist Dalit icon, Dharamvir goes to the extent of declaring that 'a mosquito or a housefly could have been Kabir's guru, but not Ramanand the Brahmin.'[9] This is, at best, a statement made on faith with little regard for historical fact.

Ramanand may have been born a Brahmin, but he rebelled against the orthodox, southern Sri Vaishnava sampradaya and till date has been excluded from the list of revered persons of the sect, his spiritual achievements and significance remain unrecognised. In the northern tradition, though, he is hugely revered as the guru of Kabir, among others. Mowbad Shah, in *Dabistan-e-Mazahib*, describes Kabir as one of the Bairagis (as Ramanandi Vaishnavas were and are still called) and explains that 'they describe their path as different from both the Veda and the Koran and declare, "We are neither Hindus nor Muslims."'[10] Denying Ramanand's role in Kabir's spiritual insights, as Dharamvir does, for ideological or political reasons, can feel radical but opens up a Pandora's box.

The response of reactionary forces, of every political and religious stripe, to the film *Padmaavat* was to browbeat a simplistic, faith and sentiment-based assessment onto a more complex historical narrative. The Supreme Court dismissed the complaint against the movie on the grounds of freedom of speech, but equally important is the distortion and reduction of history. If we base our analysis of figures like Kabir on our assumptions and prejudices, how can we complain when someone argues, say, that it's impossible that a practising Sufi Muslim like Malik Muhammad Jayasi could have written the sixteenth-century epic poem glorifying a Hindu queen and her husband that only a Hindu poet could have written?

Our past, present and future are of course connected, but confusing one with the other and erasing the autonomous existence of each is disastrous.

Coming back to Kabir's family roots, none of his contemporaries—admirers or detractors—ever tried to prove that, he, socially speaking, was anything other than a Muslim weaver. Such prominent contemporaries as Pipa and Ravidas categorically refer to Kabir's family as one that observed Eid, performed ritual sacrifices and venerated sheikhs and pirs. There was little doubt within the public sphere of Bhakti and also in the wider community: 'Kabir—the sadhu and great thinker—is born of the womb of a Julaha woman,' (जुलाहा ग्रभे उत्पन्नो साध कबीर महामुनी।) writes Rajab Ali Khan, the author of *Sarvangi* and favourite disciple of the saint Dadu Dayal, who had a great influence in Gujarat and what is today Rajasthan.

The story of 'a Brahmin widow' being Kabir's biological mother entered the scene only after the establishment of the Kabir panth. As mentioned in Chapter Two, the very first reference to this unfortunate widowed mother occurs as late as in 1776, in *Bhaktigunadamchitrini Tika* by Balakdas, a commentary on Nabhadas's *Bhaktamal*. If one of Kabir's contemporaries had been forced to speculate on the poet's religion, they would probably have said that he was 'born a Muslim weaver, had both knowledge and experience of Tantra, Nath panth, Puranic Hinduism and Islam, and had finally chosen to immerse himself into "Naradi bhakti".'

If this was early modern India, the present-day modernity in the country suffers from the dissociation of sensibility caused by colonial rule. It has deprived itself of seeing the dynamics of its own vernacular modernity. As a result, Kabir is now disowned by Muslims for going beyond the boundaries of the religion, as one young man told the filmmaker Virmani, and is accepted by Hindus only as the offspring of an embarrassed Brahmin widow.

Then, there is the category of 'educated people with urban backgrounds', as Stanford scholar Linda Hess describes them, 'who are interested in Kabir as a social critic and ally in the political struggle'.[11] Kabir's constant interrogation of the social structures and prejudices of his time makes him an icon for progressive, secular and liberal voices, but they tend to gloss over or maintain a calculated silence about the spiritual and mystical aspects of his thought and his personality. Hess cites her conversation with an activist tremendously fond of Kabir's famous song *Nirbhay Nirgun Gun Re Gaunga* (I Will Fearlessly Sing of Nirgun), but is shocked when Hess points out that the song is not about social rebellion but about yoga. Kabir is reassuring yogis who find themselves in the wilder reaches of their practice and often have strange, even frightening, experiences to tackle their fears with confidence.

The essential, in fact, existential problem with well-meaning 'educated people with urban backgrounds' in India is that their idea of 'secularism' takes no notice of the specific features of the Indian cultural experience. Their liberalism has made no space for the teachings of vernacular modernity of India. It has become commonplace to believe that 'reason' dismisses any alternative to itself as pathology. This is hardly true even of the European Enlightenment and is most certainly untrue of the idea of vivek as propounded by Kabir and other Nirgunis. This conception of vivek had wide-ranging impact, as we have already seen in the case of Akbar's grand vizier Abul Fazl's attempt to articulate 'rationality immersed in religiosity'. In the West, the rationalists had to 'fight' god; in India, though, Nirgunis, the empirical rationalists, had god on their side.

Kabir privileges human reason but does not reject intuition, mysticism and the idiom of mythology and miracles. His stinging social criticism emanated from his insight that his Ram permeated the whole universe. He saw the presence of divinity in each and every iota of existence, including in oneself. His identification with universal consciousness is quite categorical—'I am in everything and everything is within me.' (हम सब मांहिं, सकल हम मांहिं; हम थैं और दूसरा नाहीं।) This sentiment is repeatedly expressed in Kabir's work and is obviously evocative of Upanishadic monistic wisdom. The originality of Kabir, however, lies in his insistence on taking this spiritual realisation to its logical culmination in the realm of human relations. His query is simple and fundamental: 'If Ram is everywhere, if he is Jagjivan and can be reached by purity of heart and mind, if he and I are essentially the same, then how are some people "untouchable" for no crime of theirs and some venerated with no achievement to their credit?'

Vernacular modernity did not recoil from asking these

questions of what was presented as ancient wisdom. In early modern India, a variety of public figures and intellectuals engaged with the 'golden' past and attempted to find thought-provoking answers to their own questions. My advice to educated, urban, liberal Indians today is to go back and listen to the vernacular voices of that period to enrich one's sense of self and one's surroundings. At an academic level too, ideas rooted in the European Enlightenment of the long eighteenth century will become even more exciting and inspiring in tandem with the vivek of Kabir and other Bhaktas.

For Kabir, vivek, a kind of self-directed enlightenment, was the foundation for all claims to knowledge, whether pragmatic and 'secular' or mysterious and 'spiritual'. His sadhana was intended at making vivek a natural, spontaneous aspect of life, sahaj. Kabir, of course, was only too aware of the work and effort involved in making wisdom appear so effortless, so intrinsic to one's persona. His words bear witness to that rigour.

The Philosopher's Enlightenment and the Poet's Vivek

'Enlightenment is man's emergence from his self-imposed nonage,' reads the opening sentence of the essay 'What Is Enlightenment?' by the eighteenth-century philosopher Immanuel Kant. 'Nonage is the inability to use one's own understanding without another's guidance.' Kant goes on to identify 'indecision' and 'lack of courage' to use our own minds as the ills that prevent us from turning ourselves into enlightened individuals.[12]

Coming out from under the shadow of authority—parental, professional or scriptural—is a re-constructive exercise. Your parents remain important, even into adulthood, though you are on your own and not under their tutelage. Your religious and cultural tradition, similarly, remain dear to you even after you have acquired a comparative and evaluative perspective of it. Any society at any point in history, be it eighteenth-century Europe or nineteenth-century India, can be said to have gone through a period of enlightenment, of awakening. But in the sense of a broadening of mental horizons, surely, enlightenment is a perpetually ongoing process.

Until some centuries ago, ritual human sacrifice was a practice across diverse cultures and societies, something universally abhorred now. Human rights, we now agree, ought to be standard practice everywhere, but it took millennia of history and intellectual progress for our current understanding of rights to evolve—that process of evolution is vivek, how human knowledge and wisdom come to be. Humans, unlike other animals, learn not only from their own direct experiences but also from the cumulative experience across cultures and civilisations. Modern democracy cannot be ignored by non-Europeans merely due to its largely European provenance. And it is not for Germans alone to learn from the human disaster caused by the mass endorsement of Nazism.

In the case of individuals we celebrate and revere as 'enlightened', we have a tendency to identify a particular moment as a turning point, the precise moment at which enlightenment 'arrives'. Significantly, unlike with the Buddha and Mahavira, Kabir legends do not identify any moment as *the* moment of his enlightenment. In his case, vivek is a human process, not a divine boon.

Vivek is one of his four key words, as we have seen before. Kabir's life and poetry imply that instead of looking for *the* moment, every moment has to be lived as a step in the journey towards expanding one's mental horizons and acquiring moral agency; Kantian enlightenment is the closest equivalent to what Kabir meant by vivek. And just like Ram—Kabir's favourite name for transcendental experience—is always to be sought, so is vivek; the search is constant, helped by all experience and all forms of knowledge. Kabir learnt from whatever was available in his environment—Islam, Puranic Hinduism and the Nath panth, for instance. Being an artisan who sold his goods in the market, Kabir must have had basic reading and mathematical skills. But he was not a scholar of Hindu or Islamic theology and was not interested in the scholarly splitting of hairs, a standard practice among scholars that goes back centuries—a display of pedantry, a clinging on to obscurantist 'learning' while remaining aloof from and uninterested in everyday life.

Kabir could not be and would not have wanted to be part of such a scholastic enterprise, though he appeared to have had a fair understanding of the various theological positions and mythological narratives of Puranic Hinduism, Islam and the Nath path. Hazari Prasad Dwivedi, in his writing, expresses disappointment with Kabir for choosing 'a country bumpkin type of Brahmin as his intellectual adversary, remaining blissfully unaware of the fact that, a Brahmin, right or wrong, has a whole theoretical framework to justify his beliefs and practices'.[13] This is a little like feeling disappointed with Copernicus, Galileo and Kepler for rejecting the geocentric model of the solar system (a stationary earth around which revolve the sun and other planets) without engaging with the scholasticism of medieval church fathers. These astronomers rejected the geocentric model on the basis of their intuitions, observations and calculations. They could hardly make their case while remaining within the scholastic tradition and without earning the wrath of those utterly invested in upholding that tradition and the power that came with it. Galileo recanted his 'theory' under the fear of Inquisition, but as the legend goes, he still murmured, 'Yet, it [the Earth] moves.'

Kabir and other Nirgunis were converting their pain at unjust discrimination into questions they asked of the 'learned ones' and authorities. The scholarship of the time could have seriously engaged with this anguish, but it instead turned its face. That is the difference between a genuine knowledge enterprise and 'scholasticism' that privileges the church, the Brahmin priest or any other authority. A tradition of knowledge enriches and renews itself when it seriously engages with questions reflecting human concerns and anxieties. If it chooses to dismiss inquisitiveness as 'heresy' and continues to rationalise the status quo by taking recourse to punctilious argumentation, it is bound to turn in on itself, becoming an endless and barren repetition of hoary formulae, with but a few insignificant additions and deletions. Indeed, refusing to play by the rules set by scholasticism and ceasing to be awestruck by the elaborate piousness of fine argumentation is a prerequisite for the real growth of human knowledge. That is what the astronomers in Europe and the Nirgunis in India found, often at great personal cost.

To recall what Kamaali, Kabir's daughter, told the pandit Sarvajit, the great practitioner of scholastic debate:

> Kabir dwells in a high place;
> the way is too slippery even for ants.
> And some people want to negotiate it
> on a loaded bullock.

> जन कबीर का सिखरि घर, राह सलैली गैल।
> पांव न टिके पिपीलिका लोगन लादे बैल॥

As with the scholasticism of Puranic Hinduism and Islam, Kabir hardly had any patience for the esoteric ways of yogis. They spoke of experiencing a brilliant light in their sadhana, which supposedly enabled them to perform various miracles, including attaining immortality. Kabir minced no words in reminding them that being a sadhu (that is, a sadhaka, a noble soul) had nothing to do with the making of such illusory claims for oneself; even Gorakhnath himself could not escape death:

Flickering, struggling, swaying—
no one is left out
Even Gorakh got stuck in Death city
So, who is a yogi?[14]

(Translation by Linda Hess and Shukdeo Singh)

गोरख अटके कालपुर।
कौन कहावे साहु ॥

Whoever Kabir chose as his adversary or ally, a 'country bumpkin' or an accomplished scholar, it was the questions he posed that were important, not the glib 'answers' he received. Kabir gave no concessions to anybody—pandits, maulanas or Nath panthis, or even a fellow Bhakta. His persistence was similar to those early modern European astronomers who preferred fidelity to their scientific observations and mathematical calculations over false reverence for 'pious' scholarship. It was Kabir's innocence of the scholastic order, his repugnance for the necessary bowing and scraping before 'worthies', that gave him the courage to call out, 'The emperor has no clothes.'

You can have any number of rationalisations and circumlocutions, but how do you answer questions that are products of human inquisitiveness and vivek? 'As you claim special status because you are a pure Brahmin, why did you not choose a purer way of being born? If you are so proud of being a Muslim, why were you not circumcised inside the womb itself?' Kabir asks such provocative, even offensive, questions to underline his most basic perception: 'No one is inferior by birth. Inferior are those who ignore Ram.'

जो तू बाँभन बाँभनी जाया, आन बाट ह्वै काहे नहीं आया?
जो तू तुरक तुरकनी जाया, भीतर खतना काहे ना कराया?
कहै कबीर मधिम नहीं कोई, सो मधिम जा मुखि राम न होई।[15]

Kabir is also emphasising that religious identity is not divinely ordained or 'natural'—it is essentially a social construct. Rather than fight for or defend such a construct, Kabir invites you to:

Revert to your inner self
to rediscover the adventures of your spiritual quest,
which like an ocean knows no limits,
and be grateful to the merciful god.

मन उलट्या दरिया मिल्या लागा मलि मलि न्हान।
थाहत थाह न आवई तूँ पूरा रहिमान ॥[16]

Never does Kabir shy away from engaging with the pandits of Puranic Hinduism, Islam or the Nath panth on their terms. He is convinced that his questions are valid and is so confident of the strength of his bhakti that, to some, he could appear arrogant. But his 'arrogance' is only a reflection of his impatience with those who cannot empathise with the 'other' and remain indifferent to questions arising out of lived experiences. He does not hesitate to dismiss the scholastic Brahmin's claim to guru status:

The Brahmin may be a guru for others,
but not for Kabir,
as the Brahmin is hopelessly entangled
in the web of the four Vedas.

ब्राह्मण गुरु जगत का, साधूं का गुरु नाहिं।
उरझि पुरझि करि मरि रह्या,चारयूं बेदा मांहि ॥[17]

To a scholar of Muslim jurisprudence, he asks equally 'arrogantly':

Qazi, what book are you lecturing on?
Yak, yak, yak, day and night
You never had an original thought.[18]

(Translation by Hess and Singh)

काजी तुम कौन किताब बखानी।
झंखत बकत रहो निसि बासर, मति एकौ नहिं जानी॥

He also bluntly rejects the Nath panthis' claims of being miracle workers: yogis' bodies are supposed to be resistant to decay because of the constant work they put in to polish and shine their physiques.

Gorakh was yoga's connoisseur
They didn't cremate
his body
Still his meat rotted and mixed with dust. For nothing
he polished his body.[19]

(Translation by Hess and Singh)

गोरख रसिया जोग के।
मुये न जारी देह॥
मास गली माटी मिली।
कोरी मांजी देह॥

Kabir interrogated all claims to holiness and superiority. His admirers have an obligation to cultivate the same integrity and ask questions of everyone around them, including Kabir, especially about his complicated views on women. In Chapter Six, we will discuss the paradox of Kabir's adoption of a female persona in some moments and his blanket condemnation of women in others.

'Independent of the Veda and the Koran': A Wise Counsel, a Venerable Authority

Kabir must have known from his own experiences, as we come to know from our own, that sweet-talkers are not necessarily nice people. Being a straight-talker himself, Kabir preferred truthful, even if unpleasant, words. He cautions us:

> Those speaking in a sweet, friendly manner
> are not sadhus.
> Having won your confidence,
> they will leave you in troubled waters.

> जेता मीठा बोलना, तेता साध न जान।
> पहली थाह दिखाइ करि, ऊंडे देसी आन॥[20]

Honeyed words are an example of falsehood and insincerity. Kabir has a fear and loathing of all diversions from the path of truth. Intelligent and sensitive, he is keenly aware that most people are superficial and supercilious, that they are likely to be more annoyed and angered by those asking difficult questions of the authorities than by the errant authorities. He realises the enchanting power of folly, and his observation is sadly just as true in the twenty-first century as it must have been in Kabir's time:

> The intelligent person
> dies a thousand deaths,
> while the ignorant rules.
> Incapable of understanding anything,
> such fools are concerned
> only with filling their bellies.

जाण भगत का नित मरण, अनजाने का राज।
असर पसर समझै नहीं, पेट भरण सूं काज॥[21]

In these poems, Kabir is in his preacher avatar; though, he preaches as a poet and not as a dharma-guru, a religious teacher eager to win credulous followers instead of imparting real wisdom. Had Kabir been that sort of huckster, an early modern Indian version of a holy roller, we would not have been able to sense his genuine inner turmoil and immense loneliness that we do from his poetry. Despite his popularity, Kabir asks plaintively: 'With whom can I share this essence? I hardly have any friends.' (बिरले दोस्त कबीर के, यह तत्त बार-बार कासों कहिये?) Going by contemporary accounts, Kabir's loneliness was no mere literary trope. Having friends is different from having disciples. Some accounts indicate that perhaps his only friend was his senior contemporary Ravidas.

Maybe Kabir was too singular to have had friendships. He could not have been easy company. As a poet, his language permits a range of emotions and intellectual explorations. Yes, in places, he might indeed appear 'arrogant'. After all, he claims that Hari follows him as ardently as he follows god. At the same time, he is a weaver who calls himself a 'low life', albeit ironically. Self-confidence, not arrogance, is Kabir's defining characteristic. Though he does not name a guru, the poet celebrates him repeatedly in his verse, going to the extent of identifying his guru with Govind:

Guru and Govind are one;
the one that is the Other is this form.
Annihilating this form*
is the way to the creator.
*self/ego

गुर गोविंद तो एक है, दूजा यह आकार।
आपा मेटि जीवत मरै, तौ पावै करतार॥[22]

In all spiritual practices and many creative ones as well (for example in music and dance), a deep devotion to the guru is seen as a prerequisite for learning. Ideally, one needs to be grateful to one's guru as it is the teacher who shows the path of vivek. Unfortunately, this gratitude to the guru was, and continues to be, exploited until it became a weapon against enlightenment and wisdom. If such 'gurus' found a willing audience among even Kabir bhaktas and others, the highly educated of our own time too are guilty of unthinkingly submitting to religious cult personalities, disregarding vivek. And such lemming-like behaviour is justified in the name of our spiritual ancestors, including Kabir, who sang of the guru's glory.

But Kabir chose his guru only after careful consideration, and even then maintained his own moral and intellectual autonomy. Ramanand, apparently, was an idol-worshipper and believed in avatars, while Kabir did not. What attracted Kabir to Ramanand was the latter's disavowal of caste-based hierarchy and his preference for vernacular languages over Sanskrit. Ramanand was a guru who, by most accounts, entered into a relationship of mutual enrichment and respect with Kabir and his other disciples. After the Kabir panth was established, the profound gratitude for his guru of as self-conscious and evolved an individual as Kabir was used to rationalise the abject surrender of individual vivek, a seeker's responsibility to find his own path to understanding and knowledge, to serve as an armour against the onslaught of idiocy from the inside as well as the outside.

Kabir's gratitude to his guru can be reduced to mindless fawning only if you determinedly ignore everything else he said and did. While he celebrates, even glorifies the concept of the noble guru in his poems, he cautions against bad ones in his typically blunt fashion: 'An idiot is likely to take another idiot as a guru, then both are destined to doom.' These lines warn that when the blind lead the blind, both inevitably fall together into the well.

जाका गुरु आंधला, चेला है जा अंध।
अंधे अंधा ठेलिया दोनों कूप पड़ंत ॥[23]

These days, it has also become fashionable to present Kabir as a singer of love for one and all and use his rejection of scholasticism to support the anti-intellectualism that is rife today. In both cases, his spiky edges are smoothed into inane sentimentality. Kabir does not preach love for all; he is made furious by injustice and has a healthy contempt for many of the ways of humans. As for Kabir as a standard-bearer for anti-intellectualism, the following lines are cited as the essence of his entire teaching:

> Reading many volumes all your life
> will not make you a pandit.
> But reading just
> a syllable pertaining to the beloved will.

> पोथी पढ़ि पढ़ि जग मुआ, पंडित भया न कोय।
> एकै आखर पीव का, पढ़े सो पंडित होय॥[24]

If we read him beyond just this one couplet, or read even this one properly, the foolishness of making Kabir the mascot of anti-intellectualism becomes clear. The above saakhi is preceded by another which sets the context:

> The whole world seems to be reading a lot,
> but what is the point
> if it fails to create empathy
> for love, pain and suffering?

> कबीर पढ़िबा दूरि करि आथि पढ़्या संसार।
> पीड़ न उपजी प्रीत सूं तो क्यों करि पुकार॥[25]

Kabir perceives a conflict, not between love and intellect but between the most profound aspects of the human psyche and bookish knowledge. The latter, Kabir contends, is divorced from life and shies away from human emotions. He is critical of scholasticism and not of an individual's intellectual vocation.

He contrasts authentic knowledge (gyan) with knowledge systems that serve narrow, selfish interests (maya). The idea of true knowledge leading to authentic love is a recurring refrain of Kabir's. It's the perfect riposte to those critics who push the shallow, self-serving idea of an opposition between love and the intellect in his verse. Kabir articulates his position on this matter quite elaborately and unambiguously. Take the following poem, which, complete with evocative metaphors, reads like a manifesto for vivek:

> The storm of knowledge
> blew away the structures of illusion,
> splintered the pillars of self-centredness,
> brought down the thatched roof of false attachments,
> and shattered the pot of ignorance.
> To stop the seepage,
> sants have reconstructed it with tools of yoga.
> Knowing the ways of Hari,
> my body is now purified.
> The storm gave way to rain,
> I am drenched in his love.
> The sun has risen, says Kabir,
> taking away the darkness.

> संतौ, भाई आई ज्ञान की आंधी रे।
> भ्रम की टांटी सबै उड़ानी, माया रहै न बांधी रे॥
> हित चित की द्वै थूनीं गिरानी, मोह बलींडा टूटा।
> तिस्ना छानि परी धर ऊपर, कुबुधि का भांडा फूटा॥
> जोग जुगति करि संतन बांधी, निरचू चुवै पाणी।
> कूड़ कपट काया का निकस्या, गरि की गति जब जाणी॥
> आंधी पीछै जो जल बूठा, प्रेम हरी जन भीनां।
> कहै कबीर, भान के प्रगटें, उदित भया तम खीनां॥[26]

Sahaj, another of Kabir's keywords, came to connote certain esoteric Tantric practices, particularly of the sexual variety. Kabir

frees the word from this and emphasises its literal meaning—
spontaneity, a careful cultivation of compassion, curiosity,
sensitivity and critical inquiry that it becomes spontaneous, as if
an integral part of one's nature.

Perhaps because of its lingering associations with Tantric sex,
sahaj is still not entirely disassociated from hedonism. But in
Kabir's view, sahaj is impossible without disciplined sadhana, with
a clear direction and purpose. Sahaj, Kabir appears to suggest, has
to be detached from both wild abandon and extreme self-denial,
implying balance, a moving away from the extremes. Instead of
negligence or over-indulgence, Kabir says, the real way of sahaj
requires you to keep in touch with your senses and organs:

सहज सहज सब कोई कहै, सहज न चीन्हैं कोय।
पंचू राखै परसता, सहज कहिजै सोय॥[27]

Kabir's ideas of vivek and sahaj ought to be among the basic
aims of education. Before being imparted any training in either
professional or life skills, students must be taught to make vivek
a pleasant habit of the mind instead of a burden. Such vivek
would shape interrogation to be essential to any activity and

would persuade the student to assess everything, including Kabir's teachings, in line with universal human values and rationality. Kabir's vivek is flexible enough to allow for a student to buy into faith, spirituality and mythology without falling prey, for instance, to a godman charged with the rape of a child, who is nonetheless hailed by his followers just because he claims that he can postpone sunrise by forty minutes. Kabir's empirical rationalism is a challenge to authority and blind belief, but not faith. Believe, he seems to be saying, but believe for the right reasons. 'Put on the shawl of sahaj and enjoy riding the elephant of knowledge,' he writes, 'and let the dogs of the world bark.'

हसती चढिया ज्ञान कै, सहज दुलीचा डारि।
स्वान रूप संसार है, पड्या भूसौ झषि मारि ॥[28]

In the public sphere of Bhakti, Kabir's reputation as a thinker and public intellectual was influential enough to be taken seriously. We saw how aggressively Tulsidas took on Kabir, quoting his poems as an example of ideological wickedness. Kabir is extensively quoted in the Adi Granth too. Fifteen of his poems also appear in an anthology published in 1582 (within seven decades of Kabir's death), titled *Pad Surdasji ka*, compiled in Fatehpur (in present-day Rajasthan) for a prince. As the title makes clear, the anthology is mainly dedicated to the work of Surdas, a visually challenged Bhakti poet, but contains the work of other similar poets. The most revered among Kabir panthis is of course the *Bijak*, practically a holy text for them. Many Kabir panthis have composed tikas, or commentaries, on the *Bijak*, just as Sanskrit scholars write elaborate interpretations of ancient 'scripture'.

Seeing Kabir's influence in the public sphere of Bhakti dispels the absurd notion that the poet and his followers had little to do with intellectual activity. It also underlines the historical inaccuracy, and indeed disservice, of lauding Kabir as an icon of a particular brand of identity politics. He tried to create a community of Bhaktas and sants who would transcend their birth-related social identities. He, in his vivek, wanted to reach out to everyone, not just those of certain castes. Nowhere does Kabir address only weavers, or only Muslims, yogis or Vaishnavas. He imagined a community based on the purity of vivek, not blood, and it was open to all, including Brahmins.

And some of them responded positively. We already know how the Brahmin pandit Sarvajit came to defeat Kabir in debate and was so impressed and humbled by his opponent that he became Surati Gopal, perhaps the first of Kabir's disciples. Another Brahmin, Ramraj Dwivedi, became a Kabir panthi and authored *Panch Granthi*, the earliest prose commentary on the *Bijak*. His work, composed in the eighteenth century, is considered the departure point of Parakh Marg, an important branch of Kabir panth. Puran Sahib, of the Parakh Marg, wrote *Trija* (1837), a reading of the *Bijak* that is plainly influenced by Jain philosophy and which provoked a polemical rejoinder thirty years later from Vishvanath Singh Judev, a follower of the Dharamdasi branch of the panth. Such commentaries and other works were circulated through oral renderings and handwritten manuscripts. Book culture, even in those pre-printing days, was vibrant in the public sphere of Bhakti, including amongst the followers of Kabir, the supposedly 'illiterate' singer of sentimental love songs.

Starting from the seventeenth century, several works known as gosthi, meaning a small gathering, containing 'Kabir dialogues' were composed. In these, we see Kabir authoritatively enlightening figures like Gorakhnath, Guru Nanak, Ravidas and even Durvasa, famous in Hindu mythology for his hair-trigger temper. The 'teacher' image presented in these compositions were reiterated in the Bhakti public sphere. Later, many Bhaktas from all over the country claimed to have been directly initiated by Kabir. More importantly, from an intellectual point of view, was the way Kabir was cited as an apostle of knowledge and wisdom. Dadu Dayal—a sixteenth-century saint who had a panth in his name and enjoyed considerable influence among both ordinary people and the elites of present-day Rajasthan and Gujarat—quotes Kabir by name in many of his poems with a reverence appropriate for a great, wise authority. In *Dadu Janam Lila* (The Story of Dadu's Life)—composed in 1620 by Jangopal, a merchant and one of Dadu's favourite disciples—we hear Dadu quoting Kabir's couplets in conversations with both Man Singh I, who was in Akbar's royal court, as well as the emperor.

Kabir was (and continues to be) read as a friend, philosopher and guide by many. His admirers related to his positive, confident accounts of intellectual transformation:

> Using the stirrup of sahaj,
> I will mount the horse of my mind.
> I will put on the reins,
> tie up the strong saddle.
> Spurring it on with the whip of love,
> I will take my horse to the heavens, even final liberation.
> For I, Kabir, am such a rider,
> independent of the Veda and the Koran.

> अपनै विचारि असवारी कीजै।
> सहज के पावड़े पांव तब दीजै॥
> दे मुहरा लगाम पहिराऊं। सिकली जीन गगन दौराऊं॥
> चलि बैकुंठ तोहि लै तारूँ। थकहि तैं प्रेम ताजनैं मारूँ॥
> जन कबीर ऐसा असवारा। वेद कतेब दोऊं तैं न्यारा॥[29]

I brought Kant into this discussion of Kabir's vivek to underline the universality of some of the values and endeavours. The poet and the philosopher, so distant in time and space, both articulated universal aspects of modernity in their specific contexts: an emphasis on individuality instead of ascribed identity and more faith in the rational instead of the scriptural. Their concerns were similar, even if, because they were context-specific, their articulations were different. Kant was a full-fledged academic-philosopher, while Kabir was a poet with a deeply philosophical bent of mind. We find in the latter's words not only insights and reflections but also stirring emotion. He tells us a story of dramatic internal upheaval, confusion and external opprobrium, all of which is overcome.

Although, this is not expressed in the direct, intimate language of a diary. Kabir's life has not been spelt out for us by the few friends he had, or his disciples or hangers-on. But his poet's language carries within it traces of the process, the long struggle behind the pristine outcome on the page. The choice of words, metaphors and tropes help the reader come away with a profound sense of his personality.

For all Kabir's talk of the nay-sayers and doubters he overcame, he is not the sort to hold grudges. His verses contain moments of deep reflection, brooding, longing and even sadness, but his voice is essentially buoyant and his lines electric with enthusiasm, celebration and playfulness. His wit is enjoyed even by those who do not agree with him, and his sarcasm can be lethal. But Kabir doesn't use his quick-wittedness, the sharpness of his pen and tongue, to wound; his poetry is expansive, suffused with love, desire and, in an airier vein, existential, epistemological and ethical musings, and beneath it all, that omnipresent mischievous humour, most evident in his ulatbansi, 'upside-down' poems.

Kabir's poetry sparkles, a bright rainbow after the squall. His words and moods cannot be contained. But let us zero in for now on his use of the upside-down language and his moving encounter with death.

Upside Down: Talking Sense in the Idiom of Nonsense

The enigmatic side of Kabir the mystic is most impressively visible in his ulatbansi, so are his creative mischief and verbal exuberance. Things are indeed full of mystery in these poems, the familiar made strange and uncanny (centuries before Freud would coin the term 'unheimlich')—fish climb trees, lions keep affectionate watch over grazing cows, and dogs are overpowered by cats. Some images are unsettling, or cathartic, depending on your point of view: a bride, for instance, claims that she has 'brought glory to both households by devouring twelve husbands at her father's house and sixteen at her in-laws'. Some are so ludicrous you cannot help but laugh out loud—a wedding party at which an ass is dancing in full costume, with a male buffalo for the dance master and an ox playing the delicate string instrument rabab.

Kabir did not invent ulatbansi; like sahaj, it was already a familiar term, especially to those with an interest in Tantric philosophy and practice. Paradoxical expressions are found in very ancient Vedic, Buddhist and Jain texts. From the eighth century onwards, such expressions became particularly associated with Tantra. Just as Kabir freed the word 'sahaj' from its technical and hedonistic connotations, he transformed the code language of ulatbansi into poetic idiom. The strangeness of ulatbansi—or sandha-bhasha, twilight language—has attracted a lot of scholarly attention. Focussing on Kabir's use of ulatbansi, Linda Hess has written a thought-provoking and lucid essay which can be read in the appendix to her and Shukdeo Singh's translation of the *Bijak*. Hess underlines a basic point:

> Paradoxical expression in Kabir is not limited to the obvious *ulatbansi* poems. The formula *akatha katha*, Kabir's most compact little paradox, appears throughout his works. ...

Riddles and negations are common fare. Kabir repeatedly says, 'No one understands me,' 'Who can believe this?', 'A rare one figures this out,' or 'How amazing!' His teaching weaves in and out of impossible verbal and intellectual situations. *Ulatbansi* poems are merely specialists in inconceivables. Intimacy with them will have a pervasive effect on our understanding of all Kabir's poems.[30]

She also recalls a warning given her in person by Hazari Prasad Dwivedi that 'a deep and detailed study of Kabir's straightforward works must precede any effort to interpret Kabir's *ulatbansi* expressions.'[31]

This note of caution is quite valid, as Kabir is radically different from his predecessors. Those who came before him used ulatbansi to primarily, if not exclusively, convey the technicalities of esoteric spiritual and mystic practices. Ulatbansi, for instance, was a code language to limit the details of such practices to insiders and deserving seekers of Tantric knowledge. It was not used as a tool of social critique and certainly not as a medium of creative mischief.

Even if ulatbansi was used for a specific purpose rather than as a means to offer social commentary, it is true that mysticism in all religious traditions is implicitly a social critique. This is as true of Tantrikas in the Hindu and Buddhist context, as it is of Sufis in the Islamic one and the mystic saints of various Christian orders. Mysticism has led many a person of faith to be labelled heretic and sentenced to the gallows. In Hinduism and Buddhism, while the essential unity of individual and universal consciousness did not alarm the religious conservatives, the mystics' indifference to social norms did. Sahaj was intended to be a sadhana, the practice of going beyond the binary of pure and impure at all levels; digression from norms of purity in matters of caste and sexuality was particularly important for this sadhana. Sandha-bhasha served the dual purpose of keeping the esoteric truth of certain practices shrouded in code language while being sufficiently understandable to shock the conservatives incapable of appreciating the hidden truth. To this extent, there was an implicit and, in some cases, explicit critique of the social code of varnashrama dharma as well as the prevailing sexual morality.

But Kabir's critique, though it did not merely stem out of frustration with the existing arrangement, was nonetheless too explicit for the comfort of powers that be. While he has not left us a detailed blueprint of his preferred social system, there is ample evidence in his work of the direction in which he would have liked to take society. Unlike the secular utopias imagined in the nineteenth century, Kabir's utopia (sometimes called 'Amarpur', the Immortal City, or sometimes just 'that land') is not about equality alone but also about balance and moderation. 'Madhi', the middle way, and 'samata', balance, are amongst his favourite expressions. To him, social and spiritual, outer and inner, are intertwined; there is no question of antagonism or even mutual indifference.

Such a conception of spirituality, human relations and society is at the root of Kabir's repeatedly expressed dissatisfaction with most of the reality of his time. What was seen as normal (and still is today), to Kabir was abnormal or upside down: be it economic inequality or the empty symbolism of religious rituals. He calls out to his Ram desperately: 'Either me or this world of yours—one of us is out of our mind.' Wielding his irony like a sword, Kabir describes himself as a 'hopelessly gone case' and cautions others to be careful not to follow 'spoilt' Kabir, as 'he will spoil you too as the sandal tree "spoils" other trees by spreading its fragrance or the philosopher's stone "spoils" base metal by turning it into gold'.[32] Hess appositely uses a quote from one of Plato's dialogues (*Gorgias*) among the epigraphs to her essay: 'Socrates … if you're serious … won't human life have to be turned completely upside down?' Just like Socrates, Kabir too proposes to turn human life, as we know it, completely upside down.

In sandha-bhasha, various words and expressions carried specifically allotted meanings understood only by those in the know. The *Hevajra Tantra*, a Buddhist text composed somewhere between the eighth and tenth centuries, defined sandha-bhasha as a samay-sanket vistar, a code system, of the mahabhasha, meta speech, of sadhana.[33] It also, helpfully, provided an extensive glossary of code words and their meanings. As already noted, the hidden symbolism was intended to hide as well as shock, and the words were appropriately chosen. For instance, in the work of a Tantric master, you might come across an injunction to kill your guru. The text is not recommending murder; 'guru' in this case means the mind, and the instruction is a standard exhortation to tame and master the mind. Elsewhere in such a text, you might come across someone being praised for slaughtering cows; in this case, 'cow' is a reference to sexual desire. Scholars have, however, noted the lack of uniformity and consistency in the use of sandha-bhasha codes; not everyone followed the 'standard' lexicon, such as the one provided in the *Hevajra Tantra*.

This is why attempts to read every sadhaka's use of ulatbansi in the same way mostly leads to frustration rather than elucidation. In Kabir's case, he uses ulatbansi both as a mystic and as a poet. It is the poet's job to imbue even technical terms and the most prosaic of thoughts with fresh insight, to evoke with the use of that word in that spot a particular feeling in the reader. Kabir does exactly this with sahaj, taking a Tantric term and transforming it into his own. A word in a poem is never complete in itself; it acquires meaning only within the totality of the poem.

Kabir's ulatbansi poems articulate an intense feeling of being at odds with the world. To seek answers to his riddles in the glossaries provided in the likes of the *Hevajra Tantra* will only perplex the reader. So how does one crack Kabir's code? Hess tells a story about how she was presented with 'a new insight into the function of ulatbansi' while she was interviewing Dada Sitaram, 'a Tantric guru in Varanasi'. She had been, she writes, 'conducting the interview in a grave scholarly tone', when it 'suddenly dawned' on her that the poems were, as the guru-ji and his disciple chuckled with glee when they chanted the lines, intended to be 'fun!' Hess writes, 'these snapshots of animals in human guises were like a comic strip, and provided the same amusing and ironic slant on human affairs. ... We laugh as children do at a cartoon, and evoking this childlike state of mind may be one way of breaking habitual thought patterns.'[34] After all, in the story, it is a child who not only recognises that the emperor is naked but also has the courage to point it out.

In his ulatbansis, Kabir lets rip. He points out the inconstancies in the philosophical systems of the time. For instance, 'All that exists is Brahman'—सर्वं खल्विदं ब्रह्म—is a lofty sentiment about universal consciousness, Kabir acknowledges, but it appeared to mean little in practice. In the real world, it was dharma to uphold the social order based on a hierarchy not of individual qualities and achievements but accidents of birth. That to Kabir's mind was the fundamental issue—the distance between what was practised and what was, rather sententiously, preached. He was wary of even using the word 'dharma', as we shall see in the following chapter.

We are habituated to see Kabir's ulatbansis as upside down, poems that are abnormal, funny, esoteric and surreal. But what about such lines as the below, which Tulsidas makes Ram himself speak in his *Ramcharitmanas*: 'A Brahmin, even if devoid of qualities and character must be revered, while a Shudra, full of knowledge and human qualities, must not be'?[35] Is this not ulatbansi in the sense of rationality and, for that matter, rudimentary human intelligence and decency being turned upside down?

There cannot be any objection to reading ulatbansis as esoteric; but the difference between the poet who was equally concerned with the inside and the outside, the spiritual and the social, versus the sadhaka who was exclusively focussed on the spiritual must not be forgotten. Kabir brings the multilayered ambiguity of poetic language into his words. Ambiguity gives us the space to read our own meaning and experience into a poem otherwise distant from us in every way. Although such ambiguity might be seen as a weakness in the practical use of language, in poetry, it is its strength. A good poem 'suggests' much more than it explicitly says. What made Dada Sitaram chuckle in Hess's anecdote was precisely this 'suggestion' contained in the poem.

Through its apparent arrangement of words and metaphors, the poem that Hess was discussing with Sitaram actually suggests the absurdity of our everyday experiences, an absurdity which has been made to look normal through 'common sense'. The poet intends to jolt us out of our complacency through the nonsensical. Read the poem in Hess's translation; hopefully, you will join Sitaram with a chuckle of your own:

Brother, see
where humans find
security.
This tale can't be told.
Lion and tiger were yoked to a plow
sowing rice in a barren field.
The wild bear cleared the ground,
the billy goat ran the farm,
the nanny goat married a wild cat,
a cow sang festive songs.
An antelope brought the dowry
a lizard served as bridesmaid,
the crow washed all the laundry
while the heron gnashed its teeth.
The fly shaved its head, shouting

I must join the marriage party!
Kabir says, can you
figure out this
poetry?
If so, I will call you
scholar, genius,
devotee.[36]

(Translation by Hess and Singh)

If this is merely a codified manual of esoteric practice, what would be the point of calling someone who figures it out a 'scholar, genius, [true] devotee'? Having started his spiritual journey as a Shakta, Kabir knew well that this terminology would not pose a serious challenge to anyone with some knowledge of Tantra, who could then decode it with the help of the *Hevajra Tantra* or any other lexicon. He must have had his reasons for placing a premium on decoding these and similar lines.

But unmindful of this, scholars have continued to 'read' Kabir's ulatbansis with their glossaries at hand. In the standard commentaries (particularly in the ones prepared for students) on the *Bijak* and *Granthavali*, you will find such poems explained with the 'meaning' of each coded word written out. Words are thus 'explained' without any sense of the totality of the poem. The 'meaning' of the poem, its unsettling irony, the all-pervasive absurdity of the images and the challenge presented to the reader are forgotten in the smug afterglow of having cracked the 'code'.

There cannot be any objection to Kabir's ulatbansi poems being read as an aid to inner spiritual growth, but, as he warns: those on a quest must find their own way, spiritual guides are unreliable, and even the choice of a good guru ultimately depends on the proper application of one's vivek. While it is true that we read our own concerns into any poem, we cannot ignore the intentions of the poet or manipulate the words to facilitate our chosen reading. There must be an effort to maintain the delicate balance between

poetic intent and the reader's response. Now, let us read an upside-
down festive scene:

> The bull plays the mridang with confidence,
> while the ox strums as delicate an instrument as the rabab.
> An ass dances, directed by a male buffalo,
> while those who see themselves as nothing less than lions
> serve betel leaves with a rodent's assistance.
> The poor she-mouse has no choice
> but to join this unsettling celebration.

> धौल मंदिलया बैल रबाबी, कऊवा ताल बजावै।
> पहिरि चोलना गादह नाचै, भैंसा निरति करावै॥
> स्यंघ बैठा पान कतरै, घूंस गिलौरा लावे।
> उदरी बपुरी मंगल गावै, कछु एक आनंद सुनावै॥[37]

Absurd as the images may appear to be, we only have to look
around us to recognise ourselves in these animals immersed in
their ridiculous worldly activities. Are not many of us playing the
mridang like a bull and dancing like an ass in order to buttress

our oversized egos and, worse still, to curry favors with the powerful? Don't many imagine themselves to be lions while they are but betel-leaf servers of the powers that be? Do we not live in a world where the powerless are manipulated and seduced by mass media and other means of propaganda to celebrate their own ruination like the 'poor she-mouse' in this poem joining the 'celebration'?

Moksha: Living in the Presence of Death

Kabir felt sorry for those who had no sense ('khabar', or news) of themselves. His ulatbansis, for all their 'mysticism' and creative mischief, represent yet another attempt to reiterate the importance of khabar, of being well-informed and alert to oneself and one's surroundings.

And what news could be more unsettling, yet inevitable, than this: our life, so dear to us, is not forever. We have to live in the constant company of death, however hard we try to look away. Every poet worth their salt engages with death, but also love. In Kabir, love is the point of departure for social critique as well as intellectual innovation. Love in Kabir's poetry is like the invisible Saraswati at Sangam—the famed, sacred confluence of the Ganga and Yamuna in Allahabad. He engages with love in its erotic as well as spiritual form. Human love is at the core of the very idea of Bhakti, particularly in the Nirgun and Krishna-oriented sensibility.

Death, too, occurs quite frequently in Kabir's poetry, not in the abstract as it would in a philosopher's work, but through evocation, description and imagery. Kabir describes the world as the 'village of dead'. He reminds us that everyone has to die, 'even the pirs and prophets and yogis claiming immortality; not to mention kings and their subjects; the sick and the healers':

साधो, ई मुरदन का गाँव
पीर मरै, पैगम्बर मरि हैं,
मरि हैं जिंदा जोगी।
राजा मरि हैं, परजा मरि हैं,
मरि हैं बैद और रोगी॥

But, there is still hope:

Only the 'name' that cannot be named lives forever
Understand this; don't die wandering here and there

नाम अनाम अनंत रहत है,
दूजा तत्व न कोई,
कहे कबीर, सुनो भई साधो,
भटक मरो मत कोई।[38]

The expression, 'the name that cannot be named' brings to mind the Sufi idea of the hidden hundredth name of god. There is also the Chinese mystic Lao Tzu's warning: 'The Tao that can be told is not the eternal Tao. The name that can be named is not the eternal name.' We are being told that we must go our own way, choose our own preferred 'name', which would transform the abstract—love, remembrance and gratitude, for instance—into a palpable presence (as noted in Chapter One). For Kabir, that name is 'Ram'; for you, it could be another and not necessarily from a religious tradition.

A profound psychological point is presented here: we need an emotional anchor and a moral compass, and we need to give it a name. Most of us forget that no one name can monopolise the sphere of spiritual anguish and no one method can claim to have exhausted all avenues to deal with such anguish. As the other great poet Malik Muhammad Jayasi puts it: 'There are as many ways to god as there are stars in the firmament and pores in the human body.' (बिधना के मारग हैं तेते, सरग नखत तन रोआँ जेते।)

In the famous 'Yaksha Prashna' episode of the *Mahabharata*, one of the questions put to Yudhishtira—by Yama, the god of death who has assumed the guise of a yaksha, a spirit of sorts, which had earlier taken the form of a crane—is what he would think of as the most 'amazing'. The yaksha's questions are open-ended and largely philosophical, existential and metaphysical in nature. Yudhishtira—whose brothers lay dead around him, having drunk from a lake despite the yaksha (as crane) warning them that the water was poisoned and could only be drunk once its questions had been answered—thinks carefully. 'We see so many dying every day,' he says, 'yet behave as if we are never going to die. What could be more amazing?'

Does Yudhishtira express amazement at human folly? At our ability to turn our face away complacently from the hardest of facts? Or is he marvelling at human bravery, our irrepressible will to live in the face of death? The word 'kaal' means death as well as time. Intrinsic to Indic wisdom is the poignant awareness that each and every moment of time is also a moment of death. Our journey in kaal—time and death—is irreversible. It is on us to make this journey meaningful.

Like every mystic sadhaka, Kabir speaks of the transient nature of the world and our need to make space for the eternal in this very transience. But in the way of this, Kabir observes, stands maya— cosmic illusion and false attachment. 'Even gods and sages,' he says, 'are hardly beyond the grip of Maya, the great seductress (माया महाठगिनी).' We live through the body and death is its end, but it is only through the body that the human self can hope to do the things necessary to break free of maya and kaal and achieve moksha, the final liberation. Kabir devotes a lot of attention to the body, recommending and explaining practices and critiquing the ones he finds misleading. He rarely talks of any outward exercises or postures (asanas) or diet. The body's health and appearance are not his primary interest. Instead, his corporal advice is directed at our 'inner body'. Kabir has no patience with those who inflict torture on their bodies. He also cautions against over-indulgence. Excessive pride or attention on the outer body seems to Kabir to be misplaced: 'See this body burning? Just wait a moment, with all its achievements it is going to turn into ashes. Full of desire, anger and other such distortions, the world is in any case burning. Kabir says, we are already like the dead; it is only with the name of Ram that we can get rid of our conceit.'

देखहु यह तन जरता है,
घड़ी पहर बिलमो रे भाई जरता है।
काहे को एता कीया पसारा,
यहु तन जरि बरि ह्वै ह्वै छारा॥

काम क्रोध घट भरै विकारा, आपहि आप जरै संसारा।
कहै कबीर हम मृतक समाना, राम नाम छूटै अभिमाना॥[39]

Being constantly aware of death is necessary to living life meaningfully, argues Kabir. We are, after all, alone in death. Take, for instance, a widow atop her husband's pyre addressing her only friend:

Sitting on the pyre, the sati calls out,
'Listen, dear crematorium,
everyone has left, and only two remain:
you and I.'

सती पुकारे सलि चढ़ि, सुन रे मीत मसान।
लोग बटाऊ चलि गये, हम तुझ रहे निदान॥[40]

Self-awareness leading to dialogue with death makes 'jivanmrit' possible. That is true immortality—being alive in the memory of those we leave behind—not the fantasy of making the body immortal through esoteric practices.

When Yama tries to divert Nachiketa's attention from existential questions by offering him immortality, the boy responds: 'Having spoken with you in person, O Lord of Death, what value does immortality have for me?' In a similar vein, Kabir declares confidently: 'I am one with he who gives life, so where is the question of dying? Death is only for them who have not known god. If god dies, only then will I die; if he doesn't, I wouldn't either. Having met him within myself, I have attained the ocean of bliss, I have become immortal.' Even at this moment of supreme self-realisation, Kabir takes a dig at the Shaktas: 'The true Bhakta fortified by the elixir of Ram is going to live, while the Shakta is certainly going to die.'

हम न मरिहैं मरिहै संसारा,
हम कूं मिला जियावनहारा।
अब न मरूँ करनैं मन माना। तेई मुये जिनि राम न जाना॥
साकत मरैं, संत जन जीवैं। भरि भरि राम रसाइन पीवैं॥
हरि मरिहै तौ हमहूं मरिहैं। हरि न मरै हम काहे कूं मरिहैं॥
कहै कबीर मन मनहिं मिलावा। अमर भये सुख सागर पावा॥[41]

Moksha to Kabir is not a post-death phenomenon. Just as there is no single moment of enlightenment, similarly, moksha is a constant process—of being in the state of jivanmrit, in constant awareness of death. Despite being reconciled to death, there is still the physical fact of life coming to an end. The body is destined to wither away. And even the most liberated souls among the poets want to be remembered, to leave behind traces of their struggles, frustrations and realisations. And so, Kabir confesses:

This life and body are transitory,
hence Kabir composes poetry.

छिन में बितसै यहै सरीरा, तिहि कारन पद रचै कबीरा।[42]

V

Bhakti: Morality and Moksha in Everyday Life

Rational vs Spiritual?

In July 2019, an infamous godman, currently a fugitive from Indian justice for crimes of sexual assault, made the ridiculous claim that he commanded the sun to rise forty minutes later than it normally would have risen, so he could complete a dawn ritual. Naturally, according to him, the sun obliged. In the video, his disciples clap wildly, beatific smiles wreathed across their faces, their faith absolute in their guru-ji's capacity to work miracles.[1] In an earlier video, this same godman is in 'deep' public conversation with a US-based businessman of Indian origin, a self-appointed guardian angel of Sanatan dharma. The businessman had come up with a plan. With the powers and the knowledge assured to the two by their devout faith, they could enable the wealthiest people in the world, in return for a payment, of course, up to half their net worth, to take their riches into their next life and be spared the ignominy of being born paupers 'in some African village'. With the swami's help and the use of a 'jeevatama GPS', they could locate the wealthy in their next life and give them their money, or rather, a portion of it. For a correspondingly greater fee, this Hindu committee could guarantee these billionaires, so concerned about the future of their wealth after their death, a rebirth in a place of their choosing.[2]

The admirers and followers of these supposed standard-bearers of Hinduism are not 'uneducated' people, but often English-speaking professionals trained in management, technology or other fields. And yet, how conveniently they discard rationality in favour of ersatz spirituality. Even schoolchildren know, as did the ancient inhabitants of this country, that sunrise and sunset are caused by the earth's revolution around the sun. Even a nanosecond's break in the earth's perpetual rotation on its axis and revolution around the sun would cause cosmic disorder, or Mahapralaya. Surely, those applauding the 'swami' for the miracle of postponing sunrise knew better. The same goes for the audience applauding the 'swami' and his businessman interlocutor for their 'Hindu' spin on the Catholic church's sale of indulgences and pardons, a corrupt practice that helped catalyse the Protestant reformation.

Such absurd claims and their enthusiastic acceptance by highly educated, elite followers can be found in every contemporary religion. A Muslim televangelist trots out verses from the Koran to buttress his flights of fancy and regressive ideas. A trained medical doctor, he rubbishes the theory of evolution before his huge audience purely based on faith in the 'final divine word'. His Christian counterparts, meanwhile, treat chronic diseases and disabilities with a few florid hand gestures in full view of cheering, hyperventilating crowds. On a 2019 visit to the Grand Canyon in Arizona, I was offered a tour with a 'Biblical view'. Alas, I could not take up the offer, but committed, no doubt, intelligent Christians reject the geologists' scientifically backed view that the canyon developed through millions of years of erosion in favour of a much shorter Bible-inspired timeline. One guide, quoted in the *New York Times* for his Creationist revision of the Canyon's history, wrote in an online article: 'If we look at the Canyon through the eyes of a biblical, or scriptural, geologist (those who believe in the Bible's timeline of a young earth), we will see a very different Canyon. These geologists see a young canyon carved with a massive amount of water, likely in a matter of just days, shortly after the global flood of Noah's day about 4,300 years ago.'[3]

Is it necessary to be credulous in order to be religious? Is there such an unresolvable conflict between the rational and the spiritual? Admittedly, in matters of faith and gratitude, rationality has to be applied with empathy and care. We are, after all, humans, not robots. But the question remains: to what extent can reason be denied? Without rationality, emotions like gratitude and devotion can be exploited; don't we have enough examples of political figures, businessmen and religious leaders who misuse the faith placed on them? And then there is the question of universal human values. Can we uphold violence and injustice in the name of faith? Can we buy racism and sexism and other such prejudices if they come packaged in spirituality? Is it not sad to see educated and otherwise 'rational' people defend utter nonsense as demonstrable truth just because the nonsense emanates from their 'own' faith or from their 'teachers'?

The human mind experiences spiritual anguish precisely because of its capacity for rational thought. Our anguish should certainly not be dismissed as some kind of illusion. Indeed, such anxious seeking is integral to the human self. Our minds are programmed to find meaning. We use our rational faculties to connect the dots, as best as we can, and imbue a seemingly unconnected, random world with order, perspective and meaning. For instance, we don't know what happens after death but, as a

species, we have imagined every kind of possibility—cycles of birth and rebirth, the day of judgement, heaven and hell, and of course the void, a total end with no kind of afterlife. In any case, the idea of the afterlife is a result of our refusal to see the death of the body as an end. Various forms of afterlife described across religions may not be acceptable to everyone, but afterlife through the act of remembrance is a universal desire. As Kabir writes, 'Life is transitory, hence Kabir composes poetry.'

Here is the essential paradox of being human: our desire for immortality alongside the certainty of death. There are other similar ironies: As humans, we must love ourselves but must make space to love others too. We desire freedom but need some bonds. We want desperately to be rooted but to be able, at will, to wander into the unknown. No wonder that as we live our mundane, pragmatic lives, we long, too, for the sacred and mysterious. What we believe to be 'sacred' gives us the tools to explain or rationalise certain experiences and fragments of our life. It also provides us with community, the fellowship of like-minded people. Why else, despite the leaps we make in our knowledge and understanding of the world, do we continue to seek out god (or whatever we hold sacred) to find answers to the unexplainable?

The twenty-first century is faced with the development of technology at an unprecedented pace and, intriguingly, a pronounced return of religiosity across large parts of the world. Everyone seems to have become acutely sensitive about their religious identity and sentiments. But, this apparent religiosity can hardly cover the all-pervasive spiritual emptiness expressing itself in ever-increasing stress and trauma. The lacuna between religion and spirituality is widening by the day, as is the quotient of anxiety and aggression. Our very sanity appears at stake.

And the mantra of 'being positive', routinely trotted out by so many gurus and counsellors, is ineffective for the simple reason that the spread of negativity is not merely an 'inner' phenomenon. It has an integral 'outer' dimension as well. You cannot feel positive unless you have some rational hold of the issues afflicting the world around you. The same is true of the other side of this: no meaningful social or political act can ignore the inner, spiritual aspect of human beings. The issue of transcending the binary of spiritual and rational has always been important; for us in the twenty-first century, it has become critical. We need a rational idea of spirituality that is sensitive to the inner world of the individual and, at the same time, is mindful of collective, social challenges and external issues.

Does Kabir help us in articulating a 'rational spirituality'? Yes, indeed, he does. He calls it 'bhakti'.

To begin with, his idea of 'profound' truth itself is based on a clear rejection of the binary. It is both within and without, both need to be experienced. Truth requires the interaction of the inner and outer worlds:

> How do I convey the profound truth I have come to know?
> If I say it's within, where does the world around me go?
> If I claim it to be outside, then it is a lie.
> It is both inside and outside; a constant flux.
> Mind and non-mind; visible and invisible;
> it cannot be held or beheld
> and is impossible to convey through mere words.

> ऐसा लो नहीं तैसा लो मैं, केहि बिधि कथौं गंभीरा लो।
> भीतर कहूं तो जगमय लाजै, बाहर कहूं तो झूठा लो॥
> बाहर-भीतर सकल निरंतर, चित-अचित दोउ पीठा लो।
> दृष्टि न मुष्टि परगट अगोचर, बातन कहा न जाई लो॥[4]

Recognition of the interconnected nature of the 'inside' and 'outside' leads to the rejection of either/or choices between the pleasures of life (bhoga) and the attempts to connect with the supreme consciousness (yoga). Kabir confidently assures us that 'both can be pursued simultaneously through bhakti and love'. He reaches this conclusion as a result of his own reflections on the Brahman, the ultimate truth:

You can either
have a blissful union with the ultimate truth
or enjoy the pleasures of this life—
so goes the popular wisdom.
But by doing yoga of the name of Ram,
you can indeed attain both.
Practise bhakti through the path of love,
your speech will have a nectar-like sweetness.
Just imagine the bliss.
My words are no ordinary songs,
in these is contained my reflections on the Brahman.
I have simply put forth
the essence of self-realisation.

एक जुगति एक ही मिलै, किंवा जोग कि भोग।
इन दुन्यूँ फर पाइए, राम नाम सिधि जोग रे।
प्रेम भगति ऐसी कीजिए, मुखि अमृत बरसै चंद।
आप ही आप बिचारिए, तब केता होइ अनंद रे।
तुम्ह जिनि जानो गीत है, यह तो निज ब्रह्म बिचार रे।
केवल कहि समझाइया, आतम साधन सार रे॥[5]

The word 'yoga' is used here in its etymological sense
of 'combining': bringing together bhakti with everyday life
diminishes the day-to-day stresses. He is talking of the coexistence
of yoga (discipline) and bhoga (pleasure) in the framework of
bhakti rooted in love. Notably, he describes his reflection as that
on Brahman, or transcendental reality, not on dharma. In all, this
poem is about the essence of the realisation of the self. It covers
artha, kama and moksha, but where is dharma? Why is Kabir wary
of using the word 'dharma'?

Not Dharma, but Bhakti

In the four purushartha schemes, you achieve moksha (liberation from karma and the cycle of birth-rebirth) by following dharma (one's ethical and moral duty) diligently in your pursuit of kama (needs and desires) and artha (resources). But Kabir insists on bhakti, not dharma, as a way to moksha and as the prime measure of the moral worth of life.

But, is devotion not an integral part of every religious practice in any case? Did Kabir himself not establish a new religious order? Was he not a dharma-guru as Hazari Prasad Dwivedi and many other scholars believe?

Such observations would have been valid had Kabir really propagated a new religion, as Buddha did, or had he, like Tulsidas, tried to conserve and rejuvenate the available notion of dharma. But he did neither. Far from religious tradition, new or old, Kabir's bhakti, instead, is a forceful interrogation of it all. Ironically, this persistent questioning is presented as irrefutable evidence of him being the founder of his own peculiar panth or even an altogether new religion.

From what was discussed in the previous two chapters, we can start to uncover the assumptions that underlie attempts to present Kabir as a dharma-guru. When everything was predetermined by family lineage, religious affiliation, caste and so on, when there was no question of individual choice and moral agency, the only motivation behind a sharp critique of Hinduism and Islam must have been the desire to establish one's own religious panth.

The interrogation of the very idea of religion is very modern, and that is precisely what Kabir did. An early modern Indian, his criticism was not confined to any specific religion but was directed at the very idea of organised religion. His Nirgun bhakti, far from being religious, is in fact the touchstone of his critique.

Nabhadas had correctly summed up Kabir's position—'Any dharmic (religious) act bereft of bhakti is in fact an adharmic (irreligious) one.' Kabir's ambition was far greater than merely establishing a new religion or sect. Religion's hold over human consciousness is made tighter by its monopoly over spirituality. In Kabir's poems, we hear an anguished soul trying to articulate spirituality beyond religion.

Kabir panthis of course claim that their panth was established by 'sahib' (as they call Kabir) himself. But this claim is not supported by any historical evidence. In Kabir's own poems, we find no hint that he ever saw himself as the founder of any new religious order, as a prophet or an incarnation. He speaks of his 'immortality' not as a god but with the confidence of a man who has achieved identification with the ultimate truth—death—and has overcome his fear of it. He suggests the way to this eternal life:

Hindus die chanting 'Ram'
Muslims die chanting 'Khuda'
Kabir tells you, only he who avoids both, lives

कबीर हिंदू मूये राम कहि, मुसलमान खुदाइ।
कहै कबीर सो जीवता, दुइ में कदै न जाइ ॥[6]

In other words, in order to live, it is better to keep one's distance from organised religion. He would have added Christianity to the list had he been around in nineteenth-century India instead of in the fifteenth and sixteenth centuries.

But, is it really possible for an individual to keep an arm's length from all organised religion? Kabir's own ironical fate suggests not. He tried to break free of its chains and ended up being seen as the—for some, divine—founder of a new sect. So, what is the way out? Rationality coupled with compassion is at the core of Kabir's notion of spirituality. He calls it 'bhakti', a word which in various forms and with many derivatives occurs innumerable times in his poems. He incessantly speaks of its glory as well as its challenges.

On the other hand, dharma is conspicuous by its near absence in the Kabir compilation *Granthavali*, which literally means 'series of books' and carries the connotation of 'collected works'. Shyam Sundar Das, a professor of Hindi literature at Banaras Hindu University prepared this 'collected works' of Kabir in 1928 on the basis of two manuscripts. A better-edited version of the same material was published just over forty years later by Mata Prasad Gupta.

Granthavali is the most comprehensive Kabir collection. Its value was underlined as recently as the year 2000 when Winand Callewaert, professor at the Belgian university KU Leuven and eminent scholar known for his work on Bhakti manuscripts, published *The Millennium Kabir Vani*, a critical edition of poems 'attributed to Kabir'. Callewaert had begun his research into the book because he was dissatisfied with the editor of the *Granthavali* for including too many poems 'without rigorous research'. He believed that the *Granthavali* had 'Vaishnavised' and softened Kabir the iconoclast.

In order to determine the Kabir text as it might have been around 1550, Callewaert took ten manuscripts, dated between 1570 and 1681, from Bihar, UP, Rajasthan and Punjab, and fashioned a 'star system' to determine the probable authenticity of poems circulating with Kabir's imprint—the more manuscripts in which a poem appeared, the more stars it received. He identifies forty-eight poems which he argues constituted the 'early Kabir core' and are probably most 'authentic'. The Kabir who emerges from these forty-eight poems is not the bitter, cutting critic of brahminism that perhaps scholars like Callewaert and the poet's political admirers want him to be. He is a more holistic figure, critical, of course, but evidently a seeker of balance between the spiritual and social. It is also apparent that, above all, he is a thoughtful and humble poet, not at all an ambitious religious guru.

But, the Kabir that emerges from Callewaert's research continues to remain 'Vaishnavised' despite the fact that the scholar

intended his work to liberate him from the image he believed
had been foisted upon him by the *Granthavali*. This was because
Callewaert's assiduous labour showed that of the 403 poems
collected in the *Granthavali*, 396 are found in the manuscripts he
consulted to determine the 'core Kabir'. On the other hand, out
of the 593 poems Callewaert found in these manuscripts only 15
are fully or partially found in the *Bijak*.[7] It appeared the editor of
the *Granthavali* had not been all that careless, even if he had not
had access to the bells and whistles of contemporary methods to
determine authenticity. The *Granthavali* contains 809 saakhis and
403 pads from Dadu-panthi manuscripts, 192 saakhis and 222 pads
from the *Adi Granth* and dozens of compositions called 'ramaini'.
So, in such a large number of poems, comprising thousands of
words, how many times does the word 'dharma' occur? A grand
total of twenty-one times.

Of these occurrences, four are references to Dharmaraj,
or Yama, the god of death. In one poem from the *Adi Granth*,
'dharma' refers to the very nature (jiva-dharma) of all living
beings; in another poem, it refers to the duties assigned to a varna,
so a 'Kshatriya performs his Kshatriya dharma'; and in yet another
instance, 'dharma' is employed to remind every householder in the
grihastha stage of his life of familial and social obligations.

In the *Bijak* too, a similar situation prevails. The term 'dharma',
in the sense of a codified spiritual and social system, is hardly
used and when it is, the tone is often sarcastic and harshly critical.
Kabir challenges the proud followers of all religions about what
constitutes authentic spirituality and proper social behaviour. He
can often sound like a preacher, but his tone is that of a family elder
or well-wisher giving occasionally unasked-for advice, not the
hectoring spiel of the proselytiser. He desires your moral, spiritual
and emotional growth, not your conversion to 'his' religion. There
is absolutely no textual evidence that can be marshalled to suggest
that he imagined himself as the prophet and founder of a new
religion. I have already noted the significance of the legend of his
last rites from this point of view: 'Not another religion please!' But,

though Kabir is sceptical of formalised religion, his sensibility and creativity breathes in the air of bhakti, of faith and devotion.

The word 'dharma' conventionally refers both to inherent nature and duty. It is fire's dharma to burn and it is a king's dharma to take good care of his subjects. It is water's dharma to flow and, apparently, it is a wife's dharma to follow her husband and a Shudra's to be ever respectful to Brahmins. The word 'dharma-sankat' (धर्म-संकट) indicates a conflict between duties, a moral dilemma.

It is often claimed that Hinduism is a way of life, not a religion, as if the two can be somehow distinguished. The thing is, every religion proposes a certain 'way of life'; it comes as a package deal with faith and ritual. The difference between Hinduism and the Abrahamic religions is that the latter insist on exclusive devotion to one theology and doctrine. The followers of the 'correct' doctrine constitute the community of believers, while the others are either to be overcome and converted or tolerated. Hinduism expects you to follow a certain code of conduct and to link yourself with the deity/deities and schools of thought of your choice within a loosely structured system containing multiple faiths, including atheism.

These differences notwithstanding, faith in some kind of

transcendental truth and the idea of a shared space of the sacred is a feature common to all religious traditions—Indic or Abrahamic. It is because of this shared space that attempts to treat religion or dharma as merely a 'private' affair cut little ice with the faithful, or even those who are not particularly religious but whose lives move to the cultural beat of organised religion. Every religion also has a system of reward and punishment for what you do in this life, whether you learn your fate on the final day of judgement or through the cycle of rebirth. This idea of reward and punishment— an example of what Max Weber thought of as 'theodicy', man's need to explain and make sense of a senseless world—also helps to project as divine the social order upheld by the religion concerned. Sharing sacred space with others who participate in a similar faith structure makes you a member of a 'religious' community. And such is the influence of religion on daily life that you remain culturally a member of a faith even after you discard its belief system.

Organised religions specify modes of worship with devotion as their crux. But, to the Bhakti poets, bhakti was not merely a form of personal devotion or a mode of worship. After Namdev reinvented bhakti in the Kali yuga, Sagun bhakti too gained a pronounced social aspect which led to many poetic innovations. But Sagunis continued to worship god in their favourite forms, that is, their traditional avatars. They saw no conflict between the existing ideas of dharma and bhakti and propagated this 'no-conflict' position in their songs. The Sagun-panthi idea of directing bhakti to one of the avatars implied a continued belief in the divinely ordained validity of the varna order. God assumes an avatar to uphold the sanctity of varna and eliminate evil-doers. This is the famous assurance of the Gita. Tulsidas's Shiva says something similar, as he explains to Parvati why gods must sometimes descend from the heavens:

> I tell you, my dear,
> the logic as I understand it:
> whenever dharma suffers
> because of despicable, arrogant, evil people gaining power

and many indulging in unspeakable excesses,
including the persecution of Brahmins and cows,
then, at such moments,
the lord himself assumes various physical forms
to eradicate the suffering of good people.

तस मैं सुमुखि सुनावउँ तोही। समुझि परइ जस कारन मोही॥
जब जब होई धरम कै हानी। बाढ़हिं असुर अधम अभिमानी॥
करहिं अनीति जाइ नहिं बरनी। सीदहिं बिप्र धेनु सुर धरनी॥
तब तब प्रभु धरि बिबिध सरीरा। हरहिं कृपानिधि सज्जन पीरा॥[8]

Sagunis also shared the idea, in varying degrees, that bhakti must
be articulated in conformity with Vedic knowledge and a Vedic
worldview—'*Bhakti ved prakasa*,' as Tulsidas puts it. Opposed to
this conformist version of bhakti, Kabir and other Nirgunis spoke
and sang of bhakti rooted in sahaj vivek, a natural, self-reflective
wisdom and knowledge. They showed remarkable indifference to
scriptural tradition, Hindu or Islamic, and felt uncomfortable with
the idea of avatars precisely because it implied a celebration of the
unjust, as they thought of it, varna order.

By avoiding the very term 'dharma', Kabir emphatically
distanced his bhakti from that of the Sagunis. In his opinion,
instead of bhakti conforming to dharma and Veda, it ought to
be the other way round. Bhakti for Ram, or rather Kabir's Ram,
should be the way to assess the worth of any dharma. As Kabir
himself put it, 'Dharma lives forever in a heart that keeps testing
it on the touchstone that is Ram.' (सदा धर्म तेहि हृदया बसई, राम कसौटी
कसतहि रहई।[9])

In no less than the Bhagavad Gita, we can find bhakti
being proposed as an alternative to dharma. Ramanujacharya,
the eleventh- and twelfth-century theologian, in his bhakti-
orientated commentary, described the sixty-sixth verse of the
Gita's eighteenth and last chapter as the 'ultimate' statement of the
divine text. In this verse, Krishna tells Arjuna categorically:

Discard all dharmas, take refuge in me.
I will free you of all sins, you need not worry.

सर्वान् धर्मान् परित्यज्य मामेकं शरणं व्रज।
अहं त्वां सर्वपापेभ्यो मोक्षयिष्यामि मा शुच: ॥

Note the use of the plural for dharma. Krishna is referring here to various theological positions and, more importantly, to general and varna-specific codes of conduct. All of them, he says, should be discarded in favour of surrender to god which, as it stands, is a precise definition of bhakti. But, in the same text, the lord admonishes Arjuna for ignoring his Kshatriya dharma and declares that the varna order had been created by none other than himself. Even if an individual (Arjuna in this case) could, with divine encouragement, discard all the dharmas, the basic sanctity of the varna hierarchy would remain intact. This ruled out any chance that Kabir might gravitate towards the Krishna avatar. Kabir could not countenance the denial of individual agency implicit in the varna hierarchy. That is why, as Nabhadas wrote, Kabir 'did not care for any of the six schools of philosophy'. He could not accept the inconsistency between the theory of 'All that exists is Brahman' and the practice of exclusions rooted in caste prejudice. That is why he dreams of reaching the stage where 'dharma, karma and veda become irrelevant'. (धर्म कर्म कछु नाहीं उहंवा, न उहां बेद विचारा।[10])

The name Ram is a stand-in for this grand dream. One must reach this stage in this very life, not in some supposed rebirth. One can understand, without much difficulty, Kabir's point of view: The next birth (if any) will not be my life, but someone else's. The story of me as me will be over as soon as I am dead. Hence, my Ram, he writes,

I must meet you in this very life;
meeting you after death is as useless
as a piece of iron being touched by a philosopher's stone
after the iron has already turned into stone.

मूवाँ पीछे जिनि मिलै, कहै कबीरा राम।
पाथर घाटा लौह, तब पारस कौणे काम॥[11]

One achieves that feeling of 'meeting Ram in this very life' only through bhakti, which to Kabir meant the unambiguous rejection of caste hierarchy and the claim of any book to divine authorship. His position naturally involved the risk of social ostracisation, persecution, even physical assault. Kabir knew of these consequences first hand and so resorted to a powerful, even frightening metaphor to forewarn those who would follow in his wake:

> Having burnt down my house,
> I carry the burning stick in my hand.
> I'm now going to burn down the house
> of anybody who intends to follow me.

हम घर जाला आपना, लिया लुकाठा हाथ।
अब घर जालूँ तास का, जो चले हमारे साथ॥[12]

> Ram-bhakti is extremely risky,
> the chicken-hearted better keep away.
> Only he who has the guts to cut off his own head
> should think of uttering Hari's name.

भगति दुहेली राम की, नहिं कायर का काम।
सीस उतारे भुँइ धरे, सो लेसि हरि का नाम॥[13]

The above saakhi is taken from a section which contains many similar ones and is aptly titled '*Soora Tan ko Ang*' (The Section of the Brave); there are many more in a similar vein spread across the *Granthavali* and the *Bijak*.

Ironically, Kabir and other Nirgunis were made to suffer precisely because they were trying to reclaim the original meaning of the term 'bhakti'. This term etymologically means 'participation' and 'belonging'; this is how the ancient glossary Yaska's *Nirukta*, from the fifth century BCE, explains it. As early as the *Rig Veda*, the verbal root 'bhaj' and its associated nouns, such as bhakti and bhakta, indicated the sharing, serving and distribution of something. 'Bhakti' soon acquired a connotation of emotional involvement as is indicated in Panini's Sanskrit grammar; in the grammar's *Ashtadhayayi* (literally meaning 'a treatise divided into eight chapters'), composed in the fourth century BCE, Panini explains words with reference to their socially prevalent use. He defines 'bhakti' as a deep emotional involvement with a deity, city or individual. This wider, generic sense of bhakti is prevalent today in expressions like 'desh-bhakti' (devotion to one's country), 'pitra-bhakti' (devotion to one's father), 'guru-bhakti' (devotion to guru) and the like.

Bhakti as 'sharing and belonging' never fully disappeared as a secondary definition but became increasingly marginalised. Later, the use of the word 'bhakti' began to suggest submission and surrender. It then came to mean 'worship' detached from everyday life and social situations. Namdev became the 'first one to capture god in Kali yuga' (as his hagiographer Anantdas says) because he once again, after a long hiatus, insisted on 'bhakti as participation'. He asks Vitthal (his preferred name for god) with anguish, 'Why have you made me of a low caste?'

Before Namdev, the idea of caste or gender being no bar for attaining moksha through bhakti was put forward in the *Srimad Bhagavata*, one of the eighteen major Puranas, but without challenging the ideology of caste. Thus, the noble idea of moksha through bhakti remained just a spiritual conceit with hardly any social implications. Bhaktas could be equal before god, but out in the world, inequality prevailed. Namdev was the first to interrogate this duality. The same sentiment was later articulated by Ramanand, who rebelled against the conservative Sri Vaishnavas of southern India, moved north and was credited with 'bringing the bhakti born in the south'.

After this, the bhakti of Kabir, Pipa, Ravidas and Tukaram became the way to moksha as well as the measure of morality. An inner life of love with god and an outer life of householder responsibilities complemented each other in Bhakti morality. Kabir celebrates hard, honest work in his poetry. In one, we find him celebrating his 'sahaj samadhi', a kind of super consciousness, by relating himself with various professions and thus finally defeating death. The message is clear—whatever your profession, making every moment of life a moment of bhakti, of moral self-awareness, helps you reach moksha in this life.

In this poem, sahaj samadhi has taken away the fear of death, and Kabir's spiritual practice is at one with work. He will now 'make utensils as a potter, wash dirt as a washerman, press both sins and virtues in the oil mill, hold the sword as a Kshatriya, handle things like a yogi, stress this body as an avadhuta (a singular saint), "kill" the mind as a butcher, sell this body as a travelling merchant and defeat Yama as a gambler.'

सहज समाधि न जम थैं डरिहूं।
कुंभरा ह्नवै करि बासन घरिहूं धोबी ह्वै मल धोऊं।
तेली ह्वै तन कोल्हू करिहौं, पाप पुनि दोऊ पेरूं।
क्षत्री ह्वै खड़ग सँभालूँ, जोग जुगति दोउ साधूँ।
अवधू ह्वै करि यह तन धूतौं, वधिक ह्वै मन मारूँ।
बनिजारा ह्वै तन कूँ बनिजूं जुवारी ह्वै जम हारूं।[14]

Typically, Kabir does not imagine himself as a Brahmin or a maulana; he did not don, even as a creative exercise, the self-important mantle of religious authority. By transforming the poet's own self into a dynamic signifier, this poem becomes a particularly imaginative critique of the rigid hierarchical society in which the self is trapped.

So far as 'taking refuge in god' (as suggested in the Gita) is concerned, the Nirgunis had no problem, as long as it did not imply the acceptance of an unjust social hierarchy. That is why they steadfastly rejected the worship of avatars, while happily borrowing

words, legends and metaphors from their poetic narratives. Kabir
had the same approach to Islam. He did not uphold the finality of
the Prophet and the Koran, despite the free use of Islamic language
and tropes. The Nirgunis went to god and to the people with
probing questions about structured injustice and prejudices. In
their poetry and songs, we come across an abundance of metaphors
and images that show their willingness to surrender themselves,
to abandon themselves before god. But this faith, this love, is not
entirely unconditional. The Nirgunis want answers and do not
accept varna, in the way Sagunis could, as simply the handiwork
of god.

Kabir takes all these aspects of Nirgun bhakti to great heights.
He articulates his longing for god while showing the moral courage
to take on scholars and religious authorities on their versions and
interpretations of the 'laws of god'. This questioning of authority
was integral to his very being, as it should be, he believed, for all
of us. Such integrity is paradoxical: on the one hand it is 'pure
bliss' and on the other it is 'like walking on the edge of a sword'.
One must be prepared though for the exhilaration of a life lived in
bhakti, because, Kabir said, bhakti was not a tap you could turn on
or off, it had to suffuse your being:

> Sahaj samadhi by grace of the guru
> is the best and everlasting.
> Now, every walk of mine is a holy circumambulation,
> whatever I do is an act of worship.
> My sleeping posture is a ritual act of prostrating before god,
> I need not worship a deity anymore.
> Each utterance of mine is a chant of his name,
> listening is to remember him,
> eating a meal is to offer one to him.
> I don't need to renounce the world for my sadhana:
> the difference
> between a householder and a renunciate
> has been eliminated.

साधो सहज समाधि भली।
गुरु प्रताप सैं जा दिन तैं उपजी, दिन दिन अधिक चली॥
जहाँ जहाँ डोलो सोइ परिकरमा, जो कुछ करूं सो सेवा।
जब सोवों तब करों दंडवत, पूजों और न देवा॥
कहौं सो नाम सुनौं सो सुमरन, खाँव पियों सो पूजा।
गिरह उजाड़ एक सम लेखों, भाव न राखौं दूजा॥[15]

Kabir is conscious of the uniqueness of his bhakti and uses irony to emphasise it. He speaks to his Ram as if in confusion: 'Either I or this world of yours, one has surely gone mad.' Then, he says of god's worshippers, 'They worship god without reflecting on what kind of worship he likes. If worship means love, then certainly there is a gap. They worship god, but love someone (or something) else.' Finally, Kabir makes worshippers an offer that they can take or refuse: 'Keep all the paraphernalia aside, worship the worshipper, that is yourself. I would love to sing the praises of such a wise worshipper.'

रांम राइ भई विकल मति मोरी,
कै यह दुनी दीवानी तोरी।
जे पूजा हरि नहीं भावै, सो पूजनहार चढ़ावे।
जिहि पूजा हरि भल मानैं, सो पूजनहार न जानैं।
भाव प्रेम की पूजा, ताथैं देव थैं दूजा।
का कीजे बहुत पसारा, पूजी जे पूजनहारा।
कहै कबीर मैं गावा, मैं गावा आप लखावा।
जो इहि पद मांहि समाना, सो पूजनहार सयांना।[16]

Such a wise worshipper would indeed be worthy of praise, for the worship Kabir recommends implies keeping oneself 'clean' and above reproach. After all, nobody worships filth. Kabir's self-worship is not self-indulgence, it is a morally and spiritually rigorous bhakti, it demands that you live up to an exalted idea of yourself.

Kabir braved a number of attempts to drown (one of them quite literally) his truth-seeking and plain-speaking spirit. He enriched his inherent courage and dignity by interacting with many sources,

as we gather from his poems. But, amongst all these sources, he
mentions only one by name, telling everyone:

> Your claims of dancing to the tune of anhad are pointless
> if there is no real love for Hari in your heart.
> Get rid of this fakery;
> the only way to negotiate the ocean of existence
> is to become immersed in Naradi bhakti.

हिरदै कपट हरि सूं नहीं साचो, कहा भयो जे अनहद नाच्यौ।
भगति नारदी मगन सरीरा, इहि बिधि भव तिरि कहै कबीरा॥[17]

Even while challenging 'Pande' the Brahmin rather aggressively,
Kabir invokes Narada as the authority to validate his own
position—'What nonsense has taken over you that you don't chant
the name of Ram, you carry your reading of the Vedas and Puranas,
just like an ass carries its load of sandalwood. Reading the Vedas is
meaningful only if you see Ram as permeating everyone. You don't
believe me? Please go and ask Narada, Vyas and Shukadeva.'[18]
      Why is Narada and his form of bhakti so crucial to Kabir?

Immersed in Naradi Bhakti

Narada is the great archetype of Vaishnava bhakti. Malik
Muhammad Jayasi was paying Kabir the greatest compliment
when he described Narada lamenting his defeat in bhakti at the
hands of a weaver. Also recall that in Anantdas's description of
Kabir's welcome to Vishnu's vaikuntha, the poet's most preferred
company is that of Narada. His affinity with the worldview of the
Vaishnava (not the specific sect but the larger philosophy) is well

known, but he describes his bhakti as particularly Naradi, not Vaishnava in general. Why?

The answer to this once again underlines that despite the persistent rumours of Kabir being 'illiterate', he had a nuanced understanding of the various deliberations on bhakti. There are two collections of sutras (aphorisms) about bhakti, one attributed to the sage Shandilya and the other to Narada. Shandilya sutras are more inclined to scriptural wisdom and are supposed to be more philosophical in nature. Narada sutras are anchored in love and rule out the necessity of judging bhakti on the basis of scriptural authority. According to Narada, bhakti 'is proof of itself, it doesn't require any other proof'. (प्रमाणांतरस्यानपेक्षत्वात् स्वयं प्रमाणत्वात्। sutra 59).

Hindu tradition accords the privilege of being proof in itself only to the Vedas. All other philosophical and theological positions seek validity by claiming to be in accordance with the Vedas. Those who don't (like Buddha and Mahavira) are considered outside the fold—nastikas.

Narada is doing something remarkably radical while remaining within the fold. He is putting bhakti on the pedestal with Veda—

in other words, bhakti need not bother itself with Vedic authority and approval. Put in practice, this indicated bhakti's indifference to scholastic deliberations and debates. This was in tune with the way Narada defined bhakti from the very beginning. Bhakti, declares Narada, is the 'embodiment of ultimate love for it'. (सात्वस्मिनपरमप्रेमरूपा । sutra 2). By using 'it' instead of 'that' or simply 'god' (as Shandilya does in his sutras: 'Bhakti is love for god'), Narada is highlighting the essential unity of the individual and universal selves. To love in the sense of bhakti is to love the universal self that is inherent in all of existence. Having known this essential unity 'one feels "intoxicated" with achievement, becomes peaceful, becomes bliss personified'. (यज्ज्ञात्वा मत्तो भवति, स्तब्धो भवति, आत्मारामो भवति । sutra 6). Unlike Kabir's words, Narada's idiom is polite yet the message is clear: in his bhakti, hierarchies of 'birth, education, beauty, lineage and wealth are totally irrelevant. There is no point in argumentation as well.' (नास्ति तेषु जातिविद्यारूपकुलधनक्रियादि भेद: । यतस्तदीया: । वादो नावलम्ब्य: । sutras 72, 73, 74).

But Kabir vehemently disagrees with this last sutra.

Historically, these sutras have been dated to around the tenth and eleventh centuries—a couple of hundred years before Namdev. The great sadhaka of love and bhakti who composed these moving sutras must have achieved the total erasure of ego to have attributed such a remarkable work to the mythical Narada. The *Srimad Bhagavata* was composed some time before these sutras. In contrast to the *Mahabharata*'s philosophical, pragmatic, adult Krishna, the *Srimad Bhagavata* is primarily a celebration of the child, of naughty Krishna's 'loving and loved' personality. It celebrates human love in an uninhibited manner and insists on bhakti as the best, in fact, only way of relating with the supreme reality, the ultimate truth—god who is fully manifested in the persona of Krishna.

As with the *Mahabharata*, the *Srimad Bhagavata* too was composed by Vyasa.

The *Mahabharata* is a deeply disturbing story of a fratricidal war which resulted in all-round destruction and decay. At the end of it, Vyasa grows doubtful if people would listen to the voice of sanity anymore. The author of the great epic finds himself traumatised and shares his anguish with Narada. The way out of his anguish, Narada suggests, is to celebrate the love of ordinary people—cowherds, say, or even sinners. Reflect on bhakti, love in its most sublime form. Vyasa had, Narada tells him, faithfully recorded and reflected on the horrors of hatred. Now it was time to turn his attention to the antidote—love. Vyasa follows that advice, and we got the *Srimad Bhagavata.*

Why was Narada so insistent on having Vyasa compose a text celebrating ordinary human, rather than celestial, love? Indeed, why did Narada, so close to Lord Vishnu, have to come down to this world in the first place? Because of his infatuation with sensual desires, Narada was ordered to be born as a Shudra in this world by his father Brahma. He was born to a servant woman. Forbidden from scriptural knowledge because of his caste, he needed an alternative route to piousness that was open to all.

It made sense for the composer of these sutras to attribute them to Narada, a Shudra, as the embodiment of the common person who had no claims to the elite access to the Brahman but found a way nonetheless. The sutras describe the women who herd cows in Braj (Mathura and its surroundings) as the 'epitome and model' of true bhakti (यथा व्रजगोपिकानाम् । sutra 21). These epitomes of bhakti were doubly disqualified in the wider world from any status by virtue of their being both Shudra and female. But, starting from the *Srimad Bhagavata,* the Braj gopis are seen as role models in the Bhakti tradition, particularly in vernacular texts. These women create a relationship of amorous love and playfulness with Krishna, rather than awe and surrender. It is this friendly, even flirtatious, relationship with god that is emphasised by Kabir when he addresses and describes his Nirgun god as Gopinath—god of the cowherd women.

The author of these sutras (Narada, for convenience) goes on to recommend the 'rejection of prevalent opinions and even the Vedas'. (निरोधस्तु लोकवेदव्यापारन्यास । sutra 46). He asks, 'Who swims across (the world) and helps others swim?' The answer is unambiguous: 'The one who discards even the Vedas and focuses uninterrupted affection on god.' (वेदान्नपि सन्नयस्ति केवलमविच्छिनानुरागम् लभते। स तरति स लोकांस्तारयति। sutras 49, 50). These sutras are important in many ways. Firstly, they are another reminder that in medieval India the changes in 'ideas and attitudes' were making a difference to social and even Sanskrit intellectual life. The conservative law-givers were also innovating, but, by 'reading' ancient texts in accordance with changing social equations, Narada moved far ahead of them. He was not proposing a bhakti-orientated interpretation of the Vedas and related literature, but he was leaving these texts behind, taking a 'sanyas' from ancient wisdom.

His insistence on love is related to this sanyas. Love in this case is not merely an emotion, it is also a name given to a paradigm of knowledge which implicitly or explicitly challenges that scholastic tradition which took pride in its pedantic disputations and forgot a fundamental truth—knowledge is supposed to help explain the inner and outer worlds. That is why, in the vernacular discourse, the influence of the 'Naradian' approach is all-encompassing, even if his sutras are not often directly referenced. The echo of Narada's rejection of lok and the Vedas can clearly be heard in Pipa's expression of gratitude to Kabir: 'But for whom lok, Veda and Kali yuga would have destroyed bhakti.' By the time of Kabir and Pipa, Naradi bhakti was already known as a method that privileged love over everything else (thus distinguishing itself from the Nath panthis and various Tantric schools). It openly advocated indifference to scriptural authority and maintained a distance from self-referential scholarly disputes.

Kabir happily and correctly described his method of bhakti as Naradi. But he took it further. He was anything but indifferent to debate and argument. He was, however, indifferent to how he came across knowledge, as long as it was knowledge. Kabir was a spokesperson for no one school of thought or method. Being an inquisitive and sharp person, he gathered his material from every possible source, but the thoughts that emerged from this knowledge-gathering bore his unmistakable stamp. The baseless idea that vernacular wisdom was merely an extension (if not straight translation) of Sanskrit tradition has made it a truism to argue that Bhaktas were poetically packaging the ideas of some or other Sanskrit acharya. Modern scholars find it hard to imagine that Kabir and other Bhaktas might have been articulating their own original thinking. Fortunately, there are some exceptions to the rule.

R.D. Ranade was one such voice. On the basis of his study of Bhakti literature in Hindi, Marathi and Kannada, he observes, 'Medieval mysticism does not depend on given philosophical constructs. It stands on its own.'[19] Even 'conservative' Tulsidas, according to Ranade, devised his own way of self-realisation rather than following the philosophical schools of Shankar, Ramanuja or Nimbarka. Acharya Ramchandra Shukla would vehemently disagree with Ranade on Tulsidas, even if he at least partially agreed with his assessment of Kabir and other Nirgunis. But, while Ranade admires them for their originality, Shukla vehemently denounces the Nirgunis' audacity to ignore and rebuff the precepts of great acharyas in their poems on the self-aggrandising and unproven basis that they were original thinkers.[20] He describes attempts to look for any systematic philosophical thought in these poets as pointless, and he categorically rejects scholarly attempts to place Kabir and other Nirgunis in the philosophical tradition of Shankar, Ramanuja or even Ramanand. For him, there was no question of these Bhaktas being placed in any of the six traditional schools of philosophy. In this, Shukla was in agreement with Nabhadas, though while the latter was celebrating Kabir, the former dripped with condescension and even disdain.

The Ram Touchstone: Empirical Rationality and Rational Spirituality

Ranade and Shukla recognise that Kabir's worldview does not fit easily into any of the six philosophical systems of Vedic tradition, nor with Buddhism or Jainism. Kabir was his own man but, according to Hazari Prasad Dwivedi, he had the Nath panth in his DNA. In support of this position, as we have already seen, Dwivedi invents a new philosophical system for Kabir and other Nirgunis to occupy—'dwaitadwaitvilakshanwad' (an unwieldy term coined by him to establish that the system was distinct from both monism and dualism). According to Dwivedi, 'Nath panthis defend this position forcefully and, in this matter, Kabir is directly related to them.'[21] Dwivedi quotes extensively from Nath-panthi sources to prove that they followed dwaitadwaitvilakshanwad. But how did he prove Kabir's 'direct' relationship to this position? Not by citing any of Kabir's poems, or even a later Kabir-panthi text, but by entering a single anecdote into evidence. Once, we are told, when 'Kabir was informed about an ongoing disputation between monists and dualists, he commented with a witty chuckle, "Ask the pandits, how can one who is beyond forms, names and all such attributes be limited by numbers?"'[22]

Shukla was critical of the Nirgunis for their claims of originality implicit in their poems. Dwivedi, instead of explaining their originality, ends up 'defending' Kabir and other Nirgunis on Shukla's terms. Just as the Sagunis propagated the philosophical positions of acharyas, according to Dwivedi, not only Kabir but all the other Nirgunis as well composed their poems in order to explain 'eight divisions of yoga, however, with more emphasis on knowledge and morality than the yoga itself'.[23] So, in Dwivedi's analysis, the entire enterprise of Nirgun bhakti is reduced to the explanation and propagation of Nath-panthi yoga. Kabir, an exciting and challenging voice, is explained away as a preacher of the Nath panth, unusually gifted perhaps but not particularly original.

Namwar Singh, the eminent literary critic, in his thought-provoking book *Doosari Parampara ki Khoj* (In Search of Alternative Tradition), reflected on the historical context and philosophical positions of the Nirgun bhakta poets. The book was written as a tribute to Dwivedi, his guru, and generally upholds the positions of the venerable scholar. But on the worldview of Nirgun bhaktas, Singh is in agreement with Shukla (minus the disdain) and rejects Dwivedi's attempt to put these poets in line with the Nath-panthi metaphysics. 'These sants called mystics,' Namwar Singh writes, 'were in fact empirical rationalists. That is probably why they were called "gyani" (knowledgeable). They attacked untouchability and prejudice of high and low with the weapon of this empiricism.'[24]

The modern scholarly discussion of Nirgun philosophy has generally centred on metaphysics. Singh made a significant departure by focusing on epistemology. Metaphysics refers to the conception of ultimate reality: What is its nature, how is it related to creation and human consciousness? Are soul and god two distinct entities or somehow woven into one? These are metaphysical questions. The concerns of epistemology revolve around credibility, authenticity and knowledge of the ultimate and mundane. The value system upheld by any philosophy results from the interaction of its metaphysics and epistemology.

Brahminical epistemology treated the Vedas as the ultimate proof and authority. Every philosophical position had to be vetted against the intent and wisdom of the Vedas. But then the Vedas were not open to non-Brahmins and women, and most certainly not to Shudras like Namdev and Kabir. Shudras were not encouraged to learn Sanskrit. If they somehow managed to learn it, they would still be forbidden to access the Vedas. Unlike Shankar and Ramanuja, Namdev and Kabir had no opportunity to argue that their philosophical positions might be in accordance with the intent of some Vedic text.

If you enter such a closed epistemology on its own terms, you have no avenue to turn to and no chance to argue. Faced with such a situation, before speculating on metaphysical questions, you have to address the issue of epistemological method. Dwivedi, in his disappointment in Kabir, who 'did not engage with a knowledgeable Brahmin', misses this crucial point. Shut out from debate, Namdev and Kabir put their experiences forward as questions to the dominant epistemology. They ask, 'Being Brahmin, do you have milk flowing in your veins, while we Shudras just have blood?' (तुम कत बाँभन हम कत सूद? हम कत लोहू, तुम कत दूध?[25]) This is a completely rational question. If the Brahmin is superior due to merit, surely the way to earn that merit should be open to all; if the superiority is due to accident of birth, the difference should show. Kabir saves his most savage lines for the pretensions of the Brahmin and the mulla, both of whom claim piety as their birth right: 'If that is the case, the Brahmin should have come to this world through some other way, not by the usual dirty one, and the mulla should have been circumcised before he was born.'

The empirical rationality of the Nirgunis provides the basis with which a proper theory and system of knowledge can be evolved. Such a system would be able to adequately respond

to human curiosity and existential angst. It is this angst that various religions claim to address by offering their own spin on spirituality. This promise is the source of religion's hold on the human mind and its role in social life. In the long eighteenth century of European Enlightenment, organised religion was subject to a sustained critique that was so effective that in the nineteenth century many believed the church was going to be largely marginalised in human affairs. This supposedly rational belief was rooted in a rather irrational faith in the omnipotence of science. It was believed that science would discover the secrets of the universe as well as those of the human psyche, and so it was assumed, religion, supposedly rooted in the fear of the unknown, would gradually become irrelevant, first in the public realm and then in the private.

This belief was irrational because it did not fully account for the inexhaustible nature of the universe as well as the complexities of the human psyche. It was as if they had forgotten the wisdom and insight such as the one seen in 'Nasadiya Sukta' of the *Rig Veda*—'No one, not even the one presiding over it all, knows all the mysteries of creation.' More sophisticated, modern minds have learnt the lesson in humility—even science cannot claim to know it all; perhaps harbouring such an ambition was hubristic in the first place. The experience of the twentieth century (described as the 'age of extremes' by the historian Eric Hobsbawm) has played a critical role in reinforcing this lesson. It may have been the century of decolonisation, democratisation and the empowerment of people, but it was also a century of holocausts—the Nazi slaughter of six million Jews, of course, but also the seemingly forgotten holocausts in India (the Bengal famine) and Africa engineered by the British, the Belgians and other 'civilised' European colonial powers. It was a century of alternatives to capitalism—cherished utopias and socialist substitute—eventually turning into totalitarian nightmares.

Eurocentric modernity failed to address the crises facing the world—whether economic, social, ecological or spiritual. Religion, which was expected to recede quietly into the distance with the spread of science and technology, has returned aggressively to prominence, many of its adherents filled with anger, hate and violence. The spectre of 'hurt sentiments' is now a near-constant, palpable presence. Human rights, universal values—increasingly, these seem like relics of some past age. Creative engagement with voices of early modernity and empirical rationalism outside Europe would rejuvenate flagging ideals like universal respect for human individuality, rational dialogue and sensitivity to spiritual angst. Kabir's is such a voice, a reassuring one for dark times. Underlining the universality of the Nirgun sensibility, academic David Lorenzen writes that 'the social and religious values embodied in Nirgun texts can be understood by persons outside the movement, even by non-Indians, without the need of more than a judicious amount of commentary'.[26]

I have been reflecting on the nature of religion and related questions for two decades now. These reflections were first published in 2004 in a collection of essays titled *Nij Brahm Vichar: Dharma, Samaj aur Dharmetar Adhyatma* (A Transcendental Thought of One's Own: Religion, Society and Secular Spirituality). As you might see, the title is borrowed from a Kabir song quoted earlier in this chapter. ('Brahm' as transcendental and 'dharmetar' as secular were rendered in English by Linda Hess while engaging with my reflections a decade or so later in her book, *Bodies of Song*.) The common open-hearted generalisation of religions, that all religions are just different roads to reach one god, is considerably off the mark. If various religions are just routes to a single destination, then why do the travellers, all on their different paths, keep having such vicious fights? Every religion talks of 'love', so why is religious conflict so riddled with hate? And how cruelly religious 'love' is taught and forced upon those refusing to fall in line. It is said, rhetorically, 'Religion does not teach enmity' (मज़हब नहीं सिखाता, आपस में बैर रखना, as in Muhammad Iqbal's *Sare Jahan se Accha*). Looked at factually, this is just wishful thinking. If one were to go by historical experience, it would be more truthful to say: 'Religion only teaches enmity' (मजहब यही सिखाता, आपस में बैर रखना ।).

Humans commit violent crimes for petty personal reasons and out of passion, but the number and scale of heinous crimes committed at the altar of 'noble' causes are infinitely greater than those committed for private motives. Nation and political ideology figure amongst such noble causes, but looming largest is religion, which appears to inspire extraordinary fury, bloodletting, persecution and torture. At the same time, it is indisputable that the religious imagination is as sublime as it is violent. This is borne out not by the lives of illustrious, celebrated figures but by the lives of millions of ordinary, pious people who act with compassion, kindness and faith-imbued grace. Kabir shows us that organised religion may be worthy of criticism, of anger and sometimes even contempt, and ultimately, it is your own vivek that leads you to make the right choice. You can read the Gita in the Gandhi way, or the Godse way; you can read the Koran in the Khan Abdul Ghaffar Khan way, or the Osama Bin Laden way—the choice and responsibility are yours.

Faith, per se, cannot be the measure of morality. People can have different, even conflicting, faith systems, but their mutual interaction must be governed by a code of behaviour based on consensus across the divides of faith, emotions and opinions. For any game or activity, you need agreed-upon rules. If we were to play, say, a game of chess, it would not be fair if my knight were allowed to move in an L-shape and jump over other pieces, while yours were not. Human vivek accumulated over centuries and open to dialogue with and among all traditions can be the only basis to arrive at a consensual fair play. Such a dialogue, in turn, adds to the edifice of human vivek. Gandhi's reading of the Gita, or Martin Luther King's reading of the Bible, for instance, is not unconnected to the growth of ideas in non-Hindu and non-Christian contexts. Literalist, fundamentalist readings on the other hand reject the possibility of dialogue. Instead, such dogmatism speaks the language of hurt sentiments—though the only sentiments it is prepared to consider are its own—while seeing no contradiction in the willingness to hurt and even kill those 'guilty' of causing such 'injury'.

Violence is integral to the fundamentalist worldview; only the person who kills and dies for faith, or shows willingness to do so, is taken seriously. The tremendous significance of Kabir making his singular Ram bhakti the touchstone of his dharma should be understood in the context of what we have just discussed. 'Ram', Kabir's key word, is not the name of a historical or mythological figure/deity, as emphasised in this book, but is his preferred name for the human conscience. Connecting with Kabir's Ram is not about being Hindu but about being human and insisting on engagement (bhakti) with the divine as well as with other humans. This is what Kabir tells 'Pande' the Brahmin, specifically referring to his study of the Vedas—'Learn to see Ram in everyone.' (बेद पढ़या का यह फल पांडे, सब घटि देखै रामा ।). 'I see your reflection in every man and woman. Kabir is the child of both Allah and Ram; Hari is my pir, my lord.' (जेती औरति मर्दां कहिये, सब में रूप तुम्हारा । कबीर पंगुड़ा अलह राम का, हरि गुर पीर हमारा ॥)

With the help of Narada's bhakti sutras, we can guess why the name Ram is so crucial to Kabir. 'Ram' literally means 'soothing'. A real bhakta, according to Narada, reaches the stage of atmarama, living with a perpetual sense of soothing bliss. Kabir's Ram is at the core of his love, longing and emotions; Ram is the source of vivek. A mind obsessed with its own 'sentiments', indifferent to the suffering of others and insensitive to injustice, can never experience atmarama, Kabir might argue. He would, no doubt, find amusing those who claim to be on a perpetual quest for 'positivity' while neglecting all life around them.

How Kabir might enjoy firing some 'Kabiresque' questions at the new-age gurus who dominate our airwaves with their bland positivity formulae, which dispense with social sensitivity and basic rationality altogether and claim to teach 'spirituality, not religion'. Linda Hess makes a sobering observation: '"Religious" and "spiritual" are historically and socially intertwined. Rejecting religion and embracing spirituality is too easy. It oversimplifies the ways in which religions actually function and perpetuates the alienation of secular intellectuals from the majority of their fellow citizens.'[27]

While making this valid, valuable caution, Hess, responding to my argument, concedes: 'I accept that there can, within limits, be a distinction and that "spiritual" as distinct from "religious" may be useful in a discussion of Kabir.'

In order to understand this distinction and its implications for our troubled times, it is important to understand how the religious and spiritual are intertwined. It is important to remember that even religions without a conception of god (Buddhism and Jainism, for example) provide their followers assurances to address their existential, spiritual angst.

Spirituality is about going beyond the here and now, beyond smug self-centredness; it is about the human instinct to connect with the universal spirit, to partake in 'cosmic wonder'. And it is also about having empathy for others—to see Allah and Ram in every woman and man. That should be the logical outcome of seeing god as the Holy Father or Creator (as in Christianity and Islam) or feeling his presence in every iota of the universe (as in Hinduism). The Indic word 'adhyatama' conveys the connotation of 'going beyond' (adhi) one's own 'self' (atma) in order to better relate to others. And according to Lord Krishna in Gita (VIII, 3), this quality is not something exotic, to be obtained from the outside, it is very much your 'nature'—'Svabhavo Adhtyamam Uchyate.' (स्वभावो अध्यात्मम् उच्यते ।).

Humans, like any other animal, are insistent on their own self; when it comes to self-preservation against a real or perceived threat, our aggressive instinct comes to the fore. At the same time, sympathy for others and some conception of fairness and justice are also human instincts. Morality is an attempt to strike a balance between the two. There is no point in any religious or secular activity, according to Kabir, if you 'fail to find something like balance'. (समता सी वस्तु न पावे ।)

Every religion in its own way seeks to address the needs of human nature, seeks to provide an anchor for one's negotiation of life in its totality. There exists a whole system of rituals and practices to address existential angst. By making the human being part of a design devised by a larger, mysterious force, religion ensures a sense of human self-worth, makes us realise that we are more than the result of base biological activity. It gives our life a sense of purpose. Then, religion provides an elaborate code of social and individual conduct that comes divinely sanctioned. This code comes with a power structure to which every faithful must submit. And, finally, every religion gives its faithful a sense of solidarity, a tribal fealty to sustaining a specific group identity distinct from that of other religions.

These elements are found in other systems as well. Even finding ways to soothe spiritual angst is not unique to religion. Existentialist philosophy, for instance, deals with anxiety pertaining to the meaning and purpose of life. Albert Camus, at the very outset of *The Myth of Sisyphus*, declares, 'There is but one truly serious philosophical problem, and that is suicide. Judging whether life is or is not worth living amounts to answering the fundamental question of philosophy.'

Existentialist philosophy recognises that it is beyond science to answer questions about meaning and the worth of life, but unlike religion, existentialism doesn't offer the consolation of god or some other cosmic scheme.

The other three aspects of religion are also not unique to it: we can just as easily have a secular code of ethics, hierarchy and dogma without religion.

But what does make religion unique is that it alone offers a total narrative of life and afterlife, of the temporal and the otherworldly, and of individuality and the collective. It rolls bliss, togetherness, mystic experience and fear into one. Believers do not violate the set boundaries and parameters of their faith in part due to the fear of 'punishment' in unknown, mysterious ways. Punishment is the flip side to a religious system that otherwise promises deliverance.

Religion assures us of the possibility of elevation and liberation from the mundane. It assures believers that their existential angst can be relieved; all they have to do in exchange is follow the diktats of the one true way.

Even the worst amongst secular power structures can be dealt with as ultimately a human construct. Such a structure, however all-encompassing, does not have the privilege to describe itself as divine. It can, of course, appeal to the spiritual sense of its followers by elevating nation, class or history to an almost divine status. Hitler justified his ruthlessness in the name of nation and Mao did the same in the name of history. As dictators, they were also personality cults, which requires from the people an almost religious devotion to the leader.

There has to be some way of addressing the spiritual aspect of the human mind that is more secure against its totalitarian manipulation, whether religious or secular. There has to be a constant reminder that faith by itself is not enough to live a purposeful life, one needs to have a dynamic interaction between faith and rationality. Faith could be specific, but it must work in tandem with universal values rooted in vivek. Kabir's critique of various rituals and practices needs to be understood from this perspective. Through his poems, he is not trying to popularise ashtanga (eightfold) yoga, nor is seeking to convert you to 'his' religion. What he does is to ask ironical questions, making sarcastic remarks to wake you up to the need to put your faith in dialogue with your vivek, asking you to think for yourself, to be sceptical but not cynical. He is trying to articulate, perhaps even invent, a new 'rational spirituality'. His questions are hard-hitting as they are rooted in rational curiosity:

Brother, where did your two gods come from?
Tell me, who made you mad?
Ram, Allah, Keshav, Karim, Hari, Hazrat—
so many names.
So many ornaments, all one gold,

it has no double nature.
For conversation we make two—
this *namaz*, that *puja*,
this Mahadev, that Muhammed,
this Brahma, that Adam,
this a Hindu, that a Turk
but all belong to earth.
Vedas, Korans, all those books
those Mullas and those Brahmins—
so many names, so many names,
but the pots are all one clay.
Kabir says, nobody can find Ram,
both sides are lost in schisms.
One slaughters goats, one slaughters cows
They squander their births in isms.

(Translation by Hess and Singh)

भाई रे दो जगदीश कहाँ से आया, कहु कौने बौराया।
अल्ला राम करीमा केसव, हरि हजरत नाम धराया॥
गहना एक कनक ते गहना, जामे भाव न दूजा।
क्रहत सुनत को दुइ करि थापै, एक नमाज़ एक पूजा॥
वही महादेव वही मुहम्मद, ब्रह्मा आदम कहिये।
को हिन्दू को तुरक कहावे, एक जिमी एक रहिये॥
वेद किताब पढ़ैं वे कुतुबा, वे मौलाना वे पांडे।
बेगर बेगर नाम धराए, एक माटी के भांडे॥
कहै कबीर ये दूनो भूले, रामहि किनहु न पाया।
वै खसी वै गाय कटावैं, बादहि जनम गँवाया॥[28]

It is not hard to see why the young Muslim in Shabnam
Virmani's film accuses Kabir of crossing the 'boundations'
of Islamic practice. From an orthodox Muslim's point of
view, not only the above, but a lot of Kabir's utterances are
complete heresy. How dare he include the 'word of god'
among all those *other* books? How dare he compare the

Prophet with those Hindu gods? For a Hindu, too, while it might be acceptable to have faith in multiple gods and follow several different modes of worship, how dare he compare the faith of 'mlechchhas' (impure others) with Sanatan dharma? Kabir laments that the people who ascribe to the false binaries he describes in this poem can never reach Ram. According to Kabir, all beliefs and practices that insist on group identity in opposition to the recognition of our shared humanity are deliberate attempts to distort our vision. 'Many people talk in many ways only adding to confusion,' he notes and recommends the right 'kohl' (meaning bhakti here) for a balanced worldview:

एक कथि कथि भरम लगावै, समता सी वस्तु न पावे ।
कहै कबीर का कीजै, हरि सूझै सो अंजन दीजै ॥[29]

No wonder, the 'community leaders' of both Hindus and Muslims complained to Sikandar Lodhi: 'No one is going to listen to us, as long as this weaver continues to live in Kashi.' It would have been easier for Kabir had he tried to establish a new panth or religion. Then, the pandits and maulanas would have made peace with him and eventually left him alone. He would have been just another new brand in the great religious marketplace. But the weaver wove a different story altogether. He was equipping people to move beyond organised religion, to establish a direct line to their own Ram. The dispensing of tools to make such a large segment of the market redundant was bound to draw the ire of the shopkeepers and traders in religious wares. Kabir told anyone who listened that they could retain the identity—Hindu, Muslim, whatever—that made them comfortable, but that they should practice a rational spirituality, seek to understand the connection of the inner and the outer, to ask the right questions and be sensitive to the suffering of others. He wanted his followers to focus on their inner growth, to retreat occasionally into a creative solitude that enabled them to return to the world stronger, to claim the dignity and humanity denied them and too many others in a conventional hierarchical society.

How could such a man be allowed to continue to live in the city?

If back then, many were moved by Kabir and saw the wisdom in his words, why can't we, in our equally troubled world, find solace in these same words? Over the course of the centuries that separate us from Kabir, we have perhaps only become more aware of 'the painful tensions between love of self and duty to others that is such an obstacle to our spiritual satisfaction'.[30] Kabir clarifies this awareness. It is futile to go to him for easy formulae or for a detailed plan to overcome the various issues facing us today. But he certainly gives us clues to seek out and develop our own responses to our questions. His goal was to achieve moksha in this life and knew that the prerequisite was to live with the constant awareness of death. This awareness serves as a catalyst for the embrace of moral responsibility and one's spiritual destiny. Kabir's guideline is of course Ram—no hypocrite can pass this test, only those who live as if dead even while alive, that is with the moral urgency of each moment being their last, will satisfy Kabir's Ram:

कबीर कसौटी राम की झूठा टिका न कोई।
राम कसौटी सो सहै जो मरि जीवा होई॥[31]

Proposing bhakti as an alternative to the corruptions of organised religion, Kabir challenges the pandit on the four purusharthas:

Pandit, do some research
and let me know
how to destroy transiency.
Money, religion, pleasure, salvation—
which way do they stay, brother?
North, South, East or West?

In heaven or the underworld?
If Gopal is everywhere, where is hell?
Heaven and hell are for ignorant,
not for those who know Hari.
The fearful thing everyone fears,
I don't fear.
I'm not confused about sin and purity,
heaven and hell.
Kabir says, seekers, listen:
Wherever you are
is the entry point.

(Translation by Hess and Singh)

पंडित सोध कहौ समुझाई, जाते आवागमन नसाई।
अर्थ, धर्म, औ काम मोक्ष कहु, कवन दिसा बसे भाई।
उत्तर कि दक्षिन पूरब कि पच्छिम, स्वर्ग पताल कि नाहीं।
बिना गोपाल ठौर नहीं कतहुँ, नरक जात धौ काहीं।
अनजाने को स्वर्ग नरक है, हरि जाने को नाहीं।
जेहि डर को सब लोग डरत हैं, सो डर हमरे नाहीं।
पाप पुन्य की सका नाहीं, स्वर्ग नरक नहिं जाही।
कहै कबीर सुनो हो संतों, जहाँ का पद है तहाँ तमाही।[32]

Is it not simple, yet true and profound? Moksha is a state of
mind. It is a matter of here and now, not of some reward in the
distant future for exhausting the cycle of birth and rebirth. You too,
Kabir says, can achieve moksha in this life, if you practise bhakti
consisting of rational spirituality and morality rooted in empathy
and set a personal standard from which you resolve not to slip.
The entry point is 'wherever you are', here in this poem itself, for
example, or in any moment of profound bhakti.

VI

From the Erotic to the Divine

A Poignant Paradox

Kabir declares that 'Kama can indeed take you to Ram,' echoing
the position long held by Tantrikas on erotic love. But Kabir adds
sternly that such a journey is possible 'only if you know the trick,
if you do the right sadhana'. He follows this with a reference to
Sukhadeva, son of Vyasa, as an authority:

काम मिलावे राम सूं, जो कोई जाने राखि।
कबीर बिचारा क्या करे, सुषदेव बोले साखि॥

This saakhi is cited by Mata Prasad Gupta to support a rather
odd conclusion: 'At only one place, and then only in a suppressed
voice, has Kabir accepted that controlled and limited erotic desire
(*kām*) can also be of assistance in [trying to] join with Ram.'[1]
The august scholar appears to have forgotten, in this moment, all
those beautiful, moving instances of the pain and pleasure of love
that Kabir articulates in a very erotic idiom and in the voice of a
woman. This particular saakhi is certainly not the 'only one place'
in which Kabir writes about erotic desire and definitely not in a
'suppressed voice', but rather, it is a succinct theoretical exposition
of what Kabir practices throughout his poetry.

Bhaktas and Sufis had great insight into the nature of love. They
knew its continuity from the carnal to the sublime as expressed in
the well-known precept of Sufi tradition—from ishq majaji, carnal
love, to ishq haqiqi, true, divine love. Also, recall the ambiguity
in Narada's definition of bhakti, which he says is the 'ultimate
love for it'. In this sutra, 'it' could stand for divinity but also for a

human being. The primary form of love is sexual attraction. This understanding of the nature of love is common to Tantra, Sufism and Bhakti. In the classical Indian arts, sringara, erotic love, is one of the nine rasas; indeed, in classical dance and theatre it is the first, the mother of all emotions, and for the purpose of the assessment of a creative work, no distinction is made between its articulations in human or divine contexts. This aesthetic approach is clearly based on observations of real-life situations. Love in all its forms causes similar physical and psychological responses. One can shed tears on hearing from one's beloved, recalling one's favourite divinity or while listening to a patriotic song. The erotic, however, remains the most transformative expression of love, hence the primacy accorded to sringara.

Every person in love believes their love to be unique. Although, the aesthetic treatment and appreciation of love focuses not on this subjective feeling but on its articulation and expression. Whatever the depth of love one might feel, for the critic, the relevant questions are: How does love enrich the tradition of creativity? How does it contribute to a more humane society? Love, a private emotion, has tremendous social implications. The passions of lovers upset existing power structures and prevailing social strictures. The erotic attraction between two humans is, we know only too well, often perceived as a great threat to society, culture, tradition and even nation. We know this from history, legend and current affairs. In these 'enlightened' times, the panic erotic love can sow is evident in the verdicts of khap panchayats, in expressions like 'love jihad', in the fulminations of the religious, the conservative, the hidebound, in the pronouncements of those who speak for society and even those who are tasked with making and upholding the laws. It is not for nothing that Kabir says bluntly:

> This is the abode of love, my dear,
> not your aunt's dwelling.
> You enter here only after
> cutting off your own head.

कबीर यहु घर प्रेम का, खाला का घर नांहिं।
सीस उतारै हाथि करि, सो पैसे घर मांहिं ॥[2]

He makes countless similar statements about the courage required for love. In his understanding of this emotion, the 'social' is not just implicit, it is assertively explicit, and also complex and multilayered. Apart from the continuity of carnal and sublime expressions of love, in Kabir's poetic world, we find Ram-bhavana, spiritual longing; samaj-bhavana, social concerns; and kama-bhavana, the pleasure and pain of love, eddying around each other, their streams regularly mixing. As usual, Kabir ranges too widely for those who want him to speak to their narrow concerns. Many have tried to reduce him to a cheerleader of teenage sentimentalism, an immature love. This does the profundity of his poetry an injustice. A greater disservice to Kabir is done by those who, obsessed with using him for their political project, try to downplay the centrality of love in his poetry. For them, love is an idle pastime, secondary and inferior to the 'high-mindedness' of their political and social aims.

But for Kabir, love cannot be beholden to society and politics, nor can it turn a blind eye to the injustices and ironies of the world. Love is not private, but an example of what he describes as the 'constant interaction between the outside and the inside' (भीतर बाहर सबद निरंतर). Love too is sadhana; it too informs vivek and must become sahaj, an effortless, natural way of life, if one is to reach Ram.

Usually, poets write their own experiences of love into their verse. It is tempting for readers and critics to see through poetic devices, through the allusions and metaphors, to guess at the person or the incident—the gossip—that the poet might be signalling to. For instance, in the case of Malik Muhammad Jayasi, it is probable that his own personal experience of very real, worldly love inspired his great epic *Padmavat*. But with Kabir, though the pain, pleasure, depth, depression, excitement and anxiety are so visceral, there is no hint of any 'real-life' experience feeding into his poems.

Love was Kabir's sadhana, his discipline. His compositions

utilised Sufi tropes and language familiar from the Bhakti tradition 'brought from the south to the north' by Ramanand. In the saakhi quoted at the beginning of this chapter, Kabir mentions Shukadeva as an authority on kama. Sukhadeva narrated the *Bhagavata*, composed by his father, to the Kuru king Parikshit, grandson of Arjuna. The *Bhagavata*, we know, was composed by Vyasa at Narada's advice, as an antidote to hate and violence—the central theme of *Mahabharata*. Perhaps, by invoking Sukhadeva in his saakhi, Kabir wants to state his connection to the *Bhagavata* worldview—a desire to seek refuge in love. But, 'Kama can take you to spiritual bliss' was also an oft-stated Tantric principle. Kabir, by mentioning Sukhadeva, was also reinforcing his distance from Tantrikas and Shaktas, and his affinity with the Narada school of love and bhakti.

Love is full of paradoxes. It expands our minds and hearts just as it makes us mean with envy and jealousy. It requires us to surrender ourselves to our beloved, but our natural impulse is to hold desperately onto them, to seek to possess them and fear losing them or letting them 'escape'. Love is about the forceful assertion of the self but also its withdrawal. It requires sacrifice and gentleness but also fierce aggression. Love is desire as well as erasure.

Kabir explores and expresses these many contradictions of love. But the strange anomaly in his expression of love, and that of other Nirgunis', is that in their most doctrinaire moods, they condemn women as obstacles to sadhana, but in the most intense moments of that very sadhana, they adopt a female persona, speaking to and of their Ram as women and in the language of women. It has been argued in 'defence' of these sants by their modern interpreters and admirers that their condemnation of women must be read as a device to control and reorient their own sexual desire and that of their male audience. The evidence used is that they condemn the woman only as 'seductress', not as mother, sister or wife.

But, obviously, sexual desire is not confined to men. Then, how is it that no female Bhakti poet—Mirabai, Andal, Lal Ded, Sahjobai—is found condemning the male as a device to control and reorient their sexual desire? And does it not sound rather peculiar, even amusing, to condemn the other sex as a means to control one's own sexual desire?

This peculiarity—misogyny—is truly a universal feature of human civilisation, not excluding Kabir and other male Bhakti poets, but it's a feeble excuse. Philosophical and legal discourse in all religious traditions are full of virulence against women, a manifestation of the male fear of female sexuality. Just as Kabir describes women as the 'pit of hell', Tertullian, a second-century pastor, describes his 'sisters in Christ' as 'Eve's conspirators' and tells them bluntly, 'You are devil's gateway.'[3]

Ironically, a recognition of the creative and spiritual power of the feminine is also common to all religious traditions and is quite pronounced in mystic practices. The Sufis, for instance, construct the 'ultimate' as feminine, while it is a trope for Christian mystics (both male and female) to imagine themselves as Christ's bride, exactly like the Nirgun bhaktas. Whether one sees god as male and the human soul as female or vice-versa, in both situations, an attempt at gender-transcendence and a celebration of the creative power of the feminine is implicit.

But then, why doesn't this celebration of certain aspects of femininity evolve into a general empathy for the social plight of women? It would be impossible, for the purposes of comparison, to find a single line in a Kabir poem that could be said to be approving, or permissive, of caste prejudice. But gender prejudice is evident in his verse: A pativrata, a wife totally devoted to her husband, is one of his favourite metaphors for bhakti. In a couple of poems, he even uses sati, the image of a widow burning alive on the pier of her husband, as a metaphor for total devotion to Ram. Should we then conclude that these poets' celebration of creative feminine power was merely an update of the hoary old patriarchal archetype of a woman, which idealises submissiveness in everyday life but condemns their sexual agency?

Let me repeat the necessary caveat—more than 600 years lie between us and Kabir. In his time, both rampant misogyny and birth-based hierarchy—caste in the Hindu context; Ashraf-Ajlaf among Indian Muslims, in which 'Ashraf' indicated descent from Arabs, Turks, Afghans and so on, while 'Ajlaf' referred to local, usually 'untouchable', converts; and the European class system with the nobility at the top—were considered 'acts of god' across the world. How can we expect Kabir and others from that era to behave as if they had the entire accumulated knowledge of history at their command and access to changing mores and values, and dismiss all societal prejudice with an impervious wave of their hand, even if they were cognisant of and against some of those injustices?

In a well-known saakhi, Kabir expects wise people to act like a willow basket that separates the wheat from the chaff. (साधु ऐसा चाहिए जैसे सूप सुभाय। सार सार को गहि रहै, थोथा दे उड़ाय॥) This applies equally to Kabir himself. We should critically examine his opinions using our own vivek. Why should there be either a total acceptance of Kabir or a total rejection? Why should evidence of a strain of prejudice taint the entirety of his work?

Some streams in Kabir panth even show remarkably positive attitudes and approaches to gender-related practices. Among those who were inspired by the poet, but did not belong to the Kabir panth, there was Dadu Dayal denouncing the practice of child marriage back in the sixteenth century. Then, in the eighteenth century, there was Dariya Sahib in Bihar who seated his wife besides him while dispensing his teachings. In eighteenth-century Haryana, Charandas showed a similar respect to his disciples, the major female Bhakti poets Dayabi and Sahjobai. In fact, now, at least one Kabir-panthi math (Giridih, Jharkhand) is headed by a woman sant sadhwi, Jnananad, who also happens to be the first woman to have written a commentary, tika, on the *Bijak*. Published in 2008, it has been well received amongst Kabir panthis. As for the poet's use of the sati imagery, Kabir-panthi women in a Madhya Pradesh town told Linda Hess categorically, 'We are not fools, we don't plan to jump on our husbands' funeral pyres. We don't believe widows should do that. To us, this image is about courage and devotion.'[4]

The word 'sati' does invoke those qualities, the conviction needed to stand firm on one's principles and essential truth. Its collapse into a term for the cruel practice of women burning themselves alive on their husbands' pyres is a curious little story. In early modern north Indian literature, many Muslim poets wrote admiringly of the custom of sati. For these poets, self-immolation in the frustrated pursuit of love was a romantic gesture and, crucially, not exclusively a woman's preserve. In Jayasi's *Padmavat*, we see Ratan Sen almost committing sati in desperation and being saved by Mahadev in the nick of time. Earlier, Hasan Delhavi, a contemporary of Amir Khusrau, composed a masnavi, a poem in rhyming couplets, called 'Ishqnama', a tragic tale of love between a Muslim boy and a Hindu girl from Nagaur (in present-day Rajasthan), which ends when the boy—not the girl—commits sati on the pyre of his beloved.

Kabir's condemnation of women has no poetic value; it is pure didacticism. But in his female persona, Kabir has composed some of his most poignant verse. This creative contradiction needs to be explored. And while it is fruitless and oddly defensive to attempt to rationalise Kabir's vehemence against women, it is equally fruitless to become angry with the poet. It is better, instead, to ask him: 'If

a woman's femininity is an obstacle to spiritual practice, then why
do you articulate your pleasure at union and the pain of separation
in the voice of a woman? If the mutual sexual attraction between
man and woman is this sinful, then what is the need to drag Ram
into 'sin' by calling him "beloved"?'

Questioning the poet thus will alert us to some larger social
and psychological issues.

'Beloved, Come to Me;
Without You, My Body Hurts'

Kabir, in his female persona, expresses kamna, erotic desire,
without any inhibitions. He (or should we say 'she'?) waits
desperately for the days to arrive when 'I will embrace him to my
satisfaction, give my birth meaning, and I will play the sport of
love in its totality'. S/he tells Ram, 'It is in your power to do it.
Please fulfil my desire.'

वै दिन कब आवेंगे माइ।
जा कारनि हम देह धरी है, मिलिबौ अंग लगाइ॥
हौं जानूं हिल मिल खेलूं, तन मन प्रांन समाइ।
या कामना करौ परिपूरन समरथ हौ राम राइ॥

That request is followed up with an intoxicating invitation:

Beloved, come to me
Without you, my body hurts
Everyone calls me your woman, but am I really?
How can that be unless I sleep with you?
Become one with you?

बाल्हा आव हमारे गेह रे, तुम बिन दुखिया देह रे।
सब कोई कहैं तुम्हारी नारी, मोकों इहै संदेह रे।
एकमेक ह्वै सेज न सोवें तब लगि कैसा नेह रे।[5]

Kabir's femininity covers the many moods of sringara. He draws
images and other poetic devices from folk culture and alludes to
popular stories and established literary tropes, such as a woman
in longing, to create a moving narrative of love. This portrayal can
very well be read (as many of his commentators prefer to do) as a
metaphor for his spiritual sadhana, but due to poetic ambivalence,
it can be just as credibly read as an articulation of 'secular' human
love. Consider the following saakhis and forget for a moment that
you are reading a male mystic:

Destined to end life, burning in separation
Neither can I come to you, nor can I call out to you

आय न सकूँ तुझ पै, सकूँ न तुझ बुलाई।
जियरा यूँ ही लेओगे, बिरहा तपाई तपाई॥[6]

Either you show up, or send me death;
I can no longer put up
day and night, with this burning breath.

कै बिरहिन को मींच दै, कै आपा दिखलाई।
आठ पहर का दाझना, मोपै सहा न जाई॥[7]

Standing at the turn of the road, she asks everyone,
'Any news of his coming back, or still none?'

बिरहिन ऊभी पंथ सिरि पंथी बूझै धाई।
एक सबद कहि रे पीव का कब रे मिलेंगे आई॥[8]

Could these not be the expressions of a woman gripped with
longing for her man? This is the power of great poetry—work

intended as purely secular can also lead to a transcendental experience and vice versa. In these poems, Kabir explores not only longing, pain and anticipation but also the joy and exhilaration of fulfilment. Kabir is beside 'herself' as she describes the rapture she experiences after making love with her groom, Ram:

The pleasure has reached my mind
through my body.
Ram the groom came
in a marriage procession of five elements.
My desire to meet him
is brimming over.

तन रत कर मैं मन रत करिहुँ, पंचतत बराती।
रामदेव मोरै पाहुने आए हैं, मैं जोबन मैमाती॥

My home, my temple, glows as I am in bed with my beloved
Having lost all hope, I finally found the treasure
All your doing, my love, says Kabir
I have done nothing, Ram gave me this pleasure
And made me a happily satisfied woman

मंदिर मांहि भया उजियारा। ले सूती अपना कंत पियारा॥
मैं निरासी जे निधि पाई। हमहिं कहा यह तुमहि बड़ाई॥
कहै कबीर मैं कछू न कीन्हां। सखी सुहाग राम मोहि दीन्हा॥

My dear Ram
Now, you aren't to go anywhere else
I will not let you
Take whatever you desire, but be mine
You came after making me wait for long
Dwell in my heart now
I will serve you in every possible way
But going to someone else? No way

अब तोहि जान न दैहूं राम पियारे। ज्यूँ भावै त्यूँ होह हमारे॥
बहुत दिनी के बिछुरै हरि पाये। भाग बड़े हरि बैठें आये॥
चरननि लागि करौं बरियाई। प्रेम प्रीति राखौं उरझाई॥
इत मन मंदिर रहौ नित चोखे। कहै कबीर परहु मति धोखे॥[9]

Kabir's poetry overflows with such uninhibited and stirring expressions of erotic desire from a woman's point of view. This is, of course, only a select sample from hundreds of padas and saakhis that articulate many aspects of the erotic. But, a conscious reader of Kabir cannot shy away from other samples of his writings on women:

A desirable woman is like a cobra
Only those with Ram's love can be saved
She is bound to devour the rest

कामिणी काली नागणी तीन्यूं लोक मंझारि।
राम स्नेही ऊबरे, विषयी खाए झारि॥

Your own woman, or some other, leads to hell
All fire is the same, why put your hand in it?

नारी पराई आपणी, भुगत्या नरकहि जाइ।
आगि लगि सब एक हैं, तामैं हाथ न बाहि॥

A woman destroys three pleasures—
Bhakti, freedom and knowledge
You must choose either these or female company

नारि नसावैं तीन सुख, जा नर पासैं होइ।
भगति, मुक्ति, निज ग्यान में, पैसि न सकई कोइ॥

Woman: a pit of hell
Only the rare men, sadhus, can escape its fire

नारी कुंड नरक का, बिरला थंभै बाग़।
कोइ साधु जन ऊबरै, सब जग मूंवा लाग॥

If these lines of Kabir are to be subject to criticism, we must also note that his condemnations of women are formulaic, with little of the beauty and urgency that are the hallmarks of his poetry. These didactic observations come mostly in the form of curt saakhis. In padas—longer poems that give space to the imagination to enjoy a languorous stretch—there is little evidence of the ire Kabir apparently feels towards women and their siren call. As it is true of most poets, across time and space, the puritan is not poetic and the poet is not a puritan.

All of the above saakhis are taken from the chapter in the *Granthavali* titled '*Kami Nar ko Ang*' (About the Lecherous Man).[10] The condemnation of women here is intended as a caution to these men, unable to control their desire. In a couple of saakhis, these lechers too feel the rough edge of Kabir's sarcasm, although their fault is their lechery, not simply the fact of their being men. No such allowance is made for the woman, whose fault in these saakhis is that she is attractive to men, some of whom cannot contain their lust. Without producing much in the way of evidence, Kabir blames women as instigators of 'excessive' erotic desire and for seducing men to the dark side.

As noted earlier, expression of devotion to god through love was not Kabir's idea but was already established in both Bhakti and Sufi traditions. Unlike Bhakti poets, Sufi poets imagined god as female. Kabir's specific imagery of himself as the 'bride of Ram' is inherited from the Vaishnavism of the south, where the adoption of a female persona by males was a longstanding practice. According to the poet and scholar A.K. Ramanujan, 'of the thousand or so poems of Nammalvar, 270 are in female voices. (In this practice of taking on female personae, he has classical precedents in Cankam poetry, where male poets frequently write in female voices.)'

In the same essay, 'Men, Women, and Saints', Ramanujan notes:

> Thus, in the course of constituting or reconstituting them-
> selves in this new way of being, men may take on feminine
> roles, speak through female personae and yearn for their male
> god as women do for their lovers. Women saints may take
> on the characteristics of men: they leave the house questing
> for their personal god (not their husband's or father's) and a
> community of their own choosing, in ways that shatter rule
> after rule in Manu's code book. They become the third gender
> of my title: men, women, and saints.[11]

But Ramanujan does not ask the crucial question: why do women, in the process of becoming sants, the 'third gender' of his title, not find it necessary to condemn men as distractions from the path of bhakti? The male sants' condemnation of women is excused as a deliberate measure to warn Bhaktas off the obstacles in their path. How strange that female Bhaktas and sants do not see men as obstacles.

Mirabai, the great Bhakti poet (from the region today known as Rajasthan), for instance, had to pay a price for ignoring the patriarchal norms of her society. But we do not find rancour in her verse; she does not rail against men as Kabir does against women in those saakhis, nor does she train her anger on the men who tormented her. She reports even attempts on her life in the most phlegmatic manner: 'Ranaji sends me a poisoned cup, drinking which Mira only laughs.' She shrugs off obstacles to her bhakti and humiliations heaped on her person, saying, 'Ranaji, I like being given a bad name, whether in condemnation or in praise. I insist on taking my strange way!' There are similar legends about the twelfth-century Kannada poet Akka Mahadevi and Lal Ded in fourteenth-century Kashmir.

The problem, then, lies with men, not with human sexuality. The lesson to be learnt from female poets and sants is basic: if you want to control your sexual desire, work on yourself instead of blaming your weakness on the other sex.

While distancing ourselves from Kabir's broad-brush slurs against women, let us also grant that he, in other poems, alongside other male Bhakti and Sufi poets, perhaps acknowledged this paradox in his own way by adopting a female voice both in his sadhana and poetry. Those men who cite lines from Kabir to justify their own hatred or fear of women could also take a leaf from his book and try to speak and feel as a woman might and attempt to build some empathy. It should also be noted that while Bhakti poets were persecuted for their interrogation of caste, their impersonation of women in their poetry rarely raised an eyebrow. Indic tradition was what we might describe as 'progressive' when it came to the nature of human sexuality, best exemplified in the idea and image of the Ardhanarishvara—god as half-woman, half-man.

'As Many Women and Men
As There May Be, in All Lies Your Presence':
Going Beyond Binaries

Milan Kundera, in his novel *Immortality*, writes:

> Woman is the future of man. That means that the world which
> was once formed in man's image will now be transformed to
> the image of woman. The more technical and mechanical,
> cold and metallic it becomes, the more it will need the type of
> warmth that only the woman can give. If we want to save the
> world, we must adapt to the woman, let ourselves be led by the
> woman, let ourselves be penetrated by the *Ewig-Weibliche*, the
> eternally feminine!

The pagan (polytheistic, pantheistic) cultures that thrived
before the arrival of monotheistic Abrahamic faiths had the
concept of the 'eternally feminine' and acknowledged the
coexistence of male and female principles in the universe. Not that
this awareness resulted in more equal social structures, at least
so long as the patriarchy controlled (and continues to control)
political power and systems of production. Still, at least in the Indic
tradition, the importance of the female principle has never been
completely lost or abandoned. Hinduism holds the female principle
in high esteem and revers many manifestations of it—Parvati,
Durga, Kali, Lakshmi and, of course, Sita and Radha, among others,
including new deities—male and female—added to the pantheon.
Acceptance of the coexistence of male and female principles helps
avoid the unnecessary valorisation or condemnation of people
on the basis of biological sex. More importantly, it leads to the
recognition of the simultaneous existence of a female within every
male and vice versa. There are certain positive characteristics

popularly equated with women (as we saw in the quote from Kundera); on the other hand, many negative characteristics are also associated with women in traditional worldviews and mythologies. Both these need to be examined critically, keeping the centrality of the individual in mind. Not every woman, Kabir knew, is a pit of hell, nor is she always the embodiment of human warmth, just as not every man is either a lech or a paragon of virtue.

The Ardhanarishvara gives celestial form to this notion of the male and the female each forming a part of the other. The story of why Shiva chooses to adopt this particular form has been explained in various Puranas with some variations, which throws light on how it entered the popular imagination. We need not go into those details here. For the moment, let us just note that the idea of the Ardhanarishvara helps us greatly to reflect on the problem underlined by Germaine Greer in *The Female Eunuch*:

> In fact, men and women love differently, and much of the behaviour that we describe by the term is so far from benevolence, and so antisocial, that it must be understood to be inimical to the essential nature of love. Our life-style contains more Thanatos than Eros, for egotism, exploitation, deception, obsession and addiction have more place in us than eroticism, joy, generosity and spontaneity.[12]

Greer was one of the most celebrated figures of the women's liberation movement in the 1970s; her idea of liberation is defined by her insistence on 'uniquely female differences' as opposed to arguing that women are just 'like men'. Her point is valid, even if too much focus on 'differences' could blind us to the obvious fact that the two are more alike than different. This is the chief weakness of the identity politics that has become so insistent over the last three decades or so—a need to delineate differences so starkly that there is little room for the blurring and nuance that is much more typical and accurate of the miscegenated human life. In the context of gender discourse, the Ardhanarishvara serves as a valuable and conscious departure from the standard binaries of sex and gender.

This idea, along with reverence for the female principle, actively present in mythology and cultural memory, has certainly saved Indian religions and culture from becoming hopelessly puritan. Or 'saved' until Indians began to treat the Christian, Victorian puritanism introduced by the British colonialists to India as an integral part of Sanatan Dharma and 'Bharatiya sanskriti'.

Along with Indic religious traditions, early modern India was enriched by its encounter with Islam. In the Islamic context, poets, Sufi or not, had long challenged the authoritarian, censorious and vindictive nature of religious and political power structures. Only in such an enriched context, in which poets resisted authority, could a Jayasi have celebrated love and beauty in so uninhibited a manner without causing outrage. In fact, the poet was greatly admired and respected. Apart from Kabir, many poets across the country adopted the voices of women without provoking widespread anger. Today, would they be spared the attention of internet trolls or those who believe they alone should judge who gets to tell what story in whose voice?

Greer is concerned about Thanatos (death) occupying more space than Eros (love and desire). In the half-century since she published *The Female Eunuch*, Eros has conceded much more space to Thanatos. Egotism, exploitation, deception, obsession and addiction have overpowered eroticism, joy, generosity and spontaneity within us. The insistence on 'difference' has led to religions, for instance, jealously and violently nurturing these differences, as if they are all that matter. The age of information seems to be giving way to the age of disinformation. Dialogue is fast giving way to monologue and anger is becoming second nature.

The feminist political-philosopher Judith Butler in her 1990 book *Gender Trouble: Feminism and the Subversion of Identity* gives a rallying cry for the disruption of the binary view of sex. She would have approved of Kabir's exploration of his 'feminine' self, his desire to mix genders and speak in a hybrid voice. But what would Butler have made of Kabir's rote condemnation of the 'seductive wiles of women'? A serious engagement with Kabir's paradoxical stance, and that of other Nirgunis, can show us how gender binaries can be both perpetuated and transcended.

This tension is not present in the work of female Bhakti poets or Sagun poets. Women did not need to adopt the male persona for the simple reason that bhakti is supposed to be about dedication and surrender which were, and are, known as 'female characteristics'. And amongst the male Sagunis, the Krishna-orientated ones articulated their bhakti in the idiom of kama both creatively and without inhibition, but they rarely took on the female voice. The Sagun bhaktas belonging to the Rasik school—a branch of Ramanandis—are an exception. They went substantially further than the Nirgunis in their adoption of the female persona. These Bhaktas not only wrote from the female perspective in their poetry but also dressed and behaved like women in real life. But none of them made enough of a mark with their poetry for their experiments to have been studied or analysed.

However eccentric, these poets, whether Sufi or Rasik, articulated their love within the boundaries of Islam or Vedic and Puranic Hinduism. They did, of course, expand the traditional religious imagination and were polarising figures, but they were recognisably of their religions. They remained close to their scriptures and to traditional belief systems. Despite their 'strange' behaviour, there was no question of them denying the ultimate authority of the Vedas or the Koran.

On the other hand, the Nirgunis' articulation of love was a radical transformation not only in their dismissal of gender binaries but also in their insistence that love (bhakti, to use their word) is the touchstone for everything. Instead of the 'divine', they emphasised the 'shabd', or word, that emerged from their own instinct, experience and wisdom. They agreed with Narada that bhakti is its own proof, it need not be attested by any scripture. All Nirgunis, in varying degrees, were indifferent to holy scriptures and to the assessment of bhakti in any context other than its own. They were so self-assured because they took love to its logical conclusion.

Their attempt to transcend the gender binary needs to be seen alongside their interrogation of power structures and the question that underpins all their social interactions. 'If all humans are children of god,' the Nirgun poet in love asks, 'then how can structured inequality and the persecution of non-believers be justified?' Similarly, 'If all existence is permeated by the Brahman, then how can you practice untouchability?'

By mixing love with empirical rationality, the Nirgunis evolved a method of cognition, a distinctive perception of the world. When Kabir sees the world this way, he finds each and every thing, the 'vessel', fragrant with god's presence. Realising this, the poet is filled with supreme bliss:

> Just as fragrance is inherent in flowers,
> so is Hari, Govind, in everyone.
> Having achieved the life-breath of the universe,
> I have attained bliss.

फूलों में जैसे रहती बास। घट घट गोविन्द हरि निवास॥
कहे कबीर भया मन आनंद। जग-जीवन पायो परमानंद॥[13]

Contemplating religion through the looking glass of love, Nirgunis found it flawed and lacking. Their polemical interrogation of various ideas, attitudes and practices was rooted in the love-cognition that made them inclusive and open and inspired them to embrace the other—figuratively and literally. Kabir is the fountainhead of this Nirgun sensibility; it is in him that we find the strongest criticism of the world as it is and it is in him that some of the most significant Nirgun ideas and innovations originated.

The most significant of these is the very idea of Ram as expounded by Kabir. His Ram is not the avatar but an abstraction. 'How can you love an abstraction?' Kabir asks. An abstraction may be the subject of philosophical reflection and speculation, but love? Surely, you can love only a tangible 'other', be it human, animal or thing. Kabir, a great poet, knows this and so unhesitatingly draws on the names and stories of the avatars, though he rejects the idea itself. But he shows that it is the depth and strength of his love that turns the Nirgun Ram into a tangible human presence. In Kabir's compositions, philosophically speaking, Ram signifies the essence of existence. But in the language Kabir uses, the words of a woman in love, this essence of Ram is turned into a human beloved, whom the possessive woman forewarns:

> Come, enter me through my eyes
> And stay there
> I will then close my eyes
> And will not see anyone else
> Nor let anyone see you

> नैनाँ आंतरि आव तू, ज्यों हौं नैन झंपेऊँ।
> ना हौं देखो और कूँ, न तुझ देखन देऊँ॥[14]

Besides being a normal human presence (this kind of possessiveness is so integral to ordinary human love), Kabir's Ram also serves as a metaphor for the poet's utopian vision of a more humane world, just as he uses femininity as a metaphor for the agency of and capacity to love. The humanisation of the abstract Nirgun Ram situates him within the context of actual human love and the metaphorical Ram makes him a suitable object of spiritual contemplation as well as a reference point for the critique of the social system and prejudice.

In Kabir's time (as in ours), Ram and Allah, to many people, signified two antagonistic groups. For such people, more than any spiritual connotation, these words carried the full force of organised religion and its power structure. Kabir challenged these groups directly, his question devastating in its simplicity: 'Where did you get two gods from?' The source of this challenge lies in his idea of love, which he mostly articulates as a woman, but also in the voice of a child.

In one particularly moving poem, Kabir uses the compound 'Allah-Ram' to underline the unity of the divine. He describes himself as a child, new to this entity called Allah-Ram, unsure of how to approach him. This poem is one of the most holistic articulations of Kabir's worldview:

> Allah-Ram, I live for you
> My master, please have compassion on the one who entreats you
> Should one perform wudu, chant or take ritual baths, what should one do?
> Should one keep roza, offer namaz, go on the hajj or to the Kaaba?
> The Brahmin keeps a fast, the qazi keeps Ramzan for a month
> Why do they keep the other eleven months separate, when all are equal?

If god lives in a mosque, then to whom belongs the rest of
existence?
Ram is believed to live in places of pilgrimage and idols, but
I didn't find him in either
Hari lives in the east, Allah in the west
Search inside your heart, for there lies Ram-Rahman
As many women and men as there may be, in all lies your
presence
Kabir is Allah-Ram's child, because Hari is our guru, our pir

अलह राम जीऊँ तेरे ताई, बंदे उपरि मेहर करि मेरे साँई।
क्या ऊजू जप मंजन कीयें, क्या मसीत सिर नांयें।
रोज़ा करें निमाज गुजारें, क्या हज काबे जायें॥
ब्राह्मण गियारस करे चौबीसों, काजी माह रमज़ान।
ग्यारह मास जुदे क्यों कीये, एकहि मांहि समान॥
जो रे खुदाई मसीति बसत है, और मुलिक किस केरा।
तीरथ मूरति राम निवासा, दुहु मैं किनहूं न हेरा॥
पूरबि दिसा हरि का बासा, पछिम अलह मुकाँमा।
दिल ही खोज दिलै भीतर, इहाँ राम रहिमांना॥
जेती औरति मरदाँ कहिये, सब में रूप तुम्हारा।
कबीर पंगुड़ा अलह राम का, हरि गुर पीर हमारा॥[15]

This, in a nutshell, is Kabir. As we flounder in the twenty-first
century, we would do well to recall his message of a self-reliant,
self-generated spirituality. Instead of rituals and symbols, instead
of differences, let us imbibe the musk, the heady fragrance of
Kabir's enlightened love:

पिंजर प्रेम प्रकास्या, आंतरि भया उजास।
मुख कस्तूरी महमही बानी फूटी बास॥[16]

Select Bibliography

There are many English translations of Kabir's poems, the most well-known being by Rabindranath Tagore (1915). But in my opinion, the best translation is by Linda Hess and Shukdeo Singh in *The Bijak of Kabir* (Oxford University Press, New York, 2002). Essays by Hess have further added to the value of this collection.

The reader can also consult translations by Arvind Krishna Mehrotra, *Songs of Kabir* (Hachette, New Delhi, 2011) and by Chandan Sinha, *The Vision of Wisdom: Kabir—Selected Sakhis* (Rupa, New Delhi, 2020).

Robert Bly's reconstructions of Kabir's poems in *Kabir: Ecstatic Poems* (Beacon Press, Boston, 2007) are interesting, with the expected strengths and limitations of a reconstruction.

In Hindi, *Kabir Granthavali* edited by Shyam Sundar Das (the better-printed edition is from Lok Bharti Prakashan, Allahabad, 2011) is the most comprehensive; it also includes poems found in the Adi Granth. Being based on other rather old manuscripts, it is considered the most authentic in academic circles.

On the other hand, *Kabir Granthavali* (Lok Bharti Prakashan, Allahabad, 2011) by Mata Prasad Gupta is a better-edited version of the same material, but does not include the poems from the Adi Granth.

Kabir panthis value the *Kabir Bijak* more than any other collection. Shukdeo Singh's is the most well-edited version of it (Neelabh Prakashan, Allahabad, 1972).

The general reader might find my compilation of Kabir's poems in *Kabir: Saakhi aur Sabad* (National Book Trust, New Delhi, 2017) more accessible.

Other recommended books are:

Hindi

1. Hazari Prasad Dwivedi, *Kabir*, Rajkamal Prakshan, New Delhi, 2000.
2. Namvar Singh, *Doosari Parampara ki Khoj*, Rajkamal Prakashan, New Delhi, 1982.
3. Parashuram Chaturvedi, *Uttari Bharat ki Sant Parampara*, Bharti Bhandar, Allahabad, 2019.
4. Ramvilas Sharma, *Bharat mein Angrezi Raj aur Marxwad*, Rajkamal Prakashan, New Delhi, 2004.
5. Purushottam Agrawal, *Akath Kahani Prem ki: Kabir ki Kavita aur Unka Samay*, Rajkamal Prakashan, New Delhi, 2019.

English

1. David Lorenzen, *Who Invented Hinduism?: Essays on Religion in History*, Yoda Press, New Delhi, 2006.
2. *Religious Movements in South Asia 600-1800: Debates in Indian History and Society*, ed. David Lorenzen, Oxford University Press, New Delhi, 2005.
3. David Lorenzen, *Praises to a Formless God: Nirguni Texts from North India*, State University of New York Press, Albany, 1996.
4. Linda Hess, *Bodies of Song: Kabir Oral Traditions and Performative Worlds in North India*, Oxford University Press, New York, 2015.
5. J. H. Hawley, *The Three Bhakti Voices: Mirabai, Surdas and Kabir in Their Times and Ours*, Oxford University Press, New Delhi, 2012.
6. *From Ancient to Modern: Religion, Power and Community in India*, ed. Ishita Bannerjee-Dube and Saurabh Dube, Oxford University press, New Delhi, 2009.

7. *After Timur Left: Culture and Circulation in Fifteenth-Century North India*, ed. Francesca Orsini and Samira Sheikh, Oxford University Press, New Delhi, 2014.

8. Nicholas Dirks, *Castes of Mind: Colonialism and the Making*, Permanent Black, Ranikhet, 2003.

9. Christian Lee Novtezke, *The Quotidian Revolution: Vernacularization, Religion and the Premodern Public Sphere in India*, Columbia University Press, New York, 2016.

10. Jack Goody, *The Theft of History*, Cambridge University Press, Cambridge, 2007.

11. *The Cambridge Economic History of India: Volume 1*, ed. Tapan Raychaudhuri and Irfan Habib, Cambridge University Press, New Delhi, 1982.

12. Peter van der Veer, *Imperial Encounters: Religion and Modernity in India and Britain*, Permanent Black, Ranikhet, 2001.

13. *China, India and Alternative Asian Modernities*, ed. Sanjay Kumar, Satya P. Mohanty, Archana Kumar and Raj Kumar, Routledge, New Delhi, 2020.

14. Utsa Patnaik and Prabhat Patnaik, *A Theory of Imperialism*, Tulika Books, 2016.

Endnotes

Kabir and I
A Note to the Reader

1 economictimes.indiatimes.com/news/international/trip-to-india-as-teen-was-a-life-changer-for-steve-jobs/articleshow/10264889.cms?from=mdr.

2 Walter Issacson, *Steve Jobs*, London, Hachette, 2011, p. 48.

I

1 Unless indicated otherwise, all translations are by the author.

2 Some scholars have doubted the guru-disciple relationship between Ramanand and Kabir despite the consensus within the Bhakti tradition and evidence of other, earlier sources that do not doubt this whatsoever. The making of this doubt in itself is instructive of the problems involved in reading Indian cultural experience solely on the basis of Sanskrit sources while ignoring vernacular ones. Having researched this vexed issue for decades, I have no doubt that the traditional consensus on the Ramanand-Kabir relation is quite valid historically. For details, see Chapter Five in my *Akath Kahani Prem ki: Kabir ki Kavita aur Unka Samay*, Rajkamal Prakashan, New Delhi, 2009. Also see my essays in *From Ancient to Modern: Religion, Power and Community in India*, ed. Saurabh Dube and Ishita Banerjee Dube, Oxford University Press, New Delhi, 2008 and in *Literature and Nationalist Ideology: Writing Histories of Modern Indian Languages*, ed. Hans Herder, Routledge, London, 2017. My argument on this subject is also available at pratilipi.in/2008/10/01/in-search-of-ramanand-purushottam-agrawal/5/.

3 Winand Callewaert, *The Sarvangi of Gopaldas*, Manohar, New Delhi, 1993, p. 261.

4 Raymond Schwab, *The Oriental Renaissance: Europe's Rediscovery of India and the East, 1680-1880*, Columbia University Press, New York, 1984, p. 6.

5 Quoted in Michael S. Dodson, *Orientalism, Empire and National Culture: India, 1770-1880*, Cambridge University Press, New Delhi, 2010, p. 125.

6 Peter van der Veer, *Gods on Earth: Religious Experience and Identity in Ayodhya*, Oxford University Press, New Delhi, 1988, p. 56.

7 Poem 186 in *Raidas Bani*, ed. Shukdeo Singh, Radhakrishna Prakashan, New Delhi, 2003, p. 229.

8 Harbans Mukhia, 'A Rationality Immersed in Religiosity: Reason and Religiosity in Abu'l Fazl's Oeuvre', *Medieval History Journal*, ed. Harbans Mukhia, volume 23, issue 1, pp. 50-73.

9   *Kabir Granthavali*, ed. Shyam Sundar Das, Lok Bharti Prakashan, Allahabad, 2011, p. 303.

10 Doha 114 in Bal-Kand (Canto One) of *Ramcharitmanas*, in *The Epic of Ram*, trans. Philip Lutgendorf, Murty Classical Library of India, Harvard University Press, Cambridge, Massachusetts, 2016, pp. 234–236.

11 *The Hagiographies of Anantdas*, ed. Winand Callewaert and Swapna Sharma, Curzon Press, Surrey, 2000, p. 32.

12 For some elaboration, see my paper, 'Vernacular Modernity and the Public Sphere of Bhakti', *China, India and Alternative Asian Modernities*, ed. Sanjay Kumar, Satya P. Mohanty, Archana Kumar and Raj Kumar, Routledge, New York, 2019.

13 See Christian Lee Novetzke, *The Quotidian Revolution: Vernacularisation, Religion and the Premodern Public Sphere in India*, Columbia University Press, New York, 2016.

14 *Kabir Vachnavali*, ed. Ayodhya Singh Upadhayay 'Harioudh', Nagri Pracharini Sabha, Varanasi, 1987, p. 83.

15 David Lorenzen, *Praises to a Formless God: Nirguni Texts from North India*, State University of New York Press, Albany, 1996, p. 208.

16 Nabadas, *Shri Bhaktmal*, Gangavishnu Shrikrishnadas Prakashan, Mumbai, 1989, p. 67.

17 *Kabir Granthavali*, ed. Mata Prasad Gupta, Lok Bharti Prakashan, Allahabad, 2019, p. 25.

18 See my *Padmavat: An Epic Love Story*, Rupa Publications, New Delhi, 2018.

19 *Granthavali*, Gupta, p. 10.

20 *Kabir Granthavali*, ed. Parasnath Tiwari, Raka Prakashan, Allahabad, 1989, p. 207.

21 *Granthavali*, Gupta, p. 78.

22 *Granthavali*, Gupta, p. 70.

23 *Granthavali*, Gupta, p. 324.

II

1   *Kabir Bijak*, ed. Shukdeo Singh, Neelabh Prakashan, Allahabad, 1972, p. 141.

2   *Kabir Legends and Anantdas's Kabir Parchai*, trans. David Lorenzen (with a brilliant introduction by him), Indian Book Centre, Delhi, 1991, pp. 205–206. Translation of all passages from Lorenzen are by the author, unless otherwise specified.

3   Mowbad Shah, *Dabistan-e-Mazahib*, trans. David Shea and Anthony Troyer, Khalil and Co., Lahore, 1973 (first published in Paris, 1873), p. 266.

4   *Kabir Legends*, Lorenzen, p. 206.

5   *Kabir Legends*, Lorenzen, pp. 207–208.

6   *Kabir Legends*, Lorenzen, p. 129.

7   From the oral tradition.

8   *Vyas Vani*, Hitashram Satsang Bhumi, Vrindavan, 2013, p. 40.

9   *Jayasi Granthavali*, ed. Ramchandra Shukla, Nagri Pracharini Sabha, Varanasi, 1951, p. 374.

10 *Kabir Legends*, Lorenzen, p. 130.

11 *Kabir Legends*, Lorenzen, p. 131.

12 *Raidas Bani*, ed. Shukdeo Singh, Radhakrishna Prakashan, New Delhi, p. 229; Shahabuddin Iraqi, *The Sarvangi of Rajjabdas*, Granthayan, Aligarh, 1985, p. 173.

13 *Kabir Granthavali*, ed. Mata Prasad Gupta, Lok Bharti Prakashan, Allahabad, 2019, p. 54.

14 *Granthavali*, Gupta, p. 277.

15 *Shri Guru Granth Sahib: Volume 1*, ed. Winand Callewaert, Manohar, New Delhi, 1996, p. 479, in Raag Aasa.

16 *Granthavali*, Gupta, p. 153.

17 *Granthavali*, Gupta, p. 110.

18 Charlotte Vaudville, *A Weaver Named Kabir: Selected Verses with Detailed Historical Introduction*, Oxford University Press, New Delhi, 1993, p. 47.

19 *Dabistan-e-Mazahib*, Shea and Troyer, p. 262.

20 *Indo-Persian Travels in the Age of Discoveries, 1400–1800*, Cambridge University Press, New Delhi, 2007, p. 140.

21 *Dabistan-e-Mazahib*, Shea and Troyer, p. 262.

22 *Shri Guru Granth Sahib: Volume 1*, Callewaert, p. 856, in Raag Bilwal.

23 *Granthavali*, Gupta, p. 157.

24 *Granthavali*, Gupta, p. 230.

25 *Granthavali*, Gupta, p. 308.

26 *Kabir Legends*, Lorenzen, pp. 165–167.

27 David Lorenzen has analysed Kabir and other vernacular sources to convincingly argue that 'Hinduism' was not 'invented' during the British period. See his essay in the eponymous collection *Who Invented Hinduism: Essays on Religion in History*, Yoda Press, New Delhi, 2006.

28 *Kabir Legends*, Lorenzen, p. 171

29 *Kabir Granthavali*, ed. Shaym Sundar Das, Lok Bharti Prakashan, Allahabad, 2011, p. 262.

30 *Granthavali*, Gupta, p. 8.

31 *Kabir Legends*, Lorenzen, p. 151.

32 *Kabir Legends*, Lorenzen, p. 159.

33 *Granthavali*, Gupta, pp. 359–360.

34 *Granthavali*, Gupta, pp. 382–383.

35 *Shri Guru Granth Sahib: Volume 1*, Callewaert, p. 326.

36 Poem 8 in *Pad Surdasji ka* (1582), manuscript published in facsimile, ed. Gopal Narayan Bahura and Kenneth Bryant, Maharaj Sawai Man Singh II Museum Trust, Jaipur, 1984, p. 165.

37 *The Bijak of Kabir*, trans. Linda Hess and Shukdeo Singh, Oxford University Press, 2002, p. 110.

III

1   *Muktibodh Rachnavali*, ed. Nemichandra Jain, Rajkamal Prakashan, New Delhi, 1988, pp. 288–289.

2   *The Bijak of Kabir*, trans. Linda Hess and Shukdeo Singh, Oxford University Press, New York, 2002, p. 8.

3   *Says Tuka: Selected Poetry of Tukaram*, trans. Dilip Chitre, Penguin Books, New Delhi, 1991, p. xx.

4   Immanuel Wallerstein, *The End of the World As We Know It: Social Science for the Twenty-First Century*, University of Minnesota Press, London, 1999, p. 1.

5   This book is available online at prchiz.pl/storage/app/media/pliki/Luther_On_Jews.pdf.

6   Kate Telsture, *India Inscribed: European and British Writing on India 1600–1800*, Oxford University Press, New Delhi, 1997, p. 101.

7   Hans J. Hillenbrand, 'On Book Burnings and Book Burners: Reflections on the Power (and Powerlessness) of Ideas', *Journal of American Academy of Religion*, ed. Charles Mathews, volume 7, issue 3 (September 2006), p. 600.

8   Hillenbrand, 'On Book Burnings', p. 598.

9   'A Rationality Immersed in Religiosity: Reason and Religiosity in Abu'l Fazl's Oeuvre', *Medieval History Journal*, ed. Harbans Mukhia, volume 23, issue 1 (Sage), pp. 50–73.

10 Sir Jack Goody, *The Theft of History*, Cambridge University Press, Cambridge, 2006, p. 242.

11 Peter van der Veer, *Imperial Encounters: Religion and Modernity in India and Britain*, Permanent Black, New Delhi, 2001, pp. 62–63.

12 Quoted by Anthony Giddens in the introduction to Max Weber, *The Protestant Ethic and the Spirit of Capitalism*, Routledge, New York, 1992, p. xiv.

13 Enrique Dussel, 'World System and "Trans"-Modernity', *Unbecoming Modern: Colonialism, Modernity, Colonial Modernities*, ed. Saurabh Dube and Ishita Banerjee-Dube, Social Science Press, New Delhi, 2006, pp. 170–171.

14 A. Dasgupta, 'Indian Merchants and the Trade in the Indian Ocean', *Cambridge Economic History of India: Volume 1*, ed. Tapan Raychaudhuri and Irfan Habib, Cambridge University Press, Cambridge, 1982, p. 411.

15 Jawaharlal Nehru, *The Discovery of India*, Oxford University Press, New Delhi, p. 264.

16 Sanjay Subrahmmanyam, 'Vignettes of Early Modernity in South Asia', *Early Modernities Daedalus*, ed. Shmuel N. Eisenstadt and Wolfgang Schluchter, volume 127, issue 3 (American Academy of Arts and Sciences, 1998), pp. 99–100.

17 bostonreview.net/chibber-good-empire.

18 *The Cambridge Economic History of India: Volume 2*, ed. Dharma Kumar and Tapan Raychaudhuri, Cambridge University Press, Cambridge, 1983, pp. 32–33.

19 Ashutosh Dayal Mathur, *Medieval Hindu Law: Historical Evolution and the Enlightened Rebellion*, Oxford University Press, New Delhi, 2007, p. 14.

20 Mathur, *Medieval Hindu Law*, p. 188.

21 eji.org/news/history-racial-injustice-public-spectacle-lynchings/.

22 Nicholas Dirks, *Castes of Mind: Colonialism and the Making of Modern India*, Princeton University Press, New Jersey, 2001, p. 5.

23 I would request the readers interested and patient enough to go through the 'long story' to read B.R. Ambedkar's *Who Were Shudras*, alongside Dirks's *Castes of Mind* and my *Akath Kahani Prem ki: Kabir ki Kavita aur Unka Samay*.

24 William Crooke, *The Tribes and Castes of North Western Provinces and Oudh*, Cosmo Publications, New Delhi, 1975, p. cxxxix.

25 Crooke, *The Tribes and Castes*, p. cxcii.

26 Crooke, *The Tribes and Castes*, p. xxvi.

27 Crooke, *The Tribes and Castes*, p. xxvi.

28 Jwala Prasad Mishra, *Jati Bhaskar*, Khemraj Shrikrishnadas, Mumbai, 1996, pp. 203, 237, 245 and 318.

29 Preface to *Mardumshumari Raj Marwar, 1891* (Report), Shri Jagdish Singh Gehlot Shodh Sansthan, Jodhpur, 1996 (reprint).

30 K.N. Pannikar, *Culture, Ideology and Hegemony: Intellectual and Social Consciousness in Colonial India*, Tulika, New Delhi, 1995, p. 7.

31 *Dr. Babasaheb Ambedkar Writings and Speeches: Volume 7*, Dr. Ambedkar Foundation, New Delhi, 2014, pp. 79–80.

32 Jack Goody, *The East in the West*, Cambridge University Press, Cambridge, 1996, p. 94.

33 Raymond Schwab, *The Oriental Renaissance: Europe's Rediscovery of India and the East 1680–1880*, Columbia University Press, New York, 1984, p. 133.

34 Jürgan Habermas, *The Structural Transformation of the Public Sphere: An Enquiry into a Category of Bourgeoise Society*, Polity Press, London, 1989, p. xi.

35 Tulsidas, *Dohavali*, Gita Press, Gorakhpur, 1981, p. 186.

36 C.A. Bayly, *Empire and Information: Intelligence Gathering and Social Communication in India 1780–1870*, Cambridge University Press, New Delhi, 1999, p. 181.

37 Habermas, *The Structural Transformation*, pp. 1–2.

38 Crooke, *The Tribes and Castes*, p. cixix.

39 Bayly, *Empire and Information*, p. 185.

40 An excellent translation along with the original text and an introduction has been prepared by Mukund Lath, *Half a Tale: A Study in the Interrelationship between Biography and History*, Rajsthan Prakrit Bharti Sansthan, Jaipur, 1981. Vasudha Dalmia has published a refreshing appraisal: 'Merchant Tales and the Emergence of Novel in Hindi', *Economic and Political Weekly* (23 August 2008), pp. 43–60.

41 Dirks, *Castes of Mind*, p. 219.

IV

1 *Kabir Granthavali*, ed. Mata Prasad Gupta, Lok Bharti Prakashan, Allahabad, 2019, p. 343.

2 Hazari Prasad Dwivedi, *Kabir*, Rajkamal Prakashan, New Delhi, 2000, p. 38.

3 Pitambar Dutt Barthwal, *Yoga Pravah*, Shri Kashi Vidya Peeth, Varanasi, 1945, pp. 123–127.

4 *Granthavali*, Gupta, p. 4.

5 G.H. Westcott, *Kabir and his Panth*, Sushil Gupta, Kolkata, 1953 (reprint), p. 27.

6   Chandrabali Pande, *Vichar Vimarsh*, Hindi Sahitya Sammelan, Allahabad, 2004, p. 11.

7   Achille Mbembe, *On the Postcolony*, University of California Press, 2001, pp. 10–11.

8   For details, see S.A.A. Rizwi, *A History of Sufism in India: Volume 1*, Munshiram Manoharlal, Delhi, 1978, pp. 323–353.

9   Dharamvir, *Kabir ke Alochak*, Vani Prakashan, New Delhi, 2004.

10 Mowbad Shah, *Dabistan-e-mazahib*, trans. David Shea and Anthony Troyer, Khalil and Co., Lahore, 1973 (first published in Paris, 1873), pp. 262, 285.

11 Linda Hess, *Bodies of Song: Kabir Oral Traditions and Performative Worlds in North India*, Oxford University Press, New York, 2015, p. 308.

12 columbia.edu/acis/ets/CCREAD/etscc/kant.html.

13 Dwivedi, *Kabir*, pp. 107–108.

14 *The Bijak of Kabir*, trans. Linda Hess and Shukdeo Singh, Oxford University Press, 2002, p. 94.

15 *Granthavali*, Gupta, p. 171.

16 *Granthavali*, Gupta, p. 33.

17 *Granthavali*, Gupta, p. 62.

18 *The Bijak of Kabir*, Hess and Singh, p. 69.

19 *The Bijak of Kabir*, Hess and Singh, p. 94.

20 *Granthavali*, Gupta, p. 82.

21 *Granthavali*, Gupta, p. 86.

22 *Granthavali*, Gupta, p. 5.

23 *Granthavali*, Gupta, p. 3.

24 *Granthavali*, Gupta, p. 65.

25 *Granthavali*, Gupta, p. 65.

26 *Granthavali*, Gupta, p. 154.

27 *Granthavali*, Gupta, p. 70.

28 *Kabir Granthavali*, ed. Shyam Sundar Das, Lok Bharti Prakashan, Allahabad, 2011, p. 94.

29 *Granthavali*, Gupta, p. 160.

30 *The Bijak of Kabir*, Hess and Singh, p. 136.

31 *The Bijak of Kabir*, Hess and Singh, p. 146.

32 *Granthavali*, Gupta, p. 310.

33 P.C. Bagchi, *Studies in Tantras: Volume 1*, University of Calcutta Press, Kolkata, 1939, p. 27.

34 *The Bijak of Kabir*, Hess and Singh, p. 148.

35 Tulsidas, *Ramcharitmanas*, Gita Press, Gorakhpur, 2011, p. 610.

36 Poem 55 in *The Bijak of Kabir*, Hess and Singh, p. 147.

37 *Granthavali*, Gupta, p. 150.

38 *Shabdavali*, ed. Gangasharan Shastri, Kabir Vani Prakashan Kendra, Varanasi, 1988, pp. 244–245.

39 *Granthavali*, Gupta. p. 201.

40 *Granthavali*, Gupta, p. 118.

41 *Granthavali*, Gupta, p. 172.

42 *Pad Surdasji ka* (1582), manuscript published in facsimile, ed. Gopal Narayan Bahura and Kenneth Bryant, Maharaj Sawai Man Singh II Museum Trust, Jaipur, 1984, p. 166.

V

1 youtube.com/watch?v=RQLIIx9cBIc.

2 scroll.in/article/907211/new-year-smiles-rajiv-malhotra-s-proposal-to-make-hindus-the-richest-people-in-the-world.

3 answersingenesis.org/geology/grand-canyon-facts/grand-canyon-what-is-the-message/.

4 Hazari Prasad Dwivedi, *Kabir,* New Delhi, Rajkamal Prakashan, 2000, p. 184.

5 *Kabir Granthavali*, ed. Mata Prasad Gupta, Lok Bharti Prakashan, Allahabad, 2019, p. 143.

6 *Granthavali,* Gupta, p. 92.

7 Winand M. Callewaert, Swapana Sharma, Dieter Tailleu, *Millennium Kabir Vani: A Collection of Pad-s*, Manohar, New Delhi, 2000, pp. 3, 4, 11 and 24.

8 Tulsidas, Bal-Kand 120/3.4 in *Ramcharitmanas,* Gita Press, Gorakhpur, 2011.

9 Ramaini 64 in *Kabir Bijak*, ed. Shukdeo Singh, Neelabh Prakashan, Allahabad, 1972, p. 101.

10 Pada 43 in *Bijak*, Singh, p. 126.

11 *Granthavali*, Gupta, p. 14.

12 *Granthavali*, Gupta, p. 112.

13 *Granthavali*, Gupta, p. 117.

14 *Granthavali*, Gupta, p. 376.

15 *Shabdavali*, ed. Ganga Sharan Shastri, Kabir Vani Prakash Kendra, Varanasi, 1988, p. 3.

16 *Granthavali*, Gupta, p. 311.

17 *Granthavali*, Gupta, p. 312.

18 *Granthavali*, Gupta, p. 169.

19 R.D. Ranade, *Pathway to God in Marathi Literature*, Bhartiya Vidya Bhawan, Mumbai, 1961, p. 1.

20 Ramchandra Shukla, *Surdas*, Nagri Pracharini Sabha, Varanasi, pp. 16–18.

21 Dwivedi, *Kabir*, p. 38.

22 Dwivedi, *Kabir*, pp. 38–39.

23 Hazari Prasad Dwivedi, *Granthavali: Volume 5*, Rajkamal Prakashan, New Delhi, 1981, p. 253.

24 Namwar Singh, *Doosari Parampara ki Khoj*, Rajkamal Prakashan, New Delhi, 1982, p. 82.

25 *Kabir Granthavali*, ed. Shyam Sundar Das, Lok Bharti Prakashan, Allahabad, 2011, p. 127.

26 David Lorenzen, *Praises to a Formless God: Nirguni Texts from North India*, State

University of New York Press, Albany, 1996, p. 3.

27 Linda Hess, *Bodies of Song: Kabir Oral Traditions and Performative Worlds in North India*, Oxford University Press, New York, 2015, pp. 352–353.

28 Pada 30 in *Bijak*, Hess, pp. 50–51.

29 *Granthavali*, Gupta, p. 311.

30 Bernard Yak, *The Longing for Total Revolution: Philosophical Sources of Social Discontent from Rousseau to Marx and Nietzsche*, New Jersey, Princeton University Press, 1986, p. 75.

31 *Granthavali*, Das, p. 238.

32 *Bijak*, Hess, p. 42.

VI

1 'Introduction', *Kabir Granthavali*, ed. Mata Prasad Gupta, Lok Bharti Prakashan, Allahabad, 2019, p. 50.

2 *Granthavali*, Gupta, p. 116.

3 Quoted in Elaine Pagles, *Why Religion: A Personal Story*, HarperCollins, New York, 2018, p. 55.

4 Linda Hess, *Bodies of Song: Kabir Oral Traditions and Performative Worlds in North India*, Oxford University Press, New York, 2015, p. 102.

5 *Granthavali*, Gupta, p. 328.

6 *Granthavali*, Gupta, p. 15.

7 *Granthavali*, Gupta, p. 18.

8 *Granthavali*, Gupta, p. 13.

9 *Granthavali*, Gupta, pp. 140–141.

10 *Granthavali*, Gupta, pp. 60–70.

11 A.K. Ramanujan, *The Collected Essays of A.K. Ramanujan*, Oxford University Press, Delhi, 1999, p. 291.

12 Germaine Greer, *The Female Eunuch*, McGraw Hill, New York, 1971, p. 144.

13 *Granthavali*, Gupta, p. 371.

14 *Granthavali*, Gupta, p. 35.

15 *Granthavali*, Gupta, p. 179.

16 *Granthavali*, Gupta, p. 25.

Acknowledgements

Apart from those already mentioned in 'Kabir and I: A Note to the Reader', I would like to acknowledge the contribution of the following people in the making of this book.

This project would not have been possible but for the persistent insistence from my dear friend and famous mythologist Devdutt Pattanaik, who has also beautifully introduced and illustrated it. Ever since our first meeting in 2013, Devdutt has been full of exciting book ideas and thought-provoking observations. A big thank you, Devdutt.

I can't imagine this book without the very stimulating conversations I had with my son, Ritwik, a budding philosopher and doctoral candidate at the University of Arizona, during a long stay in the USA forced by the COVID-19 pandemic.

My partner, Suman, a Surdas scholar, poet and unique story-teller, and my daughter, Ritambhara, a passionate photographer and aspiring filmmaker, have been a constant source of intellectual stimulation. This book owes a lot to these two women in my life.

I am deeply grateful to V.K. Karthika, Janani Ganesan and Shougat Dasgupta for the diligent editing, Sonia Madan and Pallavi Singh for the careful proofing, and Saurabh Garge for the lovely cover.

I have been able to clarify my ideas on Kabir and Bhakti poetry with the help of critical comments from the professors Nand Kishore Acharya, Monika Boehm-Tettelbach, Francesca Orsini, Awadhesh Pradhan and Sudhir Chandra, as well as Prabhat Tripathi and Karmendu Shishir. My research students

Awadhesh Pande and Sudha Ranjani, through their works on the Parakh Marg and Dariya Sahib respectively, have helped me gain significant insights into the Bhakti phenomenon. Neelakshi Tewari, a researcher at the Arizona State University, has been one of the very first readers and commentators on this book. Koslendradas Shastri, a young Ramanandi and talented Sanskrit scholar, has also been a big help in my research.

For some years now, I have been conducting a course on Kabir and Vernacular Modernity for the Young India Fellows (YIF) at Ashoka University, Sonipat. This interaction with inquisitive young minds has been a wonderful opportunity to constantly revisit my ideas. I am grateful to Aniha Brar for inviting me to conduct this course. Her comments on some portions of the book were insightful. I thank everyone associated with the YIF, particularly my teaching assistants Tannishtha, Mudra and Ashok, and wish them the very best in their ambition of expanding their knowledge horizons.

Maria, a fellow at this programme, was thought-provokingly persistent in her challenging queries; I hope she finds some of her questions addressed here.

Surya, Mathew, Rekha and Apurva enriched my thought process with their questions and comments. I wish all of them the very best.

And, our lovely, naughty cats merit a loving and grateful mention.